ACID
RAIN

Archie M. Kahan
ACID
RAIN
Reign of Controversy

FULCRUM INC.

Cover and Book Design
by Bob Schram

LIBRARY OF CONGRESS CATALOGING-IN-PUBLICATION DATA

Kahan, Archie M., 1917-
Acid Rain: Reign of Controversy

Bibliography: p.
Includes Index
1. Acid rain—Environmental aspects. I. Title.
TD196.A25K35 1986 363.7'386 86-7688
ISBN 1-55591-003-3

FULCRUM, INC.
GOLDEN, COLORADO

Dedicated to
Harriet,
Hunter, Bob
and Anne

Table of Contents

What's Going On Here?

Forest trees that once were healthy and thriving now are dying or are already dead in Scandinavia, Germany, Canada, and the United States. Lakes that once offered fishermen exciting sport now are devoid of fish, or are nearly so. Faces on ancient marble statues that once inspired awe with their beauty have become shapeless blobs, devoid of noses and ears. Steel bridges and other expensive structures are deteriorating more rapidly than expected.

These clearly-undesirable developments have something in common. They have all happened in places where airborne chemicals have been deposited on affected surfaces. One of several effective mechanisms for depositing these chemicals from the overiding air is rainfall. Raindrops that fall through heavily-polluted air scavenge a load of airborne materials. Included in the load are acid gases and acid particles. And that, Dear Reader, is how we come to have ACID RAIN!

Just in case you are someone whose consciousness hasn't already been overly impacted by discussions of acid rain, it may help to mention that raindrops do an efficient job of absorbing acidic gases and particles in falling through polluted air, and, as a result, become quite acidic. Exactly how acidic, or sour, a raindrop has to get before it is entitled to be called acid rain is a subject of some controversy, but there is agreement that rain sour enough to taste something like tomato juice or Coca Cola is not apt to be as kind to the nose of a marble statue or a newly-hatched fish as those beverages are to your stomach. Later on I'll introduce you to the measure of acidity chemists call pH. When rain is acid enough to have a pH of 5.0, most atmospheric chemists would call it acid rain.

Acid rain appears to be a problem. A recommended way of solving any problem is to begin by making sure that the problem is real. Once this crucial step has been taken, defining just what the problem is becomes highly desirable. After the definition is well-established, identification of the ingredients required to cook up a solution becomes possible. When the list of required ingredients is well in hand, it is sensible to take time out to compare the total cost of acquiring those ingredients to the value of having the problem solved. This can be a very difficult step to accomplish wisely because what is important to one person may be trivial to another. Values are by no means universal. Living with the problem may be an acceptable alternative to some and an intolerable burden to others.

Problem solving isn't always approached in the above-outlined orderly manner. Sometimes stereotypical solutions become fashionable. An elite group, expert in applying a particularly favored solution, springs up. There follows a process that can best be described as "a solution looking for a problem." If the solution doesn't fit a particular problem well, efforts are apt to be made to reshape the problem rather than the solution.

Both approaches to problem solving are being applied to acid rain.

Acidity in rain is widely considered to have caused the adverse effects on forests, lakes, statues and structures. An impressive chain of evidence, mostly circumstantial in nature, has convinced a large number of thinking citizens that there is imminent danger of widespread, irreversible environmental damage unless corrective steps are promptly taken. Human health and even human lives seem threatened. A need is seen for immediate, legally compelled, reductions in the amounts of acid-forming pollutants allowed to be emitted to the atmosphere. Advocates of this approach consider the early application of existing pollution control technology, imperfect and expensive though it may be, to be fully justified *now*.

Other thinking citizens, prepared to agree that something needs to be done, are not convinced that enough is known about the causes of the perceived problems to justify immediate corrective action. They consider that a major investment of time and money in research is required if the understanding needed to produce reliable, economically justified, solutions is to exist.

Others, including some who feel threatened by the major economic impacts associated with presently-proposed solutions, aren't convinced that any action is really needed. Their perception is that acid rain is, at worst, only a potential problem. They point out that the deposition of acid on soils, lakes, streams, forests, statues, bridges, and buildings is not some recent innovation resulting from man's use of the atmosphere for waste disposal purposes. From time immemorial entirely natural processes of respiration, decay, decomposition of rock, evaporation of sea spray, lightning discharge, and volcanic eruption have added oxides of carbon, sulfur and nitrogen to the atmosphere. Several quantitative estimates of global releases of acid-forming oxides hold natural emissions to be in excess of man-made emissions. There is also evidence that pollution is decreasing in some areas. "Why worry," they ask, "about the loss of a few acid sensitive bacteria or trees? Acid-tolerant species of bacteria and trees already exist and more could develop. Acid-resistant materials can be substituted for acid-vulnerable materials where necessary."

For people from this school of thought more stringent legislation regarding pollution control is definitely not needed. In their view, implementation of currently-suggested control legislation would do more harm than good.

The intensely emotional interaction of these three quite disparate attitudes, underlain as they are by differing value systems, has replaced the reign of reason with a reign of controversy.

Controversy has arisen around many issues relating to acid rain. Some of these started out as scientific issues which might have been expected to be resolved in a calm, impersonal, scientific manner. Contrary to that expectation, rival groups of scientists have indulged in verbal dart-throwing, impugning each other's motives and methods, while leaving issues still unresolved. Controversy over what should be done about acid rain exists between industries and between factions within a single industry. Controversy has arisen between adjoining states, adjoining regions, and adjoining countries.

There is controversy about acid rain's past, present and future. There is controversy about how much is known about acid rain and controversy about how much needs to be known about acid rain. There is controversy about how urgent is the need for additional acid-rain-control legislation. There is controversy about the effectiveness of presently-available control equipment. There is controversy about who should pay for reducing the impact of acid rain. There may even be controversy over whether or not there is controversy.

Sometimes both sides of the controversy turn out to be right, or wrong, as the case might be. Take fly ash as an example. Some years ago there was an effort made by environmental interests to force additional cleanup of the smoke plumes issuing from western coal-burning power plants. Electrostatic precipitators were not doing enough. The goal was to make the plume invisible before the plume reached the boundary fence around the power plant. The aim was to minimize the negative impact on visibility that could impair the breath-taking beauty of nearby vistas. Costly scrubbers and filters were added to plant designs to capture more of the pollutants and fly ash that were partly to blame for making the plume so visible.

There was also a concurrent effort to encourage the building of smoke stacks to heights that would ensure greater downwind transport and plume dilution. A stack in western Arizona was built to a height of 750 feet after public hearings found the original design height of 600 feet "inadequate."

All this went on before the interest in acid rain had developed to its present level. Later it came to be recognized that the filter-equipped high stacks were not an unmitigated blessing. The pollution dilution that many sought came to be seen as having an unanticipated price attached to it. Increased residence time of the pollution in the atmosphere, caused by the increased stack heights, clearly allowed greater time for adverse chemical reactions to occur, and the extended downwind transport was seen as possibly resulting in acid being deposited at more sensitive sites than otherwise would have been the case. It was further stated that the removal of alkaline fly ash from the smoke plumes had let more acid-forming sulfur dioxide into the atmosphere than would have otherwise escaped. "Not so," said opponents. "Fly ash cannot effectively neutralize sulfur dioxide in the stack. Its transit time through the stack is too brief and, besides, fly ash is not all that alkaline."

It turns out that the argument about fly ash has a lot in common with the argument the blind men had when they stood at opposite ends of the elephant and described what their hands were feeling. Fly ash isn't a single chemical substance. The fly ash produced from burning some eastern coals is quite acidic, while western fly ash can be quite alkaline. It pays to be sure of facts before starting to generalize or argue.

When an issue has such far-reaching social, environmental and economic implications as those associated with acid rain, controversy is not surprising. This is especially true where there is uncertainty about what is happening and what is causing it to happen. Presently, there are uncertainties about the extent of current damages. There are uncertainties about the probability of future damages. There are uncertainties about whether the damages are reversible. There are uncertainties about where damaging pollution originates. There are uncertainties about what reduction in emissions is necessary to produce a required reduction in pollution. To top it all off, there are uncertainties about whether research can really reduce the other uncertainties.

Controversy Leads to Polarization

Controversy can easily develop into polarization when differing viewpoints are held by people who lack trust in and mutual respect for one another. Trust and mutual respect have not been overly abundant, in the past, when environmental activists have confronted industrialists whose businesses pollute air and water. One subject that they do seem to agree on, however, has to do with how much, or how little, trust and mutual respect is warranted when dealing with people who work in the federal government, especially the regulatory agencies. What gets overlooked in all the polarization is the common bond of human fallibility that characterizes all the separate camps.

Environmental activists, industrialists and government agency officials all have roles to play in resolving the acid rain issue. One would hope that as increasing knowledge reduces the uncertainties, polarization about acid rain will eventually subside.

Partly as a result of intense polarization there is a great deal of both information and misinformation available to the person who is still trying to make up his or her mind about acid rain. The fact that you are reading this book identifies you as a person with some interest in enlarging your understanding of the subject. You do not stand alone. Acid rain is a hot topic. Not since the concerns about ozone depletion, due to unbridled use of aerosol sprays, or the fear that the "Greenhouse Effect" could cause the polar ice caps to melt and inundate continental coastlines has so much attention been paid to an environmental issue having to do with the atmosphere.

People who write or talk about the news are giving acid rain a lot of attention. The newspapers, the weekly news magazines and the evening television news shows are all allotting prime space and time to reports about the latest developments. When President Reagan met with Canadian Prime Minister Mulroney in March, 1985 — in what has been called the Shamrock Summit — their extensive talks about acid rain were reported quite fully by both print and electronic news media. At least 16 books have already been written on the subject of acid rain.

Unfortunately much of what has been written and said about acid rain for popular consumption seems more suited to recruiting adherents to a polarized point of view than it does to providing the concerned public with understandable information that is relatively free of bias. The words "relatively free of bias" arise from a conviction that even the "facts" of acid rain, let alone the opinions, have acquired biases that were probably introduced unconsciously. In the process of learning something about anything, bias is very apt to be acquired. The most this author hopes for, in pursuit of that elusive quality called "objectivity," is to avoid the conscious introduction of "special interest" bias. None of the polarized positions that has been taken on acid-rain issues is totally lacking in merit. Hence it follows that none of the opposing positions is fully meritorious. A balanced discussion of each side of the important issues, if it can be achieved, could contribute to wider understanding and wiser decisions.

It is the objective of this book to provide just such a balanced discussion. Candid, authoritative information will be offered, free of as much special-interest bias as possible. When the positions of special-interest groups are presented, they will be in the form of direct quotations taken from published statements.

Understanding the discussions presented here isn't going to require that you be some sort of scientist. When technical terms and scientific concepts are unavoidable, I will explain them. A glossary has been included to expedite understanding for those readers who have had better things to do with their time than master the esoteric vocabularies of chemistry, mathematics, meteorology, biology, limnology, geology, and any other "ology" that might creep into the discussions. If you are an expert in any of the above fields and find the discussions too simplified for your taste, please realize, in your most charitable manner, that this book was written to help inform interested non-experts.

An immediately noticeable aspect of the discussion of the issues associated with acid rain is the frequent use of qualifying words like "may," "possible," and "potential." These "weasel words" can be frustrating to the person used to dealing with unassailable facts. Unfortunately, many of the natural processes associated with acid rain are poorly understood. Incomplete understanding gives rise to uncertainty. Uncertainty permits multiple interpretations of observations.

Multiple interpretations provide the basis for differing viewpoints. Hard and fast statements about acid rain may be well suited to the partisan bent on selling a biased point of view, but, for that very reason, qualified statements are used frequently in this presentation.

Intelligent decision-making about acid rain will require clear understanding of the difference between what is known and what is merely suspected. Polarization and incomplete knowledge have erected a complex maze around the subject. Some of the complexity may have been introduced unnecessarily. This book is intended to promote understanding by reducing complexity without going to the extreme of oversimplification.

In concept, the problem of acid rain can be simply stated. Chemical waste is emitted, transported, transformed and eventually deposited. What the transformed chemicals do to the the surfaces upon which they land is not so simple to answer. The question is being vigorously studied and even more vigorously debated.

Answers to the question "What should be done about acid rain?" are not hard to come by, but unfortunately there are, as yet, no generally-accepted answers. The search for those answers can offer exciting adventure.

Come join me in reviewing what's going on with acid rain. Together we'll look at the "who," "what," "where," "when," and "why" of acid rain and its attendant controversies, with a passing glance or two at the "how" and "how much."

This book is intended to provide interested people a painless means of acquiring improved understanding of the controversial subject of acid rain. When scientific concepts are introduced, you will find they are discussed in terms intended to be understood by people who find remembering their own names a challenge.

Our joint adventure will start out with a discussion of the developments that have focused attention on acid rain, moves on to a few essential chemical concepts, and then looks at acid rain's environmental, economic, and social implications. Then we will look at the quantitative aspects of pollution and where acid rain is occurring. Next we'll meet the groups that have a special interest in acid rain and learn their positions on the question of what should be done about it. After that we'll look at the political aspects of the problem, and, finally, discuss possible solutions. I hope you find the prospect attractive.

Why All This Fuss About Acid Rain?

Acid Rain. Acid Rain! Acid Rain? How did those two words get placed together and become so newsworthy? The answer isn't immediately obvious. Let's spend a few minutes exploring the possibilities. It is well known that rain can pick up a number of noxious chemicals as it makes its way through a layer of polluted air. Why is it that only the acid component of this chemical collection seems to have made its way into public prominence? Some years ago a sample of rainfall collected in the Chicago Loop was found to have a lead content that greatly exceeded drinking-water standards. Why were there no headlines about Leaded Rain in the evening papers? Radioactive iodine — a very hazardous fission product — has been washed from the atmosphere by rainfall. What kept Iodized Rain from becoming a national concern?

Yet "acid rain" is frequently in the news. News is the name we give to recent developments that are unusual or notable. Much news concerns itself with the latest events that human beings have caused to happen. But deposition of acids onto the surfaces of Earth is by no means a recent development that man has initiated. Eons before mankind showed up acid rain was falling on much of the earth. Acids and acid precursors get into the atmosphere, and back out again, by some processes that man doesn't even influence, let alone control. Volcanic eruption, rock weathering, lightning, sea spray, and the decay of organic materials all contribute acids to the atmosphere and have been doing so for a long time now. Polar ice cores composed of precipitation laid down about 1350 B.C. have been recovered. These cores exhibit acidities comparable to the values that are causing widespread environmental concerns today.

In view of these major, long-standing, natural, acid depositions, why is so much attention suddenly being focused on acid rain? Are people just becoming aware of conditions that have gone unnoticed before? Is nostalgia for "the good old days" stimulating a desire for a return to an imagined pristine condition which may have never existed? Or is acid rain "fear" a deliberate conspiracy that is underway to disrupt our industrial economy? Is coal-burning for electric power being portrayed as a villainous practice in order to promote the use of some other energy technology? Is media hype, in greedy pursuit of readership or audience ratings, responsible? Each of these explanations has been offered by concerned people, all of whom seemed convinced of the correctness of their analyses.

Before we go much farther it will be well to recognize that the term "acid rain" is now generally considered to be a misnomer. The term is used to cover all the mechanisms for transferring acids and acid precursors from the atmosphere to the Earth's surface, regardless of whether or not rain has had anything to do with the transfer. Scientific types, with a penchant for careful speech, now speak of *acid deposition* instead of acid rain. There are good reasons for making a distinction between acid rain and acid deposition. Rainfall washout is by no means the sole acid-deposition process. A number of water-related deposition mechanisms, in addition to rainfall, operate in the acid-deposition arena. Snow, hail, drizzle, dew and fog are all effective in bringing atmospheric acids down to Earth. In New York and California, fogs have been sampled that were 10 to 100 times as acid as the rains in the same area, but this doesn't seem to have reduced the frequency with which "acid rain" is brought to our attention by the news media.

Another important fact, that has received very little attention outside the scientific community, is that a major portion of the acid and acid-forming stuff which reaches the ground does so without involvement with any form of precipitation whatsoever. That process is called *dry deposition.*

In spite of all the impressive reasons just listed for not calling all acid deposition "acid rain," it is still happening. It is a popular and easily-recognized term. I am not about to try to swim upstream against such an overpowering current of popular usage and familiarity. In the pages that follow you will find "acid rain" and "acid deposition" used interchangeably.

What is it about acid rain that has caused the focusing on it of so much popular notice? The intense attention currently being paid to acid rain seems to be part of a fairly complicated picture. In the foreground, there is the matter of familiar experience. Most of the world's population lives in the temperate zones. In the temperate zones industrial activity and its accompanying air pollution, are familiar sights to people. In the temperate zones rain falls over large areas, during all four seasons, with attention-commanding frequency and intensity. As a consequence, rain is a much more familiar part of the human experience than are the other forms of precipitation. Collection of a water sample and determination of its acidity is comparatively easy in the case of rainfall and quite difficult for the other forms of acid deposition. As a result, past data on the acidity of rainfall, while not plentiful, are much more readily available for study than are data on other forms of acid deposition.

In the background of the picture is the reality of intensifying environmental interest on the part of people in many walks of life. These interests have developed comparatively recently and have played a role in changing nearly-universal indifference to present widespread concern.

Environmental awareness came to most of us along with the space age. Only a few decades ago most people were enthusiastically supporting the idea of an ever-expanding economy based on coal-burning heavy industry. Generating more and more "inexpensive" electric power was perceived to be good for everybody. Most of us were happily buying "better things for better living through chemistry." Synthetic pesticides offered comfortable freedom from insect-borne disease and a "low-cost" pathway to greatly increased agricultural production. Smoke-belching stacks were welcome signs of a healthy economy. The noxious, unsightly smoke seemed a small price to pay for the many good-paying jobs.

For many of us, the world then seemed to be endowed with an inexhaustible abundance of natural resources. What difference did it make if we poisoned our air and water? Technology, it was assumed, would soon provide us the capability of renewing the purity of air and water indefinitely. The land, the atmosphere, and the oceans appeared to offer an unlimited capacity for swallowing and digesting all the inconvenient chemical by-products of our "healthy economy."

And then perceptions began to change. Post World War II prosperity played a role in the change. More and more people found themselves with the leisure and wherewithal to escape the confines of their polluted urban environment. People, who had never before spent a night away from home, found themselves competing for parking space at crowded campgrounds. They developed an intense appreciation of the difference between clean air and the air they were used to breathing. The spiritual renewal provided by fragrant forests became a common experience. Sparkling streams and lakes, where fish could be seen leaping for fishing lures gave enjoyment to ever-increasing multitudes. A public love affair with out-of-the way places flourished. As might be expected, anything that threatened to impair or destroy these newly-appreciated blessings came to be viewed as definitely undesirable.

Rachel Carson wrote the best seller *Silent Spring,* and the previously unrecognized costs of using the wonderfully efficient insecticides, which chemistry had made available, rose to public attention. The interconnections among living things and their vulnerability to hostile environments became increasingly understood. The word "ecology" was suddenly part of the national vocabulary. Many people used the word; some even understood what it meant.

The widely-published colored picture of our planet Earth, taken from an orbiting Apollo spacecraft, drove home to many people the realization that the planet we all share is itself only a populated, orbiting spacecraft. Earth's continents, oceans, and atmosphere — when viewed in their entirety — were seen to be only vast, not infinite. Appreciation of the desirability of conserving limited natural resources was no longer confined to the minds of a thoughtful few.

Then more and more scientists began to go public about their environmental concerns.

Ellis B. Cowling, associate dean of the School of Forestry at North Carolina State University and chairman of the National Atmospheric Deposition Program, has written a fascinating account of the history of scientific interest in acid rain. Entitled "Acid Precipitation in Historical Perspective," Cowling's article (published in *Environmental Science and Technology*, Volume 16, No. 2, 1982) provides rewarding reading to anyone interested in learning more about how the subject of acid rain came to its present prominence. The following paragraphs draw heavily on Cowling's excellent article.

Scientific Interest in Acid Rain Acid rain had been a matter of interest to several branches of science for a long time before any space was allocated to it in the newspapers of the world. England and Sweden were centers of early interest. Atmospheric chemists, agricultural scientists, ecologists, limnologists, and meteorologists all had reasons for studying acid rain. (Just in case limnology hasn't been one of your consuming interests, I'll mention that limnologists are people who are concerned with understanding the life and phenomena associated with lakes, ponds, and streams.) Unfortunately, the above-mentioned scientists didn't spend much time communicating across the boundaries of their individual specialties. Understanding of the phenomenon and its effects could have been accelerated by more interdisciplinary exchanges.

The adverse effects of industrial air-pollution on the health of plants and people had been the object of scientific discussion in England as early as 1661. By 1727 it was known that dew and rain washed acid and sulphurous particles from polluted air. An English chemist, Robert Angus Smith, first used the words "acid rain" in a book that was published in 1872. He called it *Air and Rain: The Beginnings of a Chemical Climatology*. The book reflected his consuming interest in the chemical content of rain and its effects. It was an interest that had lasted for over 20 years. A paper Smith published in 1852 reported findings about the chemistry of rain, based on observations he had made near Manchester, England. Much of what is now understood about acid rain was first described by Smith. He was the first to tell us how natural processes combined with the burning of coal to add acids to precipitation. He also reported on the damage to plants and materials that resulted from the acids and metals brought down to Earth's surface by rainfall.

Smith deserves fame for his pioneering understanding of acid rain, but fate has failed to make his name a household word. His work went largely unnoticed until it was brought to light in 1981 in connection with a study conducted by the United States National Academy of Sciences.

Evidence of early awareness of acid rain can be found in the literature of several quite separate fields of science. Limnologists have long had an interest in acid rain and its effects. Eville Gorman, a Canadian who did much of his work in England, deserves special mention. His research, begun over three decades ago, has added much to the understanding of how acid rain affects life in aquatic ecosystems. As in the case of Robert Angus Smith, Gorham's work received underwhelming attention from fellow scientists until recently.

Agricultural scientists also made major contributions. The first modern network for collecting data on the acidity of rainfall was established in Sweden in the mid 1940s by a soil scientist, Hans Egner. He was interested in how chemicals deposited from the atmosphere might fertilize crops. Egner's Swedish network was subsequently expanded, first to Norway, Denmark, and Finland, then to most of western and central Europe, and, by 1957, to Poland and the Soviet Union. His inspired effort initiated the organized acquisition of acid-rain data over large areas.

Meteorologists also deserve mention in the subject of acid rain. Carl Gustave Rossby, whose name is associated with many important developments in meteorology, used data from Egner's network to test hypotheses about turbulent diffusion and trajectories of air movement in Europe. He was also responsible for stimulating early interest in atmospheric chemistry in the United States.

In 1967, Svante Oden, a Swedish soil scientist, took the unusual step of publishing his concerns about acid rain in a Stockholm newspaper. By doing so he very effectively alerted the Swedish public to the importance of acid rain. In the manner long employed by many scientists, he stated his unproven hypotheses about the dire environmental consequences that could be expected from acid rain. Intense concern and controversy were stimulated by Oden's writings, first in Sweden and then throughout Europe. His projections of how acid precipitation could cause declining fish populations, decreased forest growth, plant-disease increases, and material damage were very impressive. It didn't take long before significant financial resources were allocated to European scientific investigations to determine the validity of the hypothesized effects.

In Canada and the United States, the adverse environmental effects associated with the operation of large smelters also attracted attention. Declining fish populations, observed in the lakes of Ontario and Nova Scotia, came to be associated with polluted air.

Agricultural scientists in the United States made sporadic attempts to study precipitation chemistry in the 1950s and 1960s, but these efforts suffered from inadequate funding. Interest in acid rain was stimulated significantly in 1971 by a series of 14 lectures presented by Oden in the United States. By the mid-1970s numerous publications about acid rain were appearing in technical journals as well as in such popular magazines as *Scientific American.*

The Search for Solutions As interest in acid rain has grown, so has appreciation of the difficulty of solving the problem. Research programs undertaken in pursuit of the understanding that might result in cost-effective solutions have produced high levels of frustration in some circles. Not only are the required studies both costly and time-consuming, but, as is frequently the case in science, the pursuit of understanding can uncover more uncertainty than was originally recognized when the studies began. *The Acid Rain Information Book,* by Frank A Record, David V. Bubenick, and Robert J. Kindya contains an analysis of 43 major scientific or technical items and issues associated with acid rain. Several of the major items cover lists of subsidiary items or issues. The level of uncertainty applicable to each major issue and its need for further research has been identified and described as either low, moderate, moderate-high, or high.

The authors considered 19 different topics to merit the "High Level of Uncertainty" designation:

1) The magnitude assessment of naturally produced sulfur oxides relative to manmade sulfur oxide emissions.

2) The magnitude assessment of anthropogenically produced (man-made) sulfur oxides and nitrogen oxides.

3) The effect of combustion variables on source emissions.

4) Oil-fired burners as direct sources of sulfur trioxide, sulfate ion, and sulfuric acid.

5) Effect of control technology on source emissions.

6) The role of airborne particulates in catalytic oxidation of sulfur oxides to sulfates.

7) Deposition rates.

8) Transformation rates.

9) Regional modeling.

10) Evidence of trends toward increasingly acidic rain over increasing area of influence.

11) Source determination of acidic components of precipitation.

12) Evidence of a trend toward increasing acidity in North American lakes.

13) Relative role of acid precipitation in contributing to acidity of lakes.

14) Continuity of monitoring programs.

15) How we can evaluate whether acidification of a lake has occurred and what effects can be predicted.

16) How fast will a given lake become acid and how and why do lakes vary in their susceptibility to acidification.

17) Mechanisms and quantitative effects of acidification on aquatic and terrestrial ecosystems.

18) Long-term effects of rainfall acidity on soil and soil/plant systems.

19) What are the impacts of acidic precipitation on human health and well being?

Most of the issues that were assigned a high uncertainty designation were also considered to have a high need for further research. Now pause a moment to consider what you believe to be true about the above listed issues? I find it interesting to note how many of the acid-rain effects that are frequently discussed in the popular press, as if they were well-established facts, were assigned both high-uncertainty and high-further-research-needed designations.

Some people, concerned about the damage to the environment being reported on an almost-daily basis, decry the continued postponing of corrective action. Many of them see the research programs as boondoggles that are being used to delay the enactment of the legislation which would force immediate corrective action.

To many others immediate action equates to ill-advised action. They see measures taken before sufficient understanding has been achieved as having a high probability of creating worse problems than the ones intended to be solved. The controversy between the "Do-it-now" portion of the public and the "let's-don't-go-off-half-cocked" portion is only one of many involving acid rain.

The limited understanding of the natural processes involved in the production of atmospheric acids, the complexity surrounding their subsequent transport and the uncertainty about their ultimate impacts combine to feed fears about the future. Controversy is quite likely to develop whenever fear of the uncertain future overshadows confidence in the ability to cope.

Confidence in the ability of science and technology to solve the important environmental problems of the future is not nearly as widespread today as it once was. It has been replaced, in the minds of many people, by the conviction that too much reliance on science and technology has put mankind on a fast track to catastrophe. This diminished confidence in society's ability to cope contributes to the sense of urgency about acid rain.

There are also many unanswered economic questions and unaddressed policy considerations that are themselves productive of controversy. Selection of a national strategy for coping with acid deposition will require willingness to make decisions in spite of uncertainty. Examination of some of these issues in detail should help define the real scope and complexity of the acid rain problem. With this in hand we may be better prepared to understand what all the fuss is about.

The Chemistry of Acid Rain

If you plan to do much thinking, talking, discussing, or arguing about acid rain, it will be useful to feel comfortable with a little bit of simple chemistry and the chemical concepts relevant to acid rain. Those of you with a good background in chemistry may wish to skip this whole chapter. It won't teach you much you don't already know. This chapter is addressed to those of you who had better things to do with your time than to go to chemistry classes.

Most of you probably already know much more about chemistry than you realize. If you know that baking soda is also called sodium bicarbonate, you are well on your way. Even if that second name of baking soda comes as a surprise to you, don't despair. The paragraphs that follow are going to be quite painless. They may even turn out to be fun. Are you still out there? Hang in a little longer while we look at some elementary chemistry that will help us understand how acid rain gets that way. Some fascinating chemical processes operate in the production of acid rain. Let's spend a little time identifying them and discussing the role each plays.

Chemistry, like most sciences, is really a grown-up's form of child's play. It is a form of play that adults are permitted to indulge in, free of the risk of becoming socially unacceptable for failing to grow up. Occasionally, circumstances contrive to preserve into adult life the curiosity, imagination, and creativity with which most of us are born. Even though some aspects of the educational process seem designed to stamp out these qualities, you have clearly escaped that tragedy with some part of your original allotment intact. If this were not true, why would you be reading this book? You can rest assured that you have all it takes to understand the chemistry that is about to be laid on you.

Chemists play with building blocks. They call their building blocks *elements*. The smallest possible chunk of an element is called an *atom*. Atoms contain one or more positively-charged particles called *protons*. Some atoms also contain *neutrons* which are heavy like protons but have no electric charge. All atoms have one or more negatively-charged particles called *electrons*. Electrons are light and flighty. They weigh only 1/1,836 as much as a proton and move about energetically. They are not above leaving one atom to join another. For our purposes, we can safely consider that every atom of a particular element is built exactly like every other atom of that element. That isn't strictly true, but there is no need to get radioactive about acid rain. There are over 100 elements in a complete set of blocks, but we are mostly going to be playing with seven of them: the gaseous elements hydrogen, oxygen, and nitrogen, and the solid elements carbon, sulfur, and calcium. We will also encounter aluminum from time to time.

Atoms of some elements have a strong affinity for atoms of different elements. When two or more such atoms get together they usually stay together as if glued to each other. The glue in this case is the attraction that exists between electric charges of opposite sign. You may recall the bit of wisdom that declares "opposites attract each other." Nowhere is that more true than in the bonding together of atoms. When chemists let two or more different atoms glue themselves together they call the resultant stack of building blocks a *compound*. The smallest possible chunk of a compound is called a *molecule*. Some molecules, called *electrolytes* dissolve in water and become temporarily unglued, forming two or more electrically charged particles called *ions* which move around in the water quite freely. The sum of all the charges involved in ionization is zero, since the positive charges are balanced by an equal number of negative charges. Most of the acid-rain chemistry we will be considering will involve compounds that ionize.

Chemists are not given to wasting time, space, or energy, so they work with a kind of shorthand. If, for example, they want to write about the element *Einsteinium* they usually settle for the symbol *Es*. Now that you have learned about Es you can begin immediately to forget about Es. You'll not encounter it again in this discussion. But you will encounter symbols for the seven elements of interest. Hydrogen is represented in chemical circles by the capital letter H, oxygen by O and nitrogen by N. Carbon is represented by a capital C and sulfur is represented by S. Calcium's shorthand symbol is Ca and aluminum's is Al. Remembering the meaning of H, O, N, C, S, Ca, and Al won't tax your mind unduly, will it?

Your knowledge of chemistry probably already includes the chemical formula for that priceless oxide of hydrogen, water. Practically everyone has had occasion at some time or other to speak of water as "Aitch two oh." Chemists write the formula for water either as H_2O or as HOH. The latter representation eases remembering the ionizing capability of water. Pure substances are electrically neutral, and water is no exception. Water can ionize weakly into hydrogen ions (H^+) and hydroxyl ions (OH^-). Remember these two ions well. We will encounter them in discussing how acid rain gets that way.

Hydrogen combines with oxygen to form more than one oxide of hydrogen. You are probably familiar with the antiseptic, hydrogen peroxide. Its formula is H_2O_2. You aren't apt to notice an encounter with hydrogen peroxide outside the vicinity of your medicine cabinet, but it does occur in the atmosphere where it plays a role as an effective oxidizing agent.

Ozone, a three-atom molecule of oxygen, is another effective oxidizing agent. And what in the world is an oxidizing agent? Glad you asked! For our purposes, it is a chemical compound that generously contributes some oxygen to another compound. Both hydrogen peroxide and ozone are chemically unstable compounds. They readily come apart at the seams and liberate a very reactive atom of oxygen, called *nascent oxygen* that combines readily with other compounds. Molecular oxygen, which chemists designate as O_2, because the molecule contains two atoms of oxygen, is not nearly as reactive as is nascent oxygen.

Oxygen combines with all the other elements that we will be playing with as we seek to understand the chemistry of acid rain. Some of the elements form more than one oxide.

Carbon combines with oxygen to form both carbon monoxide (CO) and carbon dioxide (CO_2). One molecule of carbon dioxide will join with one molecule of water to form the weakly ionized acid called carbonic acid. Symbolically that reaction looks like this: $H_2O + CO_2$ yields H_2CO_3. Carbonic acid ionizes in two stages. The first stage produces a positively-charged hydrogen ion and a negatively-charged bicarbonate ion. In symbols the first stage of ionization looks like this: H_2CO_3 yields $H^+ + HCO_3^-$. The bicarbonate ion, which chemists also classify as a radical, can ionize further into a second positively charged hydrogen ion and a doubly negatively - charged carbonate ion or radical. The second stage of ionization is represented symbolically as: HCO_3^- yields $H^+ + CO_3^{--}$.

By this time you may be wondering about the chemical meaning of the word *radical*. It has nothing to do with political philosophy when used in a chemical context. In chemical parlance a radical is an atom or group of atoms with at least one unpaired electron. Unpaired electron means there is an electron the negative charge of which is not balanced by, or paired with, the positive charge of a proton. You remember electrons and protons don't you?

Nitrogen has a very flexible mind when it gets chummy with oxygen under conditions favorable for merger. Several different oxides of nitrogen are apt to result. One of them that you may have encountered in your dentist's office is the anesthetic, nitrous oxide or "laughing gas." Its formula is N_2O. Other gaseous oxides of nitrogen are NO, NO_2, N_2O_3 and N_2O_5. You'll encounter an ill-defined mixture of these gases in discussions of acid rain. The formula for the mixture is NO_x. The "x" is a chemist's way of admitting that he really isn't sure how many oxygen atoms are involved with nitrogen atoms in a particular parcel of polluted air. When NO_x combines chemically with water, either in the atmosphere or in soil, nitric acid (HNO_3) is formed. Salts of nitric acid are called nitrates, which are frequently found in chemical fertilizers. Up to a point, acid rain containing nitric acid performs a fertilizing function.

Nitrogen also combines with hydrogen, but not eagerly. It takes a lot of energy to put that couple together. The resulting compound is the gas ammonia, which is symbolized as NH_3. Ammonia combines readily with water to form ammonium hydroxide, NH_4OH. When ammonium hydroxide ionizes it forms an ammonium ion, NH_4^+ and an hydroxl ion, OH^-. Most of the ammonia in the atmosphere gets there as a result of natural processes.

The oxides of sulfur are the real heavies in the acid-rain soap opera. When fuels containing sulfur are burned, one of the products of the combustion is sulfur dioxide (SO_2). In the presence of sunlight, sulfur dioxide isn't above picking up another atom of oxygen and turning into sulfur trioxide (SO_3) which is a very potent gas. It combines readily with water to form sulfuric acid (H_2SO_4), which can be pretty unfriendly stuff.

Since our discussion of the oxides of the non-metallic elements carbon, nitrogen, and sulfur has focused on how they all combine chemically with water to form acids, it might be a good idea at this point to define the word *acid*. Acids are compounds that ionize into positively charged hydrogen ions and corresponding negatively-charged ions. For example, sulfuric acid ionizes into two positively-charged hydrogen ions and one sulfate ion having a double negative charge. A chemist would represent this ionization symbolically as: H_2SO_4 yields $2H^+ + SO_4^{--}$.

The chemical opposite of an acid is a base. The oxide of the metallic element calcium (CaO), which you may know as lime, combines chemically with water to form calcium hydroxide, $Ca(OH)_2$, which you may know as slaked lime. In chemical circles, calcium hydroxide is called a base. Ammonium hydroxide is also a base. This means it is one of those substances which will react with an acid to form a salt and water. Chemists would describe the reaction as neutralization. The acid has been neutralized by the base, and the base has been neutralized by the acid. In symbolic form, the reaction between sulfuric acid and calcium hydroxide looks like this: H_2SO_4 + $Ca(OH)_2$ yields 2 HOH + $CaSO_4$.

The calcium compound formed in this reaction is called calcium sulfate and is spoken of as the salt of sulfuric acid and calcium hydroxide.

The Processes that Relate to Acid Rain

Be that as it may, let's get back to carbonic acid. You may be more familiar with it than you might be ready to admit. Club soda just wouldn't be the same without it. By coming apart, into carbon dioxide and water, carbonic acid put some of the bubbles in your most recent bottle of pop. It also puts some of the hydrogen ions into acid rain.

The salt formed when carbonic acid reacts with calcium hydroxide is *calcium carbonate* which is found in limestone, marble, and Tums. As you have no doubt heard, if you watch commercials on television, acids can be neutralized by calcium carbonate. This is true even if the acid isn't in your stomach. The acid in acid rain can be neutralized if the rain comes in contact with soil or rock that is rich in calcium carbonate or one of the other carbonates that occur in nature.

This brings us to the chemical concept of *buffering*. In chemistry, a *buffer* is a substance capable of maintaining the relative concentrations of hydrogen and hydroxyl ions in a solution by neutralizing, within limits, added acids or bases. A soil rich in carbonate salts is spoken of as being buffered against the acids in acid rain.

Three chemical concepts that crop up frequently in discussions of acid rain are *conductivity, alkalinity* and *pH*.

The *conductivity* of a solution is a measure of its ability to conduct an electric current. This ability depends on the three factors of ion mobility, ion concentration, and temperature of the solution. Pure (*i.e.* recently distilled) water conducts electricity very poorly. Put a little acid in the water and the highly-mobile hydrogen ions get the electricity flowing in more of a hurry. Warm the solution and things speed up even more. Conductivity measurements are made using conductivity meters. The measurements can be used to infer the buffering capacity and the acidity of surface waters.

The *alkalinity* of a solution is a measure of its ability to neutralize an acid. Another name for it is acid neutralizing capacity (ANC). Loss of alkalinity is a way of defining acidification. The alkalinity of of water can be determined by adding a few drops of a chemical which changes color in the presence of acid and then finding out how much acid is required to make the water sample change color.

pH is a piece of chemical shorthand condensed from the words *Potential of Hydrogen.* In a footnote that appears shortly after pH is first mentioned in articles about acid rain, most authors tell us "pH is the negative logarithm of the hydrogen ion concentration." If that tells you everything you want to know about pH, you can probably safely skip the next few paragraphs. You are already sufficiently expert in chemistry. If, on the other hand, you happen to be a person to whom "the negative logarithm of the hydrogen ion concentration" is not the most meaningful group of words you've encountered in recent months, take heart. Reading through the next few paragraphs should help you understand what people mean when they discuss acidity of rainfall in terms of pH values, provided they know what they mean.

Most of us experience acidity as the sour taste of vinegar or lemonade. We learn early that diluting vinegar or lemon juice with water affects the intensity of the sourness. The sense of taste does not lend itself to accurate calibration. Lemonade that tastes unacceptably sour to one person may taste just fine to another. If we ever needed to communicate precisely about how sour a particular batch of lemonade tasted, it would be essential to use some unambiguous indicator of sourness. Instead of settling for vague descriptions, like "awfully sour" or "way too weak," we could then report, "On a scale of decreasing sourness from 0 to 14, this batch of lemonade rates a 2.5."

pH is just such a numerical index of acidity, first proposed in 1909 by a Danish biochemist named Sorensen. It is a means of precisely describing the strength of an acid substance dissolved in water. Its scale of decreasing acidity ranges from 0 to 14. Very strong solutions of acid have pH values approaching the 0 end of the scale. Very alkaline or basic solutions (see Glossary) have pH values approaching the 14 end of the scale. Pure water has a pH of 7.

How does it happen that the seemingly arbitrary values 0 and 14 were chosen to represent the extreme range of acidity, and why do the numbers increase as the acidity decreases? To find the answer to those questions we need to take a quick sortie into the realm of theoretical chemistry. If the prospect of such an excursion doesn't exactly thrill you, or if you don't really care why the pH scale ends at 14, treat yourself to a three or four paragraph break. We'll pick you up again when the Ionization Express has completed its brief run.

Acids are electrolytes. That means that they belong to the class of chemical compounds which, when dissolved in water, yield solutions that can conduct electricity. The reason that solutions of electrolytes can conduct electricity is that electolytes ionize in water. *Ionize* means the compounds tend to disassociate or break up into positively- and negatively-charged particles called *ions*. Ions are active. They don't just sit around soaking themselves in the water. Like hyperactive children, they are constantly in motion. If you put positively- and negatively-charged electrodes into the solution, the positively-charged ions will migrate to the negative electrode or *cathode*. Hence, positively charged ions are called *cations*. The positively-charged electrode is called an *anode* and it attracts *anions* which are negatively charged.

Frequently two oppositely-charged ions collide and reform a molecule of the compound which gave birth to the ions in the first place. While this is going on, other molecules are disassociating into still more ions. At any given instant, an electrolytic solution is a dynamic stew of ions forming molecules, and molecules forming ions. Eventually, if the temperature of the stew is held constant, an equilibrium between association and disassociation sets in. Chemists describe this equilibrium mathematically using the ratio of two numbers. The top number of the ratio is the product of the concentrations of the ions and the bottom number is the concentration of the un-ionized electrolyte. This reasonably constant ratio is quite reasonably named the *Ionization Constant*. Each electrolyte has its own individual ionization constant. Water, HOH, ionizes into positively charged hydrogen ions, H^+ and negatively charged hydroxyl ions, OH^-. The ionization constant for water at 25 degrees Centigrade is $1.0x10^{-14}$.

In case the foregoing notation doesn't send you a clear message, let me put it in a form that may be more familiar to you. $1.0x10^{-14}$ is the same number as the very small decimal 0.00000000000001. Unwieldy, isn't it? The logarithm, to the base 10, of that tiny decimal is -14. Expressing that negative logarithm in terms of pH removes the minus sign and we are left with a pH of 14.

In view of the fact that acidity depends on the concentration of hydrogen ions, why is it necessary to horse around with a pH index that gets bigger the weaker the acid becomes? You may be wondering whether it wouldn't be more understandable if chemists just reported the number of hydrogen ions in some standard volume when describing the acidity of a solution? You are absolutely right! It is sufficient to do that, under some circumstances. When not using the pH scale to describe the strength of acid solutions, chemists report acid strengths in terms of the number of molecular weights of acid per liter of solution and the number of milliequivalents of hydrogen per liter. (See the Glossary if milliequivalent isn't a household word in your neighborhood.) Those numbers increase as the strength of the acid increases, but pH continues to be convenient to use. It is a lot easier to describe a sample of acid rainfall as having a pH of 4.0 than it would be to list the number of moles of sulfuric, nitric and carbonic acid contained in a liter of the same rainwater.

The logarithmic nature of the pH scale makes comparison of two different pH values very straightforward. An acid solution with a pH of 4.0 is ten times as strong as one with a pH of 5.0 and one tenth as strong as one with a pH of 3.0, without regard to the molecular weights of the acids being compared.

Logarithms may be something you haven't been in the habit of using lately. In the days before pocket calculators, logarithms were wonderfully adapted to expediting computation. Slide rules, that engineers carried with them in scabbards slung from their belts, were simply logarithmic scales that could be added mechanically to provide the answer to complex problems of mathematics. Even today, when it is desirable to replace inconvenient numbers by small, convenient numbers, logarithms can play a very useful role.

Logarithm is just another name for an *exponent*. You do remember exponents, don't you? Those were the little numbers that showed up in algebra class when you multiplied a quantity by itself. For example, 10 multiplied by 10 equals 100. The number 100 can be represented by 10^2. That 2 is an exponent. It tells us that 10 multiplied by itself equals 10 to the second power, or 100. If we multiply by 10 again we get 10^3 or 1000. Once more and we get 10,000 or 10^4. And so on until we arrive at the national debt. Another way of talking about these numbers is to say that the logarithm of 100 to the base 10 is 2. The logarithm of 1000 to the base 10 is 3. The logarithm of 10,000 to the base 10 is 4. The base is the number the exponent operates on. In common logarithms, the base is 10, but it could be any other number you want to use. So-called natural, or Napierian logarithms, use a base of 2.71828. Isn't that mind boggling?

But let's return to the base 10 and head toward some smaller numbers. The logarithm of 10 to the base 10 is 1. The logarithm of 1 to the base 10 is 0. When logarithms decrease past 0 they get negative. The logarithm of 0.1 is -1. The logarithm of 0.01 is -2. The logarithm of 0.001 is -3. You have already seen the decimal that has a logarithm of -14.

That is about enough to know about logarithms, unless you are planning to become an algebra teacher. Just remember that every time a pH value *increases* by 1 the acidity has dropped by a factor of 10. If the pH value *decreases* by 1 the acidity has increased by a factor of 10. A sample of rainwater that has a pH of 4.0 is twice as acid as a sample that has a pH of 4.3, four times as acid as a sample with a pH of 4.6, eight times as acid as a sample with a pH of 4.9 and ten times as acid as a sample with a pH of 5.0.

At this point, some pH values of a familiar substances might help you calibrate your acquaintance with acidity and alkalinity. The sulfuric acid in a well-charged storage battery has a pH of 1. Freshly-squeezed lime juice has a pH of about 1.8. Lemon juice runs about pH 2.2. Vinegar weighs in at about pH 2.4. Apple cider's pH is about 3.2. Coca-Cola, Classic Original Formula that is, has a pH of 4.0. Tomato juice comes in with pH 4.2. The lactic acid in milk imparts a pH of 6.5. Falling above the neutral pH of 7.0, are the alkaline substances baking soda, milk of magnesia, ammonia, and lye. They have pH values of 8.3, 10.5, 11.6, and 13.0, respectively.

How Acid is Acid Rain? Are you wondering how acid rain compares with the above-mentioned acidic substances? If you have tears, prepare to shed them now. Shakespeare's lines in the

Merchant of Venice about justice falling like the gentle rains from heaven couldn't be written with a straight face today. There are some observations of acid rain that defy belief. The most acidic rain recorded, in the literature I've read, occurred at Wheeling, West Virginia. It had a pH of 1.4 which puts it about halfway between battery acid and lemon juice. Another source awarded the acidic record to rain in Scotland, in 1974, with a pH of 2.4, an acidity level which puts that particular sample of rain on a par with vinegar. Rains with pH 3.0 are not rare, but are still considered extremely acid. Rain in the northeastern United States is frequently as acid as tomato juice, at pH 4.2. Rain further removed from centers of industrial pollution runs about pH 5.0, and in places where alkaline dust storms are common, pH values over 7.0 have been observed.

Have you begun to wonder at what pH rain qualifies to be called acid rain? We have seen that some acid rain can have a pH below 2.0, but what is the pH of rain that doesn't merit being called acid rain? If you are expecting natural rain (whatever that is) to have the pH of 7.0 normally quoted for pure, recently-distilled water, you are in for a surprise. Even if rain absorbed nothing but carbon dioxide from the air, the pH of rainfall would usually be many times more acid than pH 7.0. The pH of rain is computed to be 5.6 when all of its acidity is due to carbonic acid formed in the raindrop. This assumes normal concentrations and pressures of carbon dioxide in the atmosphere. In the early years of concern about acid rain, the pH 5.6 determination was taken as the definition of the boundary between acid rain and "clean rain." It was assumed that pH values below 5.6 constituted evidence of the impact of man-made pollution. As years have gone by, however, more data have become available from areas far removed from sources of man-made pollution. Rain in some of these areas has been found to have pH values below 5.0. pH 5.0 is a reasonable average figure for rain falling in unpolluted areas due to natural sources of acids other than carbonic. As was mentioned above, rain falling through wind-blown alkaline dust storms can achieve pH values on the basic side of 7.0.

pH can be measured in the field either colorimetrically or electrometrically. The colorimetric method was used in some of the earliest field work. It involves treating a test-tube sized sample of water with a sensitive chemical indicator, such as methyl orange, that changes color with changing acidity. The sample is then compared to a number of tubes containing standard solutions of known pH. The pH of the sample is either taken to be the pH of the standardized tube showing the closest color match to that of the sample, or, if the sample seems to fall in between the colors of two of the standardized tubes, a pH value can be interpolated midway between the pH values of each adjoining tube. There are also instrumental methods of making the color comparisons. These are especially useful to color-blind investigators.

Electrometric measurement of pH involves the use of a pH meter. pH meters work by measuring the difference in electropotential between a stable reference electrode and the solution of unknown pH in which the electrode is immersed. Comparison of the observed potential with the potentials obtained for solutions of known pH leads to a determination of the pH value for the sample.

The accurate measurement of pH is a much more demanding chemical procedure than most people who once measured the pH of precipitation samples in the field seemed to realize. These people's reports usually made little mention of the details of their measurement system. Differences in the details of how a pH measurement is made can result in portions taken from a single sample appearing to have pH differences greater than 0.5. The way in which the sample is collected, and how it is treated after it is collected, have a lot to do with how much faith in the final pH value is justified. If a few ants have gone for a swim in the sample while it was awaiting the observers arrival, the formic acid contributed to the sample by the ants may have as much to do with the pH value measured as did the acids scavenged from the atmosphere. Deductions about long-term trends in precipitation acidity that are based on comparisons of recent pH data with early field measurements of pH are on shaky ground. There is no way of knowing if the differences observed are true differences in acidity or differences in measurement technique.

Not only does comparison of pH values determined by different methods of measurement have some uncertainty attached to it, but also does comparison of readings made with a single instrument at different times. The pH value of a body of water has a transient nature. A slight change in temperature can affect the pH determination. The escape of volatile acid components from the solution can also introduce uncertainty. Reliable pH determinations require dedicated attention to detail under sometimes trying field conditions.

pH has come in for some de-emphasis in recent years as researchers turn away from focusing so much attention on hydrogen ion concentrations alone. There is growing recognition that the totality of precipitation chemistry is important in considering changes in ecosystems. pH does not tell the whole story. That is enough about pH for now. In a later chapter we will consider its geographic distribution.

A final chemical concept that should be included in your acid-rain lexicon is that of *catalysis*. You may already be quite familiar with catalysis. If you drive a recent-model automobile, you operate a catalytic converter as part of the pollution-control equipment. The fuel your car uses was produced in a refinery that relied on catalytic cracking of the crude oil. Catalysis involves the action of a *catalyst* to modify the rate at which a chemical reaction takes place. A catalyst is a chemical substance, frequently a metal (usually present in small amounts relative to the amount of reagents involved in the reaction) that can speed up the rate of chemical reaction without getting used up in the reaction. The catalytic converter on your automobile is a reaction chamber which contains a finely-divided platinum-iridium catalyst. The exhaust gases from your engine are passed in together with excess air so that carbon monoxide and acid-forming hydrocarbon pollutants can be rapidly oxidized to carbon dioxide and water. The platinum-iridium catalyst speeds up the completion of the oxidation process, but it doesn't get used up in the process. It just sits there quietly doing its job as you burn tank after tank of gasoline — provided, of course, that none of the gasoline was leaded. Small amounts of lead can render the platinum-iridium ineffective as a catalyst.

What has all this to do with acid-rain? The production of atmospheric acids (and some of the effects being attributed to acid rain) may be the result of chemical reactions that are being speeded up by metals acting as catalysts. If acid rain made these metals available to participate in an undesirable chemical reaction, acid rain bears some responsibility for the reaction even though the acid rain doesn't hang around to participate.

How People Contribute to Acid Rain

Man's chemical contribution to the formation of acid rain begins, in a trivial way, when he exhales carbon dioxide as part of the breathing process, but it really takes off with his use of the combustion process. Burning fuel to release its stored energy results in chemical reactions which include the formation of gaseous by-products. If the fuel is pure hydrogen burned in air (and if the temperature and pressure of combustion were high enough), the products of combustion are heat, light, water vapor, and possibly some nitrogen oxides. The water vapor might find its way into raindrops, but the raindrops would not be highly acidified by the addition of that particular water.

If the fuel is a pure hydrocarbon, a combination of hydrogen and carbon, such as methane, the principal by-products are the oxides of carbon and water vapor. Again, under suitable conditions of temperature and pressure such as are found in the internal combustion engine, some of the nitrogen in the air involved in the combustion can also be oxidized to form gaseous oxides of nitrogen. If the hydrocarbon fuel contains compounds of sulfur, as in the case of most coal and oil used in the production of electric power, the combustion by-products become considerably more acidifying and disagreeable.

The addition of the oxides of sulfur to the list of chemical by-products usually qualifies the fumes to be called *noxious*. Noxious fumes can also be formed when sulfide ores are oxidized or roasted to separate the metallic component from the bound sulfur. We can think of the roasting of ores as a close relative of fuel combustion when considering the chemistry of acid rain.

3.

The Environmental Implications of Acid Rain

Acid rain has been closely associated with some very undesirable recent changes in our environment. Acid rain has contributed its water to lakes and streams that formerly teemed with aquatic life. Acid rain has fallen on forests that now abound with dead and dying trees. Acid rain has bathed eroding stone buildings, deteriorating statues, and corroding metal bridges. There isn't much basis for a reasonable person's disagreeing with the above statements. Disagreements arise rapidly, however, when close association is equated with causal relationships.

In 1984, before a Senate committee holding hearings on acid rain, Dr. Ellis B. Cowling's testimony included the following statement:

"It is widely assumed (and I think correctly so) that air pollutants and/or acid deposition are among the stress factors that have caused or are contributing to the symptoms observed in the forests of Central Europe. But this idea is still only an hypothesis; it has not been proven unequivocally."

This statement can serve as a model for reasonable discussion of the present state of knowledge about acid rain's impact on the environment. It shows evidence of carefully considered thought, presented with proper qualifications. Notice that Dr. Cowling did not say, "It is widely recognized that acid rain is the cause of the death of forests in Central Europe."

There are several very significant points included in Cowling's statement that deserve our careful consideration.

1) His statement recognizes that an assumption is still just an assumption, even though he considers the assumption to be correct.

2) His statement allows for the possibility that air pollutants other than the acid formers may be operating as stress factors. Ozone, which is a tri-atomic form of oxygen, is an air pollutant that is very active chemically. It could turn out to be the cause of some of the environmental damage presently being attributed to acid rain. Wouldn't it be a sad development to discover, after costly means of curbing acid rain had been put in place, that trees were still dying because ozone had not been properly considered in the fix?

3) Notice that stress factors are mentioned as possibly contributing to symptoms. A stress factor may contribute to the death of a tree, or any other living organism, by reducing its ability to withstand attack by disease or unfavorable climatic change. The stress factor may or may not be, by itself, the cause of death.

4) Notice his use of the word hypothesis. An hypothesis is a conjecture that accounts, within a theory or ideational framework, for a set of facts. It can be used as a basis for further investigation, but it remains an educated guess until further investigation produces proof. Many of the hypotheses currently being offered concerning the environmental impacts of acid rain are very reasonable. They probably constitute the best available explanation for observed facts. Most of them may eventually be proven true. But until the proof is in hand, it is wise to remember that many a seemingly-reasonable hypothesis has turned out to be false after being subjected to the test of carefully designed scientific investigation. It would be a good idea to keep this in mind during discussions of the environmental implications of acid rain.

The United States Environmental Protection Agency (EPA) has given a great deal of official attention to the issue of adverse environmental effects of acid rain. In 1984 EPA published an impressive two-volume document *The Acidic Deposition Phenomenon and Its Effects: Critical Assessment Review Papers,* which subsequently acquired the acronym CARP. Volume II of the document, entitled *Effects Sciences,* consists of critical review papers prepared by 42 highly-qualified scientists drawn from universities, national laboratories, and federal agencies. The authors addressed just about every conceivable concern having to do with potential effects of acid rain on the environment. Their review papers, which covered effects on soil systems, vegetation, aquatic chemistry, aquatic biology, health and materials, totalled over 600 pages and made reference to 1,523 published scientific papers.

Does that information make your pulses pound or are you yawning? Breath easily! You aren't about to be assaulted by a detailed discussion of each of the references or, for that matter, each of the review papers. Mention of the sheer bulk of the work is only intended to give you an idea of the breadth of the interest in the subject and the magnitude of the research effort already under way. Fortunately, brief summaries of the critical assessment were provided. Taken together they offer an understandable picture of what is known and what remains to be learned. CARP was updated in August, 1985, to CAD which translates to *The Acidic Deposition Phenomenon and Its Effects: Critical Assessment Document.*

Known and Suspected Effects of Acid Rain on Lakes and Streams The association of acid rain with increases in the acidity of freshwater lakes and streams and an attendant reduction in fish populations was reported in Scandinavia as early as 1959. The acidification turns out to involve more than mere reductions in pH. The water gets clearer, the concentration of metallic ions increases, life on the bottom changes, and eventually the fish decrease in number or disappear completely. Finding out the relationships between these acidification-related developments has required a large number of research studies. Let's turn our attention to the specifics of a few of the environmental concerns which have been carefully studied.

There are many lakes and streams throughout the world that are composed of naturally-acidic waters. These fall into three type categories. The acidity of the first type arises from geothermal activity, the second from decay of organic matter, and the third from acidic bedrock such as granite.

Geothermal activity produces lakes with very high acidity. The acidity results from the oxidation of sulfides to sulfuric acid, aided by the high temperature of the water. pH values as low as 0.9 have been observed in New Zealand, and pH values of 2.0 have been found in springs in Yellowstone Park, Wyoming. Life forms found in such waters are limited to algae, fungi, bacteria, some insects, but no fish.

Brownwater lakes and streams, so-named for their dark color, comprise the second type of naturally-acid water bodies. They are the waters of peat lands, swamps, and rain forests. Their acidity results from organic acids derived from the decay of organic matter.

Brownwater pH values range from 3.5 to 5.0, and their aquatic life forms include plankton, algae, flies and some fish.

The third type of naturally-acid lakes and streams have pH values ranging from 5.5 to 6.5 due to carbonic acid. Such waters support life forms that include plankton, larvae, flies, molluscs, shellfish, and fish.

The naturally-acidic waters provide us with a useful, but not perfect, basis for understanding what levels of acidity various life forms can tolerate when they find themselves impacted by acid rain. The absence of life forms from naturally-acidic water may or may not be due to the acid. The tolerable limits of pH due to pollution-caused acidification that would be inferred from observation of naturally-acidic waters could turn out to be either too low or high. If the fish were stressed by an high aluminum content in the water, they might not survive to as low a pH as they would in the absence of aluminum.

As was mentioned above, observed decreases in fish populations were early triggers of concern about the effects of acid deposition on acquatic ecosystems. Of all the suspected effects of acid rain, the most emotionally charged attention has been directed to its impact on fresh water fish. Perhaps the concern has more to do with the welfare of fishermen than it does the welfare of fish. Altruism, which frequently exists among fishermen does not appear to be primarily directed toward the fish.

The relationship between fish population losses and the acidity of the waters involved has been extensively studied in the United States, Canada, Scandinavia, and Great Britain. Nowhere does increasing acidity appear to have benefited fish. In some places, it appears to have been deadly.

The Adirondack region of New York State has received considerable research attention. Surveys of fish populations and water quality began there in the 1920s and have continued, with varying intensity, to the present time. The region has over 2,800 ponds and lakes and about 5,800 miles of fishing streams. Twenty-two fish species are native. Acidification has been significant. Surveys performed in the 1970s revealed that 82 percent of the high-elevation lakes had no fish and 48 percent of all lakes were fishless. It does not follow, however, that acid rain is clearly to blame. Some of the lakes never did have fish. For the others, where fish populations formerly existed but do not now, demonstration that acidification is the cause remains a requirement.

Loss of fish populations in the mountain lakes along the north shore of Lake Huron has been related to intense acidification from a smelter at Sudbury, Ontario. The lakes in the area were studied during a 15 year period in the 1960s and 1970s. The acidification observed has been described as rapid, but the decline and disappearance of fish has been described both as gradual and drastic.

The relation between acidity and success of salmon fishery in Nova Scotia has also been carefully studied. Catch data over the period 1936 to 1980 were used with the first five years serving as the standard for comparison. The 22 streams for which data were available were subdivided (according to the 1980 acidity of their waters) into a low-acid group of twelve (pH greater than 5.0) and a high-acid group of ten (pH less than or equal to 5.0). While fishing success varied from year to year, the low-acid group exhibited neither an increasing nor a decreasing catch trend. The high-acid group, on the other hand, showed a decreasing trend over the period of record, with catch success in 1980 a mere 4 percent of the level for the first five years of the record. Fortunately these drastic decreases are not applicable to other salmon fishery areas in Canada.

The mechanisms that are considered to be possible causes of fish population decreases are: reduction of the quality and quantity of food, fish kills during high-acid incidents, and insufficient reproduction to provide new recruits. Of these,the food mechanism is probably the least important since fish seem to have flexible minds when it comes to deciding what prey to dine on. When acidification reduces the population of a particular prey species, fish appear able to switch to different prey. This may explain the bewildering array of flies and other artificial lures that show up on the display racks of sporting-goods shops.

A phenomenon that has been widely observed is a sudden, intense drop in pH that occurs in streams when the first meltwater arrives from the winter snowpack. This sudden increase in acidity can cause damaging stress to fish that are in a weakened condition from overwintering or from spawning. Females may fail to reproduce as a result of acid-related stress. The early stages of fish life are more sensitive to low pH than are the adult fish so even brief periods of high acidity can reduce larval and fingerling populations. The arrival of later meltwater may raise the pH back up to values that fish can tolerate, but that may happen too late. It doesn't help much to have a tolerable average acidity level if irreparable damage has occurred during a high-acid episode. The sudden surge of acidification that accompanied the first spring snowmelt in Norway, in 1975, was associated with fish kills of thousands of adult trout; however, such reports of dead and dying fish in acid-stressed waters are rare.

The failure of the reproductive process to provide sufficient recruits is the most generally accepted acid-related explanation of declining fish populations. Clearly more research is needed to pin down answers to the questions about how acid causes decreases in fish populations.

Research is going forward on three approaches for improving the odds of fish surviving in acidified waters. Genetic screening offers promise of identifying the acid-tolerant strains within a particular species. Selective breeding for acid tolerance is being investigated with some results showing promise. The third approach involves conditioning or acclimation of fish before they are introduced into heavily-acidified waters. There is some evidence that this can be done, but much remains to be learned.

The adverse impacts of acidification of lakes and streams relate to other animals beside fish and fishermen. The well-being of birds that prey on fish and aquatic insects can be affected, as can the welfare of mammals that feed on aquatic plants.

Known and Suspected Effects of Acid Rain on Forest Resources Forest decline is widespread in Europe and in North America. But the nature of the decline is not uniform. Norway spruce is behaving differently in Norway than in Germany. Some forests are dying from the top down, others from the bottom up. In the eastern United States, high-elevation forests of red spruce have experienced mortality that has been described as massive while other forest trees in the same region are not known to be suffering a similar fate. Apparently healthy trees are growing alongside trees that have already died.

The dead and dying trees in Germany's forests, such as the famous Black Forest, may be the best publicized of all the suspected terrestrial effects of acid rain. Television reporters on prime-time news programs have repeatedly discussed acid rain as their cameras pan across desolate scenes of formerly thriving Black Forest. Often the reporters have demonstrated their erudition by confidently pronouncing "Waldsterben": the German word for the forest decline which is affecting many of the forests of West Germany. Acid rain is confidently mentioned as the cause of the desolation, usually without qualification or reservation. If you have watched these newscasts and accepted what they presented as the whole truth and nothing but the truth, you may be surprised to read the next few paragraphs.

Professor Bernhard Ulrich is a member of the faculty of the Institute of Soil Science and Forest Nutrition at the University of Gottingen, in Germany. Speaking at the conference on Saving the Forests: International Pollution and Environmental Responsibility, held in Berlin at the Aspen Institute in September, 1983, Professor Ulrich said:

"It is a matter of fact that there is no scientific consensus about the causes of the forest damage, even if there is general agreement about the importance of air pollutants. It seems that this lack of consensus is not due to missing data, but to a lacking acceptance of different scientific schools of thought. This leads to scientific statements which seem to contradict each other and this leads to confusion."

A similar message was delivered in the February, 1984, hearings on acid rain held by the U.S. Senate Committee on Environment and Public Works. Dr. Arthur H. Johnson, an associate professor at the University of Pennsylvania, testified that:

"There is currently no consensus among the scientific community about the involvement of acid deposition in the anomalous growth and mortality patterns observed here and in central Europe. I stress that there is no clear evidence that acid rain is involved, and there is no clear evidence that acid rain is not involved. It is an open question."

Some results of long-term research projects may give you further pause to wonder about the confidence with which forest decline is being attributed to acid rain. In Norway, forest researchers exposed lodgepole pine, Norway spruce, silver birch, and Scots pine trees to several different acid treatments ranging from pH 2.0 to pH 6.0. After seven years, the conclusion was reached that the data gave "no substantial evidence of effects on tree growth at acidity levels presently found in precipitation." There have been similar research results in the United States. Treatments of trees with simulated acid rain have indicated effects on growth that have ranged from positive to negative with some treatments showing no effect at all. Longer-term exposure might well give different results, but at the very least these results suggest that caution should be applied when jumping to conclusions about acid rain's contribution to forest decline.

The jury is still out in the case of forest decline versus acid rain. No one can say with certainty that acid rain is innocent of killing forests, nor can a guilty verdict be rendered at the present time that will stand up on appeal.

Finding out what effects acid rain does have on forests and other vegetation will require extensive research effort on other things beside trees. Much remains to be learned about the effects of acid rain on the soils in which trees and other plants put down their roots. How soil performs as the medium for plant growth depends on such things as the chemical, physical,and biological nature of the soil. Work in these areas has been under way for a long time. Agricultural scientists were among the early acid-rain workers. They were looking at acid rain's possible positive contributions to plant growth.

The following conclusions about the effects of acid deposition on soils were drawn by the soils scientists who performed the EPA-sponsored critical assessment review of the present state of knowledge:

• Soils amended in agricultural practice will not be harmed by acidic deposition.

• Soil acidification is a natural process in humid regions. It is obvious that acidic deposition contributes to this process; however, at current levels, it is a minor contribution.

• Most soils that were easily acidified are already acid; therefore soils likely to become perceptibly more acid due to deposition are limited.

• The availability of sulfur and nitrogen to plants will be enhanced by their presence in the deposition. Because nitrogen limitations are so common and cation limitations are rare in forests of the United States it seems likely that nitric acid inputs generally will be beneficial. Exceptions may occur on sites with adequate or excessive nitrogen supplies.

• The long-term effect (i.e. over decades or centuries) of acidic deposition can be expected to remove cations from forest soils, but it is not clear whether this will reduce available cations and enhance acidification of soils.

• Assessing acidic deposition effects on forest nutrient status involves quantifying amounts of inputs involved and the sulfur, nitrogen, and cation nutrient status of specific sites. It cannot be stated that forest ecosystems, in general, respond to acidic deposition in a single predictable way.

• The most likely damage to forest productivity, and the one for which some evidence exists, would result from aluminum toxicity.

• The increased mobility of aluminum in uncultivated, acid soils is probably the most significant effect of acidic deposition on soils as they influence terrestrial plant growth and aquatic systems.

• Based upon shorter-term studies, we can expect that increased hydrogen-ion loading will generally cause increased loss of cation and organic components from forest litter. Over the longer term it appears that the biologically-mediated mineralization of organic matter in forest soils will be only slightly inhibited by acidic deposition. (Less than 1 to 2 percent decrease in decomposition rate). In general, experimental data suggest that decomposition processes are relatively unaffected by simulated precipitation pH's above 3.0. Thus, unless average precipitation inputs were to drop to pH 3.0 or below, significant impacts of acidic deposition on litter decomposition in natural systems are not expected.

• Soil microbial activity may be significantly influenced near the surface if inputs are great enough to affect pH or nutrient availability.

Acid Rain and Vegetation

The impact of acid rain on vegetation, particularly agricultural crops, has been studied in a number of different ways. These have ranged from laboratory experiments carried out in sophisticated, controlled-environment chambers to field tests under actual farming circumstances. Concepts of experimental design have ranged from simple experiments which related crop yield to the pH of simulated acid rain to consideration of the inter-relations among the many factors that can influence plant growth. Because differences in experimental design can produce differences in research results, it is chancy to try to generalize statements about what past research says about the effect of acid rain on crop production. It is also a fact that many crops have not yet been adequately studied. Indications to date are that the yield and growth of most of the crops which have been tested showed no response to treatments with simulated acid rain at pH's of 4.2 or less. A few showed negative responses to treatments, and others showed positive responses.

The potential effects on vegetation that have been hypothesized are more numerous than are the effects that have actually been observed. Eight possible effects include: leaching of nutrients from foliage; increased permeability of leaf surfaces to toxic substances, water, and disease agents; altered reproductive processes; altered root-zone relationships; erosion of protective waxes; degradation of chlorophyll; premature aging; and general alteration of the physiology of the plant. Only the first has been observed in the field. That fact does not rule out the possible validity of the other seven. What it reflects is the extreme difficulty of isolating the effect of a specific stress factor, like acid rain, from among the many other stress factors that can affect a crop. As a result, little is known about the effects of acid deposition on agricultural crops.

There is some evidence, however, that suggests that there is a crop response to acid deposition. The results of controlled-environment experiments conducted on 34 crop varieties are interesting. Seventeen crop varieties showed no effect, six showed decreased yield, eight showed increased yields, and three were fence-sitters. The three indecisive ones exhibited both increased and decreased yields, depending on hydrogen ion concentration and other conditions of exposure. The most convincing evidence that crop productivity might be affected by acid deposition comes from studies of a soybean variety called Amsoy. Consistent decreases in yields have resulted from treating this soybean variety with simulated acid rain.

Many crops have not yet been adequately studied as to their sensitivity to acid rain. The studies that have been performed leave any person who expects to find pat, definitive answers sorely disappointed. The question of whether acid rain falling on crops produces greater disadvantages than benefits is not well-answered by available evidence. The effects of acid rain on crop production are expected to be small in comparison to the effects of natural stresses.

Some of the conclusions about vegetative response to acid deposition which were reached in EPA's critical assessment review were:

• Leaf structure may play two roles in the sensitivity of foliar tissues to acidic deposition: 1) leaf morphology selectively enhance or minimize surface retention of incident precipitation, and 2) specific cells of the epidermal surface may be initial sites of foliar injury.

• Leaching mechanisms are major factors in nutrient cycling in terrestrial ecosystems and are critical to the redistribution of nutrients within these cycles.

Under laboratory conditions gaseous pollutant combinations and integration have well-defined effects. However, ozone is the single most important gas pollutant to plant life located at great distances from the industrial and urban origin of nitrogen oxides and hydrocarbon precursors. Direct effects due to ozone include foliar injury and growth and yield reductions in numerous agronomic and forest species.

• A review of the evidence on the interaction of forest trees, insect, and microbial pests, and acidic deposition does not allow generalized statements concerning stimulation or restriction of biotic stress agents or their activities by acidic deposition. Certain studies report stimulation of pest activities associated with acidic deposition treatment while other studies report restriction of pest activities following treatment.

• Performance and longevity (persistence) of certain pesticides depend on pH of the systems to which these pesticides are applied or in which they ultimately reside; thus it it likely that acidic deposition will have significant but limited effects.

• At present we have no direct evidence that acidic deposition currently limits forest growth in either North America or Europe, but we do have indications that tree growth reductions are occurring, principally in the coniferous species that have been examined to date, that these reductions are rather widespread, and that they occur in regions where rainfall acidity is generally quite high or pH is low (pH 4.3) for an annual average.

• Controlled environment studies indicate that the deposition of acidic and acidifying substances may have stimulatory, detrimental, or no apparent effects on plant growth and development. Response depends on species sensitivity, plant life cycle stage, and the nature of exposure to acidity. Some simulation studies have indicated that acidic deposition may result in simultaneous stimulation of growth and the occurrence of visible foliar injury.

• The majority of crop species studies in field and controlled-environment experiments exhibited no effect on growth or yield as a result of exposure to simulated acidic precipitation (pH 3.0). In a few studies, though, growth and yield of certain crops were negatively affected by acidic deposition, others exhibited positive responses.

• A crop's net response to acidic deposition result from a combination of the positive effects of sulfur and nitrogen fertilization, the negative effects of acidity, and the interactions between these factors and other environmental conditions such as soil type and presence of other pollutants.

• Available experimental results do not appear to indicate that the negative effects of acidic precipitation outweigh the positive effects; however, many crops and agricultural systems have not been properly or adequately studied.

Effects of Acid Rain on Nonliving Materials In addressing the issue of damage to materials, it becomes necessary to distinguish between the effects of acidic precipitation and the other forms of acidic impact that are usually lumped under the catch-all of acid rain. Historic documents, leather-bound books, oil paintings and antique tapestries located on the inside of libraries and museums don't run much risk of being rained on, but that doesn't mean that they are safe from deterioration. The gaseous forms of acidic air pollution have attacked many valuable museum pieces so drastically that expensive scrubbers have been installed on museum buildings to forestall further deterioration.

It has also been observed that exterior statuary, located so that it is exposed to air pollution but sheltered from the rain, has experienced greater damage than similar statues that are exposed to both rainfall and air pollution. The gaseous and particulate acid that damaged the sheltered statues was evidently flushed off of the unsheltered statues by the washing action of the probably acidic rainfall.

The list of materials subject to damage from air pollution is lengthy. Metals, building stone, ceramics, glass, paints, organic coatings, paper, photographic materials, textiles, dyes, leather, and rubber have all been subject to adverse impacts. In the case of rubber ozone is the principle culprit, but the acid-forming oxides of sulfur and nitrogen are the principal causes of damage to the other materials listed.

Not all the damage attributed to acid rain has been caused by acid rain. The clearest example of this has to do with "Cleopatra's Needle." This granite obelisk, moved from Egypt to New York's Central Park in 1881, has sustained damage. Acid rain was once the suspected cause of the deterioration. The venerable *New York Times* reported in 1978 that, "The city's atmosphere has done more damage than three and a half millennia in the desert, and in another dozen years the hieroglyphs will probably disappear." A subsequent careful study revealed that the damage was due to advanced salt decay coupled with New York's high humidity and some misguided attempts at preservation.

The conclusions reached in EPA's critical assessment review include:

• Several scenarios and mechanisms exist for damage to [non-living] materials from acidic deposition, including both long-range transport and local-source emissions.

• Without question acidic deposition causes significant incremental damage to [non-living] materials beyond that caused by natural environmental phenomena.

• Because very few research efforts have attempted to isolate the effects of specific acidic deposition scenarios, it is presently impossible to determine quantitatively if any one scenario is more important than another in causing material damage.

• Reliable cost estimates for material damage from acidic deposition are at present fragmentary because they deal with only selected material systems or linked geographical areas.

• Damage to cultural property from acidic deposition is a complex problem because of the high value placed upon such objects, their often irreplaceable nature, and the wide range of [non-living] material types represented. Highest priority should be placed on identifying and quantifying actual and potential damage to such artifacts and developing methods to prevent damage.

• Further research directed at isolating damage caused by specific acidic deposition processes and identifying those processes that are most important and/or amenable to control is needed.

• Studies that accurately assess damage costs associated with acidic deposition are needed.

• Further research is needed in the development of mitigating measures such as reliable surface protection systems when damage has already been observed and when protection cannot wait for improvement in air quality.

From the above discussions it is probably clear that present knowledge does not permit precise pinning down of many of the hypothesized acid rain effects on the environment. Acid rain does appear to have some impact on fish, trees, lakes, and materials, even though the exact causes and all the interactive mechanisms are not completely understood.

Economic Implications of Acid Rain

Acid rain is impacting our economy in many way. This is a defensible statement whether or not all of the many hypothesized acid-rain-related environmental impacts turn out to be valid. Even the perception that acid rain might be a problem has resulted in searches for alternative control strategies which involve an added economic burden on society. A sizeable, continuing economic impact has resulted from the multimillion dollar acid-rain research effort which some consider to be a government-sponsored effort to substitute endless study for corrective action. The process of finding out what acid rain does and doesn't do has an economic impact, as does the hectic scramble to figure out what can be done and what should be done to protect against unacceptable outcomes.

A whole book has been written on the economic implications of acid rain. It is entitled *Acid Rain — Economic Assessment.* It was edited by Paulette Mandelbaum and published by Plenum Press in 1985. The book consists of the proceedings of a conference on acid rain that was held December 4-6, 1984, in Washington, D.C. The conference was sponsored by the Acid Rain Information Clearinghouse and brought together experts in economic research and analysis. It is clear from the papers presented and the discussions that followed the presentations that a lot more remains to be learned about the economic implications of acid rain. Not all the uncertainties are scientific in nature.

Economic analysis is often employed to assist in judging the merits of a proposed action. By examining detailed analyses of the costs and benefits associated with implementing a decision to act, one can get an idea of the merit of the proposal. If the benefits of the proposed action exceed the costs, the action is usually advocated as being worth the doing. This analytical procedure can be made to seem very straightforward and objective, and occasionally it really is. Often, however, it is not. How effective the cost-benefit analysis turns out to be depends, in large measure, on how well the available basic data reflect reality and how close to the mark are the required assumptions.

Unfortunately, where acid rain is concerned the basic data currently available are sparse and dubious, and assumptions are the order of the day. Even though some thoughtfully designed and carefully-executed damage-assessment studies have been made, it is well to remember that there is an unavoidable element of guesswork involved in the best of them.

The benefits expected from reducing the damages caused by acid rain have been studied thoughtfully by Thomas D. Crocker of the University of Wyoming. He was a participant in the conference that gave rise to the book mentioned above. In a paper he published in 1983, entitled "What Economics Can Currently Say About The Benefits of Acid Deposition Control," Crocker provided a list of six steps that are required to perform a proper economic assessment of acid-deposition impacts. Crocker then commented, "Neither natural science nor economic knowledge allows completion of any one of these steps. In some instances, only empirical knowledge is lacking; in others, no organizing principles or theories to guide the acquisition of empirical knowledge have yet been widely adopted."

Crocker identified his own estimate for 1978 of $5 billion maximum annual benefit from controlling acid deposition as being no more than an educated guess. The uncertainty about acid-rain effects is perhaps at a minimum where effects on non-living materials is concerned. There isn't much room for doubt that acid deposition, acting in concert with other air pollution constituents, has caused damage to a number of natural and man-made surfaces. Marble statues, painted surfaces, and zinc-coated gutters are examples. Much of what has been written about evaluating economic costs of air pollution applies to the narrower topic of acid rain. Significant monetary losses are sustained when the service life of some material is shortened due to unanticipated acid corrosion. A related economic impact results from the selection of acid-resistant materials that are more costly than those that could be used if there were no acid rain.

Placing a Dollar Value: A Difficult Task

The following discussion of the difficulty of assessing economic costs of air pollution appeared in the previously cited *Critical Assessment Review Papers.*

"The possibility of determining the economic costs of air pollution's damaging effects has long attracted environmental policy makers. If reliable cost estimates could be developed for such effects in relation to the pollution levels that produced them, it then might be possible to compare the costs for achieving various levels of air quality control through emission control with the cost savings from reduced damage — a significant step toward developing cost-benefit relationships for air pollution control." The many attempts to estimate costs associated with air-pollution induced damage have recently been summarized by Yocum and Stankunas (1980), in *A Review of Air Pollutant Damage to Materials,* (A report to EPA, Environmental Criteria and Assessment Office (NATO-CCMS Program), Research Triangle Park, N.C.) Without exception, all of the generalized estimates of material damage costs related to all types of air pollution existing at the time of this review are of questionable value. According to the report, the reasons for this include the following:

• As was pointed out earlier, it is usually not possible to isolate the specific portion of damage and, therefore, the associated costs created by a given air pollution effect.

• Improper assumptions and inaccurate estimates of the quantities of [non-living] materials in place and exposed to pollutants.

• Unrealistic or improper scenarios of use, repair, and replacement of materials susceptible to air pollution damage, together with improper or inaccurate assignment of costs to the scenarios.

• Incomplete knowledge of substitution scenarios where more expensive material systems may replace more susceptible materials.

• Inadequate knowledge of the exposure conditions of susceptible materials — for example, coexistence of pollutants with other environmental effects such as moisture and temperature, and the physical aspects of exposure such as orientation and degree of sheltering.

• A recent study by Stankunas et al. (1981) has addressed many of the above difficulties. (Stankunas, A.R., D.F. Unites, and E.F. McCarthy. 1981. Air pollution damage to manmade materials: physical and economic estimates. Final report to the Electric Power Research Institute, Palo Alto, CA, EPRI Project No. RP 1004. (to be published)). In this study the quantities of potentially-susceptible materials were determined within 357 randomly selected 100 x 100 foot-square areas covering the Boston metropolitan area. Teams of observers using survey techniques determined the areas of various types of exposed painted surface, bare metal of several types, brick, stone, and concrete, and several other types of surfaces. Of the 357 areas selected, 183 were found to contain man-made structures. The total area of each material found at the survey sites was extrapolated to the entire Boston metropolitan area. Then, using air-quality records for SO_2 in the Boston area, together with humidity data and published air-pollution-damage functions for given materials, the researchers computed the total damage to a given material for the entire area. In the case of painted surfaces, assumptions were made on the average thickness of typical paint films. Then costs were assigned to the increase in painting frequency, based on the SO_2-related increase in paint erosion, to arrive at a total SO_2-related damage cost to paint in the Boston metropolitan area. The excess painting costs for the Boston metropolitan area attributable to SO_2 damage for the year 1978 were estimated to be $31.3 million. This is equivalent to a per-capita cost between $11 and $12. Costs for zinc-coated materials were two orders of magnitude lower.

The phrase "two orders of magnitude lower" may require a bit of translation. It is a piece of scientist talk that borders on the esoteric. "Orders of magnitude" is the way a scientist compares the size, mass, value, or whatever is of concern about two entities. If the costs of two items are said to differ by two orders of magnitude, that means that the cost of one is 100 times the cost of the other. If you are wondering where the number two comes in, recall our earlier discussion of exponents. In exponential form 100 is 10^2 and 1 is 10^0. Since the exponents of 10 differ by 2 the numbers differ by two orders of magnitude. Isn't that fascinating? Or would you have preferred that the comparison between damages to painted surfaces and damages to zinc-coatings had been reported as "zinc costs were 1/100 of paint costs"? You are not alone.

Let's leave scientific esoterica behind now and get back to economic impacts.

A study has been made of estimated costs of damage to Tennessee Valley Authority (TVA) zinc-coated transmission towers and to galvanized roofing, siding, and guttering. TVA's towers would require an annual maintenance cost of approximately 0.0132 mills/-

kilowatt hours if the SO_2 levels were allowed to reach the ambient air-quality standard of 80 micrograms per cubic meter. Using this same air-quality standard a per capita cost of $1.80 for damage to galvanized roofing, siding, and guttering was computed for the year 1980. The cost drops to between $0.60 and $1.50 with the best estimate being $1.05 per-capita for SO_2 concentrations of 30 micrograms per cubic meter.

"Acid Deposition and the Materials Damage Question" is the title of an informative article by Stephen R. Scholle published in *Environment,* Volume 25, No. 8 in 1983. He reported that the problem of degradation of marble, sandstone, and concrete due to acidic air pollutants is not a new one. While the phenomenon of material damage has become a topic of public-policy debate only recently, the problem was observed in Elizabethan times. He acknowledged that the exact extent to which various materials are affected is still largely undetermined, but he did provide some interesting estimates of damage.

Scholle's estimates of material damage from acid deposition have been summarized as follows:

Material Damages	**(U.S. dollars)**	**Year of Study**
Paint (U.S.)	$35.0 billion	1970
Galvanized Steel (U.S.)	$335,000	1983
Zinc-coated transmission towers (U.S.)	0.0028-0.0132 mills/kwh	1982
Medieval stained glass (W. Germany)	$100 million over 10 years	1983
West German Bronze monuments	$1.6 million annually	1983
Cologne Cathedral	$1-$20 million annually	1983
Other German Cathedrals and Castles	$2 million annually	1983
Ancient Roman Monuments	$200 million	1980

Acid Rain and Recreation Another important economic implication of acid rain has to do with its impact on income generated by the recreational activities of sport fishing, camping, and tourism. Very large amounts of money are involved. Minnesota's governor, Rudy Perpich, in testimony before the 1984 Senate hearings on acid rain stated, "As far as tourism is concerned, one study shows that the first signs of lake acidification in the [Boundary Water Canoe Area] BWCA could result in an annual loss of about $40 million per year and 3,000 jobs. That represents only a fraction of the total tourism and sport fishing industry in Minnesota. We are very proud of our beautiful environment in Minnesota; the many lakes, the forests, Voyaguers National Park, and the Boundary Waters Canoe Area Wilderness. So, acid deposition is an economic, environmental, and emotional issue to our state."

An analysis of the damages caused to recreational fisheries in the Adirondack region has been made by Frederick C. Menz and John K. Mullen. They place the fishery losses between $1,700,000 and $3,200,000, expressed in 1982 dollars. They placed a net economic value of $35.33 on each angler-day for the entire fishery, with lake fishery valued at $39.52 per angler-day. They conclude their report with the statement, "At the present time, there is no generally-accepted procedure for dealing adequately with these situations within the framework of cost-benefit analysis."

C.S. Russell and W.J. Vaughan published in 1982 their finding that nationwide fulfillment of best-available acid-deposition control technology standards would generate about $750 million in 1978 freshwater fishing benefits.

David Stockman, first director of the Office of Management and Budget in the Reagan administration, attracted quite a bit of attention and editorial comment during his tenure by making eyebrow-raising statements that were eagerly reported in the press. One of his classics had to do with his calculations, made in early 1984, that the acid-rain-control program proposed by William D. Ruckelshaus, administrator of the Environmental Protection Agency, would cost $6000 per pound on every fish saved and in the Northeast the figure would rise to $66,000 a pound. It isn't clear how far into his cheek Mr. Stockman had inserted his tongue when he made that pronouncement. It is unlikely that reliable fish population figures for the nation's acid-sensitive lakes were readily available to him. Whether or not he intended his calculations to be taken seriously, it is clear that the figures reported for Minnesota, and for the nation as a whole, suggest the reasonableness of considering sizeable commitments to acid rain control.

The United States forest products industry would seem to have a clear economic stake in the relation of acid rain to forest decline. A study which used the 1978 dollar as a basis for evaluating losses found that an observed five percent forest decline represented an annual loss of $600 million in timber production alone. When other forest-related items, such as outdoor recreation, water storage, and wildlife habitat were included in the analysis, the estimate of annual damage increased by an additional $1 billion.You may find it somewhat surprising, then, to learn that a representative of major forest interest has been in the forefront of those speaking out against rushing to control acid rain.

International Paper Company owns 6.6 million acres of land in the United States, 1.6 million acres of which are in the Northeast and 1.1 million of those are located in Maine. Dr. Ely Gonick, senior vice president for technology of International Paper Company ,presented his paper entitled "Acid Rain — A Forest Industry View" to the 1984 Senate hearings. In it he presented evidence that the pH of forest litter under conifers in Maine will typically run 3.0 - 3.5 which is an acidity level ten times greater than the pH 4.3 acid rain observed in the same area. He quoted a finding based on an analysis of meteorological data that severe drought in the late 1950's was a much more probable cause of red spruce decline at Camel's Hump (New Hampshire) than was acid rain. Dr. Gonick stated:

" We, in the forest products industry, have a very strong interest in knowing whether a reduction in acid deposition will affect forest productivity. If it [acid rain] is harmful, we need to know how harmful, and what remedies are needed and their cost, for we cannot afford to lose our raw material supply, but if acid deposition has little effect on the forest and waters, as we suspect, we should not have to incur costs to control acid deposition. It is clear, at this time, there is no significant data that shows acid deposition hurts trees. I think we should defer legislation until we can determine that there is real and significant adverse effects that would be remedied by a control program."

Concerns about acid rain stand to impact the economy of the coal mining industry and the coal transporting industry. The impetus to reduce emissions of sulfur dioxide by 50 percent, the target reduction usually discussed as being necessary, has triggered consideration of fuel switching. Although there are fuels that have no sulfur content at all, such as hydrogen and methanol, most of the attention is being paid to possible substitution of low-sulfur coal for high-sulfur coal. While there are deposits of low-sulfur coal being mined in the eastern United States, most eastern coal has a high-sulfur content. There are large deposits of low-sulfur coal in the western states of Utah, Wyoming and Montana. Pollution abatement laws already on the books have forced the eastern coal-producing state of Pennsylvania to import 15 million tons of coal from other states annually. According to James Scahill, executive vice president of the Pennsylvania Coal Mining Association, this coal importation has resulted in the loss of over 4000 permanent mining jobs and between 10,000 and 20,000 supporting jobs.

A study by Pennsylvania State University of the impact of reducing sulfur dioxide emission in compliance with bills that have been considered by Congress would involve loss of 12,000 jobs in Pennsylvania, 21,000 jobs in Ohio and 24,000 jobs in West Virginia. When you consider that West Virginia already has 40,000 coal miners without jobs, it is easy to understand why further job losses of the order of 24,000 would not be viewed casually. Wyoming has replaced West Virginia as the second largest producer of coal in the United States. Wyoming coal is low-sulfur coal.

The electric utility industry is a major factor in the acid-rain drama. It burns large quantities of coal, emits large quantities of both sulfur dioxide and nitrogen oxides, and it stands to experience a heavy economic impact whatever acid-rain related fixes are eventually brought to bear. Fortunately, or unfortunately, depending on whether your relationship to your friendly local electric utility is that of stockholder and ratepayer, or just ratepayer, much of that economic impact will get passed on to the rate payers. The people who get their electricity from the Tennessee Valley Authority will have an opportunity to share in defraying the cost of a $927 million investment already made and an annualized cost of about $346 million resulting from measures taken to reduce sulfur dioxide emissions 56 percent. The Southern Electric System, which is an investor-owned utility, burns between 30 and 35 million tons of coal per year and figures the minimum cost of complying with currently - considered sulfur dioxide reduction requirements at $850 million per year in 1984 dollars.

The economic and social implications of the acid-rain issue may be the real reasons that the problem remains unsolved after years of debate. Even after the scientific uncertainties are reduced to the fullest extent possible, the uncertainties of economics and sociology will still have to be addressed. In the next chapter we will look at some of the social implications of acid rain that are not primarily economic in nature.

The Social Implications of Acid Rain

A full discussion of the social implication of acid rain should include consideration of the direct impacts on society that result from acid rain and the indirect impacts that result from society's concerns about acid rain. The physical results of acid rain's impact on the environment have a social impact to the extent that quality of life is affected by the changes in the environment. Concerns about possible effects of acid rain, whether they turn out to be valid or invalid, also have an impact on the quality of life and on the economy when the concerns become strong enough to motivate corrective actions. Whenever acid rain's impact affects the economy there is an inescapable concomitant impact on society. Although it is possible to discuss economic implications as if they constitute a self-contained subject, they are not an entity unto themselves.

There is a growing concern that acid rain might have serious impacts on health. There are well-documented cases of air-pollution-caused health effects, but health effects that arise either directly or indirectly from acid rain have not yet been demonstrated insofar as human populations are concerned. This is a true statement if the words "acid rain" are taken to apply only to precipitation that is acid. If dry deposition of sulfur dioxide is considered to be part of the total acid rain picture, another view develops. According to Dr. Alfred Munzer, a lung specialist and spokesman for the American Lung Association, there are 16 million Americans — asthmatics, and hay fever sufferers included — who are hyper-reactive to sulfur dioxide. Concentrations as low as 1.0 to 2.5 parts per million can cause bronchoconstriction in healthy people. (Incidentally, Dr. Munzer reports that the human lung occupies a surface area the size of a tennis court. I find that fact fascinating!)

A health concern related to acid rain has to do with the element mercury. Inorganic mercury gets into rain and snow by the same atmospheric processes that produce acid rain. Bacteria found in the sediments of natural-water bodies have the ability to convert inorganic mercury to the form of organic mercury known as "methyl mercury." It is one of the most hazardous chemicals to be found in the natural environment, insofar as human health is concerned. It is considered possible that the acid in acid rain may play a role in making mercury more of a threat than it would be otherwise. The form of organic mercury produced by bacteria may be pH dependent. Fish pick up organic mercury in their diet and store it in their muscle tissue. A human diet, rich in fish that accumulate large amounts of mercury, could lead to the accumulation of toxic levels of mercury in the human body. This is a possibility that warrants more attention. Accumulations of toxic metals could also result from eating fruits and vegetables which have been irrigated with water containing the metals. Recently, tragic developments at the Kesterson Wildlife Refuge in the Central Valley of California have been covered on national television. Selenium, found in high concentrations in the effluent from a large irrigation project, is blamed for death and deformity among the inhabitants of the refuge. The case made against selenium was so strong that environmental interests succeeded in closing down the irrigation project.

Another concern related to acid rain has to do with the quality of drinking water. Water which has been collected into cisterns from acid-rain-impacted drainage areas is suspect. If there are people whose health has been impaired by drinking water derived from acid rain or whose diet frequently exposes them to high levels of toxic metals transported in acid rain, they have not yet been identified. But the absence of such a demonstration to date should not be equated to the absence of risk. The concerns about acid rain are too recent to have allowed for full investigation of these issues.

An issue has been raised concerning a possible link between acid rain and the dreaded Alzheimer's disease. It is known that aluminum, a very abundant element in our environment, can be leached from the soil by water. It is reasonable to expect that the more acid in the water moving through the soil mantle, the greater would be its aluminum uptake. Research performed by Dr. Leopold Liss at Ohio State University School of Medicine has related aluminum intake to the formation of neurofibrillary tangles in the brain cells of rabbits.

Similar tangles are characteristic of Alzheimer's disease. Since humans are exposed to aluminum in food, water, and dust from childhood, it is Dr. Liss' hypothesis that the human body has a protective barrier against aluminum. If this barrier is faulty, aluminum can enter the brain and cause degeneration of the brains cells called neurons. He has had some success in lowering aluminum levels in the serum of experimental subjects by administering sodium fluoride.

I called the national office of an organization dedicated to helping the families of victims of Alzheimer's disease and asked for current information on the importance of limiting aluminum intake. I was told that their position on aluminum is that it is not known whether aluminum is a cause of Alzheimer's disease or not. When I asked if they advised impacted families to limit aluminum intake by using deionized water for drinking and cooking, I was told that they leave that entirely to the family to decide.

If serious health effects from acid rain are detected in the foreseeable future, it is likely that they will be direct rather than indirect effects. To date there has been more thought given to possible mechanisms for direct effects than to mechanisms of indirect effect.

The conclusions reached in the *Critical Assessment Review Papers* relative to health effects are as follows:

• No adverse human health effects have been documented as being a consequence of metal mobilization by acidic deposition. On the other hand, interest in the phenomena of acidic deposition is recent and few investigations, if any, have been made into the possibility of indirect effects on human health.

• The substances requiring special attention are methyl mercury, due to its accumulation in aquatic food chains, and lead, due to the potential for contaminating drinking water.

• In virtually all studies published, to date, elevated methyl mercury levels in fish muscle (most notably the pike and perch) have been statistically associated with higher levels of acidity in water. However, a number of other factors influencing mercury levels in fish may also change in parallel to acidity.

• More research is needed to identify all the factors that affect mercury accumulations in fish and the relative importance of each. This need is especially urgent in the United States where few data are available at this time.

• The contamination of freshwater fish by direct discharge of mercury has been curtailed in recent years. The role of long-distance transport of mercury merits careful investigation as an explanation for high mercury levels in lakes remote from mercury-related industries.

• Potential impacts in acidic deposition of methyl mercury concentrations in freshwater are of interest for several reasons: a) Fish and fish products are the major if not only sources of methyl mercury for humans; b) consumers of freshwater fish have a greater possibility of exceeding allowable daily intakes of methyl mercury than do consumers of other forms of fish; c) pike and trout, freshwater fish among the most likely species to be affected by acidic deposition, have the highest user-consumption figures and the highest average methyl mercury levels.

• Prenatal life is a more sensitive stage of the life cycles for methyl mercury. More information is needed on fish-consumption patterns of women of child-bearing age in order to quantitatively assess the potential impact on human health of elevated methyl mercury levels in freshwater fish.

• Data on the impacts of acidic deposition on drinking-water quality are scarce. However, by using available information, tentative assessments of impacts on ground and surface water were made.

• The lack of data is greatest with respect to groundwater. Preliminary information seems to indicate that adverse impacts to drinking-water quality are possible in water supplies using shallow groundwater in areas edaphically (that impressive polysyllable has to do with how soil affects living organisms) and geologically sensitive to acidic deposition.

• Increasing corrosivity is probably the most significant impact of acidic deposition on surface water supplies. Populations are at increased risk of being exposed to higher concentrations of corrosive toxicants, such as lead and possibly cadmium, where surface water storage facilities are small, necessitating the direct use of raw water during storm flow periods and where corrosive control is not practiced in the water system.

• People receiving drinking water from roof catchment cistern systems should be considered at potential risk of increased intake of lead in areas of acidic deposition and especially if cisterns are used that have no particulate filters.

• From the point of view of human health risks, any increases in lead concentrations in drinking water should be viewed as an additional burden of lead. This is especially important in children where substantial numbers already have elevated blood lead levels.

• Acute or chronic diseases in humans have not been related to normal dietary intake of aluminum from food and drinking water. However, a potential threat exists for patients undergoing hemodyalysis if aluminum concentrations in the water used in this treatment exceed 50 micrograms of aluminum per liter.

• Generally the indirect effects on human health attributable to acidic deposition require further study. Data are very limited with regard to measurements of the toxic elements and their speciation and to the kinetics of transfer and uptake by accumulation processes. Studying less-toxic essential metals may be important in that elevated concentrations of some or all of them might affect the food chain dynamics or the toxicity of lead or mercury.

How Much Acid Rain Is Enough?

We have looked at the "why?" and "how?" of the acid rain issue. Now let's broaden our effort to understand the problem by spending some time with the "how much?" Addressing the quantitative aspects of acid rain involves considering the quantitative aspects of the pollution that provides the raw materials for acid rain, and the efficiency with which the raw materials for acid rain are converted to the finished product. It may also help to have some understanding of how the impressive numbers are arrived at, and how much, or how little, confidence should be accorded them.

Pollutants of Concern One thing that can be said with confidence is that there is little danger of our running out of raw materials for making acid rain. Many sulfur- and nitrogen-containing compounds have been identified that are either acidic or have the potential to promote acidification of the environment. The *Acid Rain Information Book* lists the following potentially acidifying compounds and radicals found in air that has been polluted, either naturally or by man:

- sulfur dioxide (SO_2), sulfur trioxide (SO_3), hydrogen sulfide (H_2S), dimethylsulfide (DMS), dimethyl disulfide (DMDS), carbonyl sulfide (COS), carbon disulfide (CS_2) sulfate ion (SO_4^{--}), sulfuric acid (H_2SO_4), and methyl mercaptan (CH_3SH). (The mercaptans stink to high heaven. Avoid them if you can!)
- nitric oxide (NO), dinitrogen oxide (N_2O), nitrogen dioxide (NO_2), nitrite ion (NO_2^-), nitrate ion (NO_3^-) nitric acid (HNO_3), ammonium ion (NH_4^+), and ammonia (NH_3).

• hydrochloric acid (HC_l), chloride ion (C_l^-), hydroflouric acid (HF_l), carbon dioxide (CO_2) and carbonic acid (H_2CO_3).

A Closer Look at Sulfur Of all the above-listed substances, sulfuric acid and its precursor, sulfur dioxide, get the most attention from people concerned about acid rain. Nitric acid and its precursor, nitrogen oxides, come in a close second and are gaining. Sulfur is, and has been, very plentiful in the environment. The plants and animals that gave their lives so that we can enjoy the benefits of fossil fuels really knew sulfur well. The sulfur content of crude oil ranges from 0.1 percent up to 3 percent. You won't hear as much concern being voiced about combustion of sulfur-containing oil as you do about sulfur-containing coal. Part of this difference in concern is due to the fact that the sulfur content of oil can be feasibly reduced to acceptable levels by chemical treatment with hydrogen.

Coal has even greater variability in sulfur content than does oil. The sulfur content in coal can run as high as 6 or 7 percent although concerns about pollution have resulted in a practical upper limit of around 3 percent sulfur in the coal that it pays to mine. The sulfur in coal occurs in two forms, organic and inorganic or pyritic. Organic sulfur is a component part of the organic compounds in coal, and constitutes a difficult-to-remove source of sulfur-related pollution. Pyritic sulfur consists of inorganic metallic sulfides. You may have come in contact with the form of pyritic sulfur known as "fools gold." It is an iron sulfide. The pyritic sulfides can be removed from coal comparatively easily by grinding and washing the coal. In a general way, the higher the total sulfur content in the coal the higher the percentage of pyritic sulfur will be. Reducing the total sulfur content of the coal becomes increasingly more feasible as the percentage of pyritic sulfur increases.

The percentage of total sulfur that is organic is higher in the young coal mined in the western United States than it is in the older coal mined in the eastern United States. Use of the terms young and old may warrant some clarification. Young western coal was laid down a mere 80-130 million years ago, while old eastern coal has been around for 600-800 million years. Sulfur in western coal runs about 80 percent organic, while the percentage of organic sulfur in eastern coal can run as low as 30 percent and as high as 70 percent.

You are apt to encounter the terms high sulfur coal and low sulfur coal frequently in discussions of acid rain. In fact those terms have already appeared in Chapter IV in the discussion of economic impact on coal mining. Have you begun to wonder how high is high and how low is low? Wonder no more! The term low sulfur coal refers to coal having a sulfur content of 1 percent or less. Any coal with more sulfur content than 1 percent is, by definition, high sulfur coal. Sulfur contents ranging up to 7 percent are known to occur, but you won't find very much of that ultra-high-sulfur coal being burned in these pollution-conscious times. But coal that is 2 percent sulfur is being burned in abundance.

With the information about the sulfur content of coal in mind, let's play some numbers games to see how reasonable some of the estimates of total emissions are. Each ton of coal containing 2 percent sulfur has 40 pounds of sulfur available for oxidation to sulfur dioxide. Burning 40 pounds of sulfur would produce almost 80 pounds of sulfur dioxide, since the added oxygen weighs almost as much as the sulfur. The 1980 production of coal for the entire United States was reported to be 830 million tons. Let's assume that all the coal produced in 1980 was burned in that same year. If each of those tons had been 2 percent sulfur coal, and hence able to put nearly 80 pounds of sulfur dioxide into the atmosphere, the emissions of sulfur dioxide from coal burning alone might have been 66.4 billion pounds, or 33.2 million tons, or 30.1 million tonnes. (*Tonne* is the way some people choose to write *metric ton* which is 1000 kilograms or about 2200 pounds). But we learn from a tabulation prepared by a joint United States-Canadian work group (See Appendix D Table 1) that they considered the total sulfur dioxide emission for the United States in 1980 to be slightly less than 24.1 million tonnes.

There are several plausible explanations for the discrepancy between the 30.1 million tonne figure and the 24.1 million tonne figure. Our assumption that 2 percent is the average sulfur content of all the coal burned in the United States in 1980 could be in error on the high side. Since western low-sulfur coal constitutes almost one fourth of the nation's total coal production and runs less than 1 percent sulfur, it wouldn't be too far out of line to guess that the correct average sulfur content figure for the United States as a whole might be closer to 1.5 percent than it is to 2 percent. Using 1.6 percent would bring us almost exactly to 24.1 million tonnes.

But our original guess of 2 percent sulfur coal as a national average might have been too low rather than too high. After all, we did assume that all the sulfur in the coal was available to produce sulfur dioxide. That might be a very poor assumption. There is good reason to expect that not all the sulfur contained in the coal being burned will make its way into the atmosphere. The amount of sulfur dioxide that gets into the air, as the result of burning a given amount of sulfur-containing coal depends on more than just how much sulfur is in the coal being burned. The type of boiler being used, its age, and the firing procedure can make a difference too.

Also there are some other chemical properties of the fuel beside the sulfur content that can affect the escape of sulfur dioxide. The amount of sulfur that stays behind in the ash differs for different coals. The combustion of anthracite and bituminous coals can result in emission of sulfur dioxide and trioxide involving something like 95 percent of the original sulfur content while some lignite coals retain as much as 60 percent of the original sulfur in the ash.

Then, too, there are somewhat-effective devices that are designed to trap the sulfur dioxide before it escapes into the air. The people who have spent a lot of money putting scrubbers on new power plants must surely believe that their investment is at least partially responsible for the lower emission figure. In view of all the uncertainties that have been mentioned, are you prepared to consider the possibility that estimating emissions is an unsure procedure?

It has been estimated that less than 5 percent of the sulfur available for emission has been emitted to date. The coal reserves of the United States alone are estimated to exceed 400 billion tons, so sulfur dioxide is apt to be with us for some time to come.

What About Nitrogen?

There isn't any shortage of nitrogen in the environment either. Gaseous nitrogen makes up about 80 percent of every breath you take. The earth's atmosphere is approximately four-fifths nitrogen and one-fifth oxygen with all the other ingredients, such as water vapor and carbon dioxide, barely adding up to enough to be counted. Nitrogen compounds also are plentiful in the environment. The proteins, whether animal or vegetable, are made up of nitrogen-containing amino acids. When proteins decay, nitrogen compounds are emitted to the atmosphere and become available to acidify the environment.

Nitrogen oxides, released to the atmosphere as a result of combustion, are the object of the major nitrogen-related concern. Unlike the emission of sulfur dioxide that results from burning coal, the production of nitrogen oxides is not significantly related to the nitrogen content of the fuel being burned. The air involved in the combustion process provides a great deal of the involved nitrogen and the necessary oxygen. The same United States-Canadian work group, which was referred to earlier estimated that in 1980 the total United States emission of NO_x was nearly 19.3 million tonnes. (See Appendix D, Table 2.) The emission of nitrogen oxides is considered to be increasing and is expected to match the emission of sulfur dioxide in the not too distant future.

Large power plants produce nitrogen oxides in amounts that depend on the nitrogen content of the fuel used, how the boiler is designed, and how much excess air is available to the flame when the boiler is fired. It is known that the quantity of nitrogen oxides formed, both from the nitrogen in the fuel and the nitrogen from the air, is related to the availability of excess oxygen. Controlling excess oxygen is a way to reduce nitrogen-oxide pollution from boilers. Nitrogen oxides are produced in other ways too. With the exception of a few electric automobiles, every car on the highway is a mobile nitrogen-oxide factory.

Lest you begin to believe that just about everything that gets into the air can contribute to the formation of acid rain, it is well to remember that there is another side to air pollution. A type of natural air pollution that can work to reduce the incidence of acid rain is the dust storm. When low-level winds produce the turbulence that lifts particles of alkaline dust to levels where dust can react with acids and acid precursors, the pH of rain formed in the dusty air will be raised.

Making Sense Out of Emission Estimates

As you have seen, if you have consulted Tables 1 and 2 in Appendix D, estimates of sulfur dioxide and nitrogen oxides emissions were made for each state in the United States and for the District of Columbia. These tables have been widely reproduced. They appear in numerous documents concerning acid rain. It is likely that a great deal of painstaking work, performed by dedicated people, went into construction of these tables. Collecting and analyzing the many items of data involved was certainly no trivial task, and the resulting presentation probably represents the best available information on the subject. It is well, however, to keep in mind that each number in the table has a zone of uncertainty surrounding it.

Each number is the result of a process that included assumptions and varying levels of attention to detail. It is, for example, unlikely that everyone in the data-collection chain came equipped with the same dedication to accuracy. It is highly advisable not to bet the farm on the infallibility of any estimate of emissions.

The role that varying assumptions can play in the production of emission estimates is well illustrated in Table 3 in Appendix D. The table presents the estimates of global emissions of sulfur made by five different investigators in the period from 1960 to 1973. The units are teragrams per year. A teragram is 10^{12} grams which equals 10^9 kilograms which equals 10^6 metric tons or a million tonnes. The estimates of man-made sulfur emissions range from 40 to 70 milion tonnes per year with an average of 53. The estimates of man's share in total global emissions of sulfur range from 10 percent to 30 percent.

Three investigators estimated that biological decay on land puts much more sulfur into the air than does industrial man, while two investigators estimated that man outdoes nature. Such is the uncertain nature of estimates. Think how much more impressed you could have been with the reliability of the estimates if the table only presented the work of one investigator. Lacking any conflicting information, it would have been easy to assume that the figures presented deserved to be believed.

Whoever has an axe to grind on the subject of acid rain can select whichever investigator's estimates best conform with an applicable bias. So it pays to be a little sceptical whenever statistics are quoted to prove a point about acid rain. Ask the statistics quoter if he is aware of what assumptions underlie the values presented. If he isn't, by all means listen politely, but reserve your judgment.

Are you wondering if it really is important to know precisely how many tonnes of sulfur dioxide were emitted in each state in 1980? What difference does it make if the estimate for any state's 1980 sulfur dioxide emission is, to pick a number out of thin air, 10 percent off of the mark? The importance of the accuracy of any estimate depends on the nature of the decisions that will be influenced by the estimate. If the decision about how to vote in the upcoming state elections is only marginally related to your state's annual sulfur dioxide emissions, you are probably prepared to live with a fairly rough estimate. But when that estimate is used to prove that there is an upward trend in air pollution which requires the imposition of stringent state controls on your business, you will probably develop an instant interest in very acccurate estimation procedures.

The historical trends and current emissions of sulfur compounds and nitrogen oxides have come in for attention as people seek answers to the questions, "How bad is it?", "Is it getting worse or better?", and "What does the future hold?" If you have some preconceptions that the trend in sulfur dioxide and nitrogen oxide emissions has been a steady climb over the past forty years, be prepared to shed them now.

The *Acid Rain Information Book*, by Record et. al. provides some historical trend information that you may find interesting.

These emission trend figures were reported in millions of tons per year. That's "tons," not the "tonnes" that were used to report the 1980 emissions previously mentioned. If the difference in units bothers you, you can convert tons to tonnes by multiplying the ton figure by 0.907.

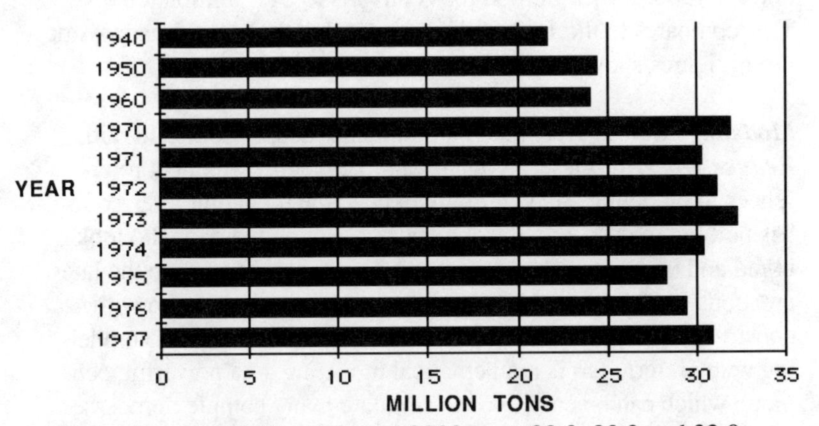

Projections for 1980, 1990, and 2000 were 29.3, 30.3 and 32.0 million tons respectively. The 29.3 megatons (26.6 megatonnes) can be compared to the 1980 estimate of 24.1 million tonnes per year made by the U.S.-Canadian work group. Do you find it surprising that the emission level projected for the year 2000, back in 1977, is about the same level that existed in 1970? It would be interesting to know what assumptions lie behind these forecasts of future emissions. A couple that come to mind as possibilities are that pollution-control regulations and technology are expected to have a salutory effect, or that future growth of the economy will not be closely linked to requirements for sulfur-containing fuels.

The comparable figures for emissions of nitrogen oxides expressed in millions of tons per year are:

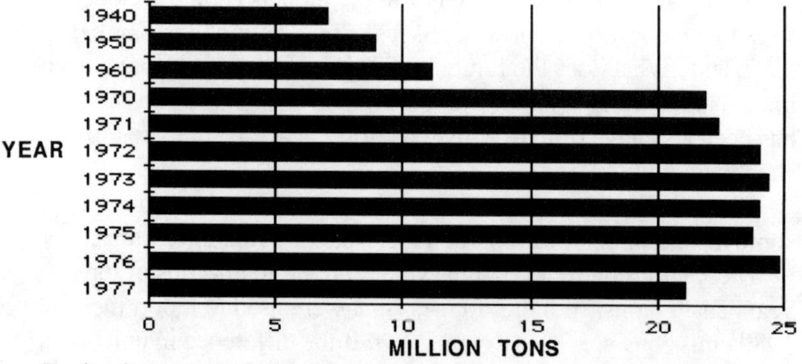

Projections made from data available through 1977 for 1980, 1990, and 2000 were 27.0, 30.0 and 34.0 respectively. The projection for 1980 of 27.0 million tons converts to 24.5 million tonnes. That compares to the 19.3 million tonnes that the U.S.-Canada work group figures show for 1980.

Modeling: Can It Help Reduce Uncertainties? If you do much reading about acid rain, you are apt to encounter frequent references to modeling. As you might expect, the modeling referred to has nothing to do with tall, sophisticated, young women who look bored and undernourished while parading back and forth in the latest creations from Paris or New York. It also has nothing to do with constructing small replicas of sailboats or automobiles. The modeling being referred to is mathematical modeling — a powerful technique which can be employed to simulate many complex processes. Modeling the processes that operate in nature has become an enjoyable pastime for many scientists with a mathematical bent and access to a powerful computer. Sometimes their efforts are quite useful.

The end product of mathematical modeling is a description of the predicted outcome of combining several variable processes, each of which partially determines the end result. How well that description will fit an actual (i.e., real world) outcome depends on how well the component processes are understood, how good are the data available for calibrating the model, and how far from reality must the modeler stray in order to fit his differential equations into the computer available to him.

The great advances made in computer technology in recent years have rendered mathematical modeling almost commonplace. Computing capacity that once filled a large air-conditioned room can now be held in the palm of the hand. But, in spite of these great advances, the computing capacity and speed required to model accurately and rapidly the more complex natural processes is not yet generally available. To get around the limitations imposed by the high cost of computer time and limited computer capacity, modelers make simplifying assumptions about the processes they are modeling. Even though a modeler knows that the outcome he is concerned with involves changes in three dimensions with time, he may be inclined to assume that one or more of the dimensions can be considered to remain constant, so that he won't exceed the available computing capacity. The instant he makes that decision he has begun to compromise with reality. The end result can turn out to be a very useful approximation to reality or it can mislead. You may recall that regional modeling of atmospheric chemistry and physics was given a high uncertainty rating by Record et al. in their analysis of acid-rain issues. Here is what they had to say about the subject of regional mathematical models:

"Models represent the link between sources and (acidic) depositions and are the only means of assessing, in advance, the effects of changing conditions. Current regional models, suitable for evaluating the acid rain problem, are preliminary and involve tentative assumptions and major simplifications, including: (1) neglect of NO_x transformation; (2) linear SO_x transformation rates; (3) elementary consideration of in-cloud chemistry; (4) the use of poorly-documented decay rates for wet removal of sulfates and nitrates; (5) prescription of regional wind and precipitation fields from existing networks; and (6) representation of the atmosphere by one well-mixed vertical layer.

"Additional development, testing, and validation will be required before models can be used with confidence. This is an iterative (repetitious) process and improvements occur gradually as a result of more realistic assumptions and more detailed monitoring data."

I have introduced a discussion of mathematical modeling at this juncture to put into proper perspective the modeling-determined estimates of future emissions that were mentioned earlier. Estimates of future emissions are playing a role in the debate about the need for more stringent controls. To the uncertainties that enter into making estimates of the present levels of pollution have been added the uncertainties about future growth, future demand, and future technology. The technique of mathematical modeling comes into play in the making of such forecasts. Give a modeler extended access to a powerful-enough computer and he will be able to provide you impressive figures about the future. How good those figures are, how much they deserve to be trusted, is heavily dependent on what assumptions have been made about the future and how well the mathematical model conforms to reality.

Emission-Deposition Relationships If the pollution we now euphemistically call *emissions* didn't go any place there wouldn't be much in the way of acid deposition to worry about. The millions of words being written and spoken about acid rain could then be reserved for other uses. But, unfortunately, emissions do go someplace. They go elsewhere. Just where elsewhere is located was not of much concern to the people involved in creating emissions until relatively recent times.

Polluters have always been sure they didn't want noxious fumes hanging around the plant. That could be downright hazardous! Safe disposal has long been the desired goal. The process for accomplishing safe disposal has involved venting the noxious fumes from as high a smokestack as necessary to ensure adequate downwind travel prior to their returning to earth. Downwind travel may not occur as expected.

Figure 1 illustrates just how complex air flow can be. It is reproduced from a photographic slide that came into my possession a good many years ago. The differing heights of adjoining smokestacks at the same power-generating station produced diametrically opposed smoke plumes at the time the picture was taken. Does that picture fit what you have been led to expect about air flow?

Adequate downwind travel was subconsciously defined as that distance which ensured that the polluter neither choked on the stuff nor got taken to task by the people who did. "Out of sight, out of mind" was the guiding philosophy. Many lived by the not-so-golden-rule, "Do it to others, preferably distant others." They were lulled by the clever poetry, "Dilution is the solution to pollution."

Unfortunately, the atmosphere in the vicinity of the dilution simultaneously undergoes the process of pollution. All the time that the fumes are traveling they are being mixed with the surrounding air by the process of turbulent diffusion. The surrounding air, which may

Figure 1 — Photo by Ralph Turcotte of the *Beverly Times*

have been relatively clean before it met the fume plume, dilutes the more-polluted air by becoming more-polluted air.

Just how much of the atmosphere gets polluted in the mixing process depends on a number of variables: the height of the smokestack, the velocity of the wind at the top level of the smoke plume rises, the temperature and moisture structure of the air layers in which the plume travels, and the topography the moving air encounters. A good many cubic miles of the atmosphere are available to be polluted. Usually the vertical component of the mixing process is confined to the lower mile or two, but entrainment of the air in a major thunderstorm cloud can increase the vertical mixing to heights of seven miles or more. The horizontal component of the mixing process can be measured in hundreds of miles.

The logic once applied was that harmful chemicals became harmless chemicals as soon as they were mixed with sufficient air to make detection difficult. That reasoning doesn't fly any more. Polluters are now considered responsible for the effects of their emissions wherever those effects occur. Finding the location of "elsewhere" has become a matter of considerable concern. Let's devote a little time to discussing what is involved in finding out where "elsewhere" is located.

Atmospheric Transport Processes When emissions leave their birthplace through the smokestack they are as free as the wind to travel, and that's what they do. If the wind is light, or nonexistent, initially the most noticeable travel is upward.

Buoyancy lifts the plume of fumes to the level where the fumes are no warmer than the surrounding air. Then the travel takes on a noticeable horizontal component and the emissions move in a direction that is usually described as *downwind.* Moving downwind sometimes involves a straight and narrow path to some distant point, but, at other times, the downwind path can rival an amusement park roller coaster in complexity of motion. The complex motion occurs when the atmosphere is in a turbulent state. Under some turbulent circumstances the plume can follow a wave-like trajectory and return to earth a short distance from its point of origin. Air-pollution experts call this condition *looping*; and if the fumes return to earth too close to the polluting plant for comfort, the condition is called *fumigation.* When deposition from the atmosphere occurs soon after the emissions entered the atmosphere, it is fashionable to speak of the pollutants as having had "a short residence time in the atmosphere." Clearly, these circumstances do not meet the expectation of *safe disposal.*

Just where the horizontal component of the wind will take the polluted air is difficult to predict. The winds aloft over most of North America blow from west to east, but only in a climatological sense. The day-to-day details of air flow are not usually that simple. On most days the pressure patterns that govern air motion exhibit alternate ridges and troughs. The air flow on the west side of a ridge is from a direction somewhat south of west, ranging from west-southwest through southwest to south-southwest. On the east side of the ridge the flow is from a direction somewhat north of west. Similarly, the flow of air on the west side of a pressure trough will have a component from north of west, and on the east side the flow will have a component from south of west. Just how much the air departs from flowing directly from west to east depends on the strength or intensity of the pressure troughs and ridges. If a low pressure trough intensifies to the point that it becomes a closed low pressure area with a counter-clockwise circulation around it, polluted air may find itself heading west instead of east.

If it is true that travel broadens one, pollution plumes stand to be quite broad. In their sometimes long residence time in the atmosphere they get to do some pretty involved traveling. The fumes may become entrained in the updraft of a fast-growing thunderstorm and be carried to heights of seven miles or more before leaving the cloud. At these heights strong winds can rapidly carry the pollutants to great distances. If their resident time in the atmosphere is of the order of several days, the wandering chemicals can end up being deposited hundreds or even thousands, of miles away from where they started, after a meandering trip that can cover more miles than the straight-line distance between the start and the finish of the trip.

Sophisticated tracer studies have been used by atmospheric chemists to identify the place of origin of deposited pollution aerosols. Just in case you have been conditioned to think that the term *aerosol* applies only to those fine sprays of insecticide or paint that come out of pressurized cans, I am moved to mention that any gaseous suspension of fine solid or liquid particles also qualifies as an aerosol.

Kenneth A. Rahn and Douglas H. Lowenthal have used neutron-activation analysis (see Glossary) to determine elemental ratios which provide a characteristic *signature* for each region studied. Taking multiple samples, they determined representative signatures for places as far removed as Barrow, Alaska; Kecskemet, Hungary; Rorvik, Sweden; Underhill, Vermont; and Narragansett, Rhode Island. Their study identified the sulfate pollution reaching Underhill, Vermont, as having originated predominantly in the Midwest. But the Midwest didn't provide all the pollution that reached the East. The same researchers found that the sulfate pollution reaching Narragansett, Rhode Island, was relatively local in origin.

The Earth's atmosphere is over 60 miles deep, but usually man-made pollutants are transported in the layer near the ground that is a mile and a half or so in depth. Meteorologists call this layer "The Planetary Boundary Layer." A wide range of atmospheric motions take place within the planetary boundary layer. These motions range in size from tiny eddies to circulations of global scale, and all of them affect the distribution of pollution at one time or another. How far the pollutants travel, and how mixed up they get, depends on the topography of the region and on several meteorological variables.

The height of the transport layer depends on the stability of the atmosphere, which, in turn, depends on the vertical distribution of temperature and moisture. The speed of travel depends on the wind velocity, which depends on the horizontal pressure gradient, which depends on the air's density distribution. While the horizontal wind plays a major role in moving the pollution toward its final resting place, it isn't the sole influence. Pollution can be dispersed at various angles to the direction of the wind, and also vertically under the influence of complex air motions produced by sudden wind shifts and turbulent eddies.

Time Scales in Pollutant Transfer The time scales that apply to the various range from diurnel to synoptic to annual. *Diurnal* is meteorologist talk for something that happens during each day. An example is the daily solar heating cycle in which convective clouds begin to develop in late morning, grow to their maximum in late afternoon, and then subside as the sun sinks slowly in the west. *Synoptic time scale* refers to the two to five days that it takes a pressure center to approach, dominate, and then depart the area where you live. During this sequence of several days the wind direction can "box the compass" — sending pollution in all directions, one after the other. The *annual time scale* is the period of time during which the differing synoptic circulation patterns of the four seasons are merged into a resultant pattern for the year.

The height to which pollution is mixed in the eastern part of the United States is somewhat more uniform than in the west. The daily peak of mixing occurs in the afternoon and the seasonal peak occurs in the summer. Much of the pollution emitted from a source is deposited relatively near to the source, and much of the total deposiion occurs during the first 24 hours after emission, usually without benefit of precipitation.

Back to Modeling: What Can We Predict? That's probably as much meteorology as we need to consider before arriving at the inescapable conclusion that predicting where, when, and how a batch of emissions will eventually come back to earth is not the simple matter we might wish it to be. Once again mathematical models enter the picture as investigators seek a means of predicting where pollution will go, when it will get there, and how concentrated it will be at various points along its journey. Both transport and diffusion processes are involved and a variety of modeling approaches are available. All have limitations. The simple models that are inexpensive to run on a computer and easy to understand depart from reality in major ways, especially if the terrain over which the pollution is travelling has a lot of topographic relief. The more sophisticated models cost a bundle to run and give results that require a great deal of interpretation. A survey of dispersion models reveals that there are more than 50 available for use in the transport range between 50 and 300 kilometers (that's 31 to 186 miles in case you haven't yet gone metric). The fact that so many models have been developed is a commentary on the uncertainty about how good each modeler's assumptions have been. Unfortunately, the relative contributions of long-range transport and local deposition to the final total are not well defined.

Some fumes are transported long distances away from their source. Others have only a brief resident time in the atmosphere before returning to earth of their own accord. Acid-rain experts call the process that returns the polluting chemicals to the earth, in the absence of moist precipitation, *dry deposition.* That seems quite logical, doesn't it?

Ideally it would be desirable to be able to describe the behavior of each parcel of air from the time it is first polluted by emissions until the processes of deposition make it into clean air once again. It would be useful to be able to trace its meandering path over the countryside, knowing where and when each portion of its changing chemical content was deposited. Unfortunately, the realities of science and economics preclude this. While it is feasible to mount occasional, localized, highly-instrumented experiments that keep scientists busy analyzing for long periods of time, continuous monitoring of acid deposition over large areas is not routinely affordable.

The upshot of all this variability in duration and direction of flow is that polluted air can meander over an involved trajectory, depositing its chemical load here and there in a haphazard and unpredictable manner. Many people would like to be able to identify precisely the source of donated pollution. Unfortunately, defining a relationship between source points and receptor points is only possible in a very general way.

Transformation Processes During the time that elapses between an emission's depature from its source and its arrival at its eventual destination, the pollution components aren't just traveling along with the breeze. They are being subjected to a lot of chemistry. Hydrocarbons in the atmosphere react with the nitrogen oxides in the presence of ultraviolet light from the sun. Both ozone and hydrogen peroxide are formed. Both of these compounds are very effective oxidizing agents. In their presence, the sulfur and nitrogen-containing compounds are transformed. Even the reduced sulfur, such as that in hydrogen sulfide, which you may know better as "rotten egg gas," gets rapidly oxidized to sulfur dioxide, which mingles in the atmosphere with the sulfur dioxide that came out of the volcanoes or smokestacks. Sulfur dioxide has an average life of three to four days before it is oxidized to sulfur trioxide and becomes eligible to combine with water to form sulfuric acid. A batch of sulfur dioxide can cover a good many miles in three to four days. The nitrogen dioxide in the emissions only lasts about 11 hours before it gets oxidized and reacts with water to form nitric acid. As a result of these timing differences, it is reasonable to expect that sulfur dioxide will be transported further from its source than will the nitrogen oxides in the same emission.

The differences in the time requirements for oxidation of the gaseous oxides to reach their strongest acidifying form has been determined in laboratories. The laboratory results match the observed results in the atmosphere fairly well. The transformation rates in power plant plumes are smaller than those for urban plumes. A difference in the concentration of the hydroxyl radicals that affect oxidation is the explanation offered for this disparity. There is a slight additional problem. The known chemical reactions do not fully explain the conversion of sulfur dioxide to sulfate ion in the quantities that are observed in the atmosphere. It has been suggested that there may be several unknown mechanisms at work in this transformation.

Considerably more than acid formation goes on during the transformation process. Vapors condense to liquids. Condensates turn into primary particles. Small primary particles coagulate and aggregate to form still larger particles. All the while this is going on, there is a very dynamic interaction among the gases, the liquid droplets, and the solid particles present. Growth, to sizes where deposition is more likely, eventually results.

Part of the activity brings natural dust particles into contact with liquid drops. It has been observed that the amount of acid that is either absorbed by the water drops or produced within the water drops is greater than can be related to the observed pH of the water drops. The pH of the water drops should be lower than it is. The explanation offered for this is the neutralization of part of the acid by either ammonia gas or by dust-size alkaline carbonates in the atmosphere, or both. (When ammonia gas combines with nitric acid the resulting compound is ammonium nitrate, which is a popular ingredient in chemical fertilizer.)

Deposition Processes After all the atmospheric transport and transformation processes have run their course, there eventually comes the time when the transported and transformed pollutants end their resident time in the atmosphere, and get back down to earth. This removal from the atmosphere can take place by either wet or dry processes.

The wet processes are easier to observe and measure, but the dry processes probably deposit more acid and acid precursors on the surfaces of interest than do the wet processes. But if it weren't for the wet processes, who would have ever heard of acid rain?

Acid and the acid-forming precursors get into precipitation in two ways. In the first case, the acid particles may serve as the condensation nuclei about which water molecules cluster to form the clouds composed of tiny cloud droplets or ice crystals. Collection of cloud droplets into drops big enough to fall out as precipitation doesn't occur casually. It takes a pretty efficient collection process to get the job done before the cloud re-evaporates and dissipates, as clouds are wont to do. Since a healthy rain-drop can have a diameter 100 times that of its constituent cloud droplets, a million cloud droplets may have gotten together form the rain-drop. The droplets have contributed more than tn just water molecules to the formation of the raindrop. Each tiny particle of acid that was at the center of a cloud droplet comes along too. A million or so acid particles ride the raindrop all the way to the ground.

But not all acid particles in the air end up at the center of tiny droplets. Many of them may be distributed in the clear air underneath a rain cloud where they are in a position to meet falling raindrops. The falling raindrop can pick up a considerable load of additional acid as particles become adsorbed onto the drop's surface.

The two processes by which a raindrop acquires its load of acid, and any other impacted chemical substances have been lumped together into what gets called *precipitation scavenging*. The process involving condensation is spoken of as *rainout* and the second form of chemical collection is called *washout*. Washout is effective in making air clean again and has long been considered to be a blessing. Only recently has disposal of the chemically laden wash water come to be recognized as a problem.

Wet acid deposition isn't limited to raindrops. Snowflakes do it, hailstones do it, even periodic frost and dew do it. The most drastic acid deposition occurs when fog, which can be thought of as a misguided cloud on the ground, impacts sensitive surfaces. Lacking the opportunity or capability to perform the scavenging function on neutralizing alkaline dust particles, fog droplets achieve acidities many times higher than those observed in precipitation. Michael R. Hoffman of the California Institute of Technology found southern California fog to be often 100 times more acid than the average rain in the same region. The ratio of fog acidity to rain acidity on Whiteface Mountain in the Adirondacks was found to be often 10 to 1 by Volker A. Mohnen of the State University of New York at Albany.

Dry deposition has been defined as the aggregate of all materials transfered to natural surfaces from the atmosphere in the absence of precipitation. It is hard to observe, measure, or predict. While the force of gravity has a lot to do with dry deposition, it isn't the only force that operates. Wind turbulence can drive to the ground many tiny particles, which would remain airborne in calm air. The acid-forming gases have an affinity for many natural surfaces, so gaseous adsorption accounts for considerable transfer of gases out of the atmosphere onto those surfaces. Measurement of amounts and rates of dry deposition has an uncertain aspect about it. Not only does the amount transferred from the atmosphere vary with the nature of the surface, but, with some surfaces, the dry deposition can easily move around and become undeposited.

The available estimates of what fraction of total acid deposition is accomplished by dry deposition processes range from 25 percent to 80 percent or more. Not exactly the kind of precision one might desire is it?

Deposition Monitoring Determining the pH of precipitation and trying to assess how much acid has been deposited from the atmosphere has been approached in a variety of ways over the years. Interest in the chemical content of rainfall surfaced as early as 1727 in England. It reappeared sporadically from time to time until 1948 when Hans Egner established the first large-scale precipitation chemistry network for collection and chemical analysis of precipitation. As noted earlier the network began in Sweden and spread to Norway, Denmark, Finland. Later on it covered much of western and central Europe.

In the United States individual scientists determined the acidity and alkalinity of occasional precipitation samples on a sporadic basis in the 1930s and 1940s. Henry G. Houghton, an M.I.T. meteorologist, is known to have measured the pH of a sample of rain in Maine in 1939, but it was not until the 1950s that an organized interest surfaced. In 1955, Christian E. Junge of the Air Force Cambridge

Research Center began the collection and analysis of precipitation over a network of 24 sites in the eastern United States. The network was abandoned in 1956. In 1959, James P. Lodge, Jr., an atmospheric chemist then with the U.S. Public Health Service, established a 30-station network of gages at the urging of Carl G. Rossby, a famous meteorologist, who was disturbed that Junge's network had been abandoned after so short a period of data collection. When Lodge moved from the Public Health Service to the National Center for Atmospheric Research he continued the operation of the network until he was forced to abandon the effort in 1966. The top management of NCAR withdrew support for the network on the grounds that operation of a network was not a proper research activity. The data collected included precipitation acidities, but the focus of attention was not primarily on acid rain. Lodge told me recently that at the time the network was operating he was doubtful about the validity of the pH data because they were determined for monthly accumulations.

In 1975-76 Gene E. Likens collected data on the pH of precipitation by contacting all the people that he knew were studying precipitation chemistry. From this effort he was able to put together what amounted to a synoptic network of 65 sampling points. Observations at 46 sites in the eastern U.S. and 19 sites in eastern Canada provided the basis for drawing isolines of acidity which indicated that the area experiencing acid rain had spread markedly since the 1955-56 period covered by Junge's observations. The validity of this evidence of increasing acidity was subsequently questioned by Stenslund and Semonin of the Illinois State Water Survey. Their studies suggest that drought in the 1950s put large amounts of alkaline dust into the atmosphere, partially neutralizing the acidity of rain in the years 1955-56. The increase in acidity suggested by Liken's data may reflect, instead, a decrease in the alkalinity of atmospheric dust.

Since 1978 Agricultural Experiment Stations have sponsored the collection of data on acid deposition as part of the National Atmospheric Deposition Program. This effort was augmented in 1982 to develop a nationwide network dedicated to observing long-term trends. This National Trends Network and the stations operated under the National Atmospheric Deposition Program combine to provide a network of more than 130 sampling sites. Canada operates 60 additional sampling sites under the Canadian Air and Precipitation Monitoring Network.

Where Has Acid Rain Been?

Considerable importance is being attached to knowing where acid rain has fallen in the past, where it is falling right now, and where it is apt to fall in the future. Large amounts of both time and money have been invested in establishing extensive instrumented networks, collecting and analyzing voluminous data, and going through mind-stretching modeling exercises all in the hope of finding out acid rain's whereabouts — past, present, and future. Clearly some sizable payoff is expected from the investment. Discussing what the hoped-for payoff is, and what the odds of hitting the jackpot are, could very well turn out to be a worthwhile expenditure of a portion of our brief time together. Let's hope so.

Maps have been published which show, for the year 1980 over North America, the geographical distributions of: 1) pH of the acid precipitation, 2) sensitivity to acid precipitation, 3) sulfate deposition, and 4) nitrate deposition. I have reproduced them here as Figures 2, 3, 4, and 5, respectively. I have chosen not to include numerous other maps which offer other depictions of the geographical distribution of some aspect of acid-rain-related variables. For the enlightenment of those whose interests are somewhat less far-flung than the entire North American continent, there are maps of the contiguous 48 states of the United States which show: 1) hardness of surface waters, 2) characterizations of the density of SO_x and NO_x emissions averaged over each state and 3) for people who are really sticklers for geographic detail, maps which summarize the same emissions on a county-by-county basis over the contiguous 48 states of the United States.

Why is all this emphasis being placed on geography? There are many questions that need to be asked and answered before real progress can be made toward resolution of the numerous dilemmas surrounding the subject of acid rain. Valid information about where acid deposition has occurred, is occurring, or will occur, would seem to be useful to anyone who hopes to make a contribution to the containment, reduction, or elimination of the problem. The final solution may turn out to be a composite of several partial solutions each of which has been fitted to the special circumstances of a geographical region. The eventual design of even a partial solution to the problem will be influenced by how accurately the geography of the problem is known or knowable.

If the resources that society allocates to coping with the effects of acid rain are too limited to permit an overall approach, knowledge of the geography of the component parts of the problem will offer some basis for setting priorities. For example, consider the first two maps mentioned above. Overlaying the map of sensitivity to acid precipitation on top of the map of pH reveals two areas that combine high sensitivity with low pH values: the New England states and one stretched along the Blue Ridge Mountains from western Virginia to northern Georgia. If sensitivity and acidity were the only important concerns, these two areas would probably be given priority attention over areas that had only high sensitivity or only low pH.

Maps depicting the geography of acid deposition could also be important to the implementation of some future dynamic solution to the acid-rain problem that involved relating day-to-day weather factors to ongoing emission patterns. It would be possible for the manager of an acid-rain mitigation program to use routinely available, up-to-the-minute maps of the current geographical distribution of acid rain as decision-making tools. The ingredients required to synthesize a reliable, synoptic picture of the geographic distribution of acid rain would include: 1) accurate information about the location of emission sources, 2) detailed information about the timing of emission releases, 3) detailed information on the quantity and quality of pollutants emitted, 4) complete understanding of the transport and transformation processes affecting the pollutants, and 5) up-to-the-minute data on precipitation and the other depositional processes. Don't hold your breath while awaiting the availability of such detailed information. Unfortunately, none of these ingredients is available, nor is it likely to become available in the near future.

Decisions that require knowledge of the geographic distribution of acid rain must presently depend on data that have been collected at

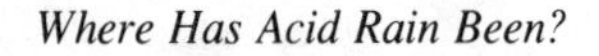

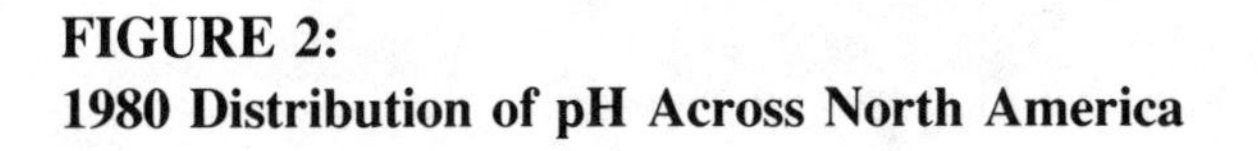

FIGURE 2:
1980 Distribution of pH Across North America

Source: Gibson, J. and Baker, C. National Atmospheric Deposition Program: Isopleth Maps, January - December, 1980. National Atmospheric Deposition Program and Canadian Network for Sampling Precipitation. March, 1982.

FIGURE 3:
Areas of North America Considered Sensitive to Acid Precipitation

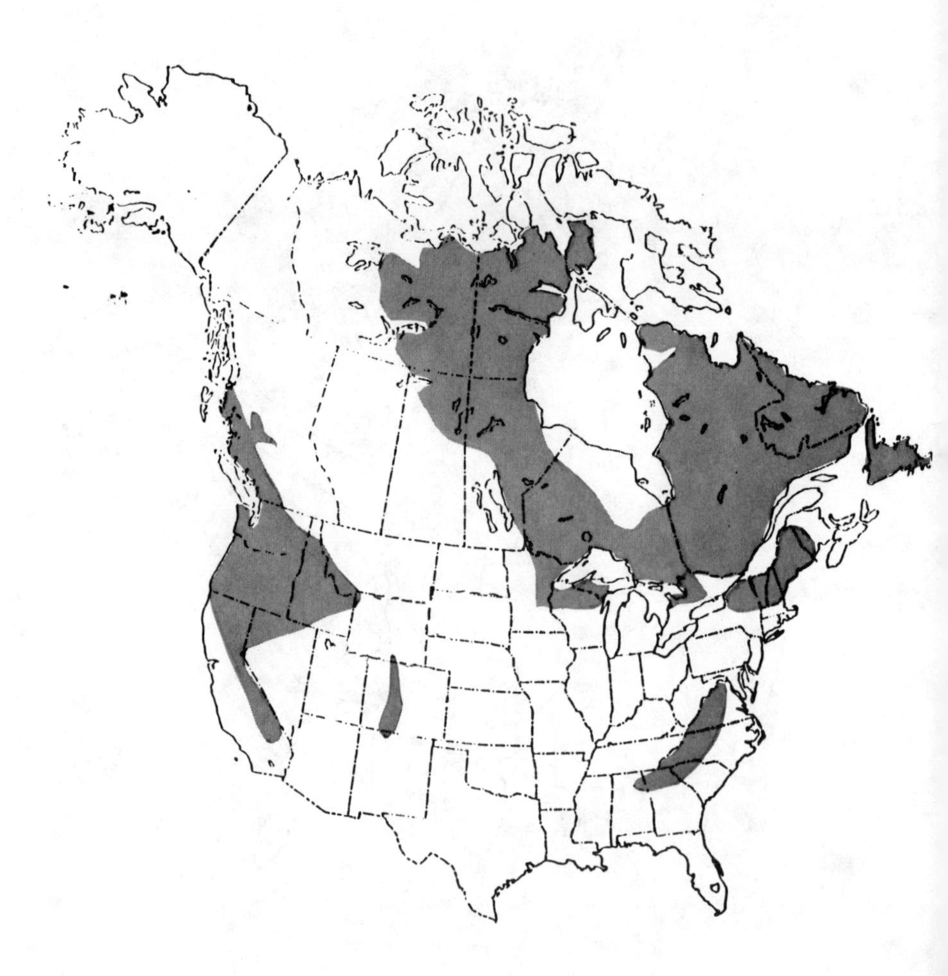

Source: Galloway, J. and E. Cowling. The Effects of Precipitation on Aquatic and Terrestrial Ecosystems: a Proposed Precipitation Chemistry Network. JAPCA, v. 28, no. 3, 1978. p. 229-235.

FIGURE 4:
1980 Distribution of Sulfate Deposition
Across North America
(milligrams/square meter)

Source: Gibson, J.H. and C.V. Baker. National Atmospheric Deposition Program: Isopleth Maps, January - December, 1980. National Atmospheric Deposition Program and Canadian Network for Sampling Precipitation. March, 1982.

FIGURE 5:
1980 Distribution of Nitrate Deposition Across North America
(milligram/square meter)

Source: Gibson, J.H. and C.V. Baker. National Atmospheric Deposition Program: Isopleth Maps, January - December, 1980. National Atmospheric Deposition Program and Canadian Network for Sampling Precipitation. March, 1982.

widely scattered sites over long periods of time. The wider the spacing between sampling sites the greater the chance for masking the fine structure of the actual distribution. The longer the period of time between successive observations, the greater will be the opportunity for masking the variability of the inputs. A picture of the geographic and temporal distribution of acid rain can be constructed from occasional observations taken over a sparse network of instrumented sites. How representative that picture will be of the actual space-time distribution of acid deposition is a matter deserving our thoughtful consideration.

Any observing network involves sampling. Sampling automatically involves possible error. As the number of samples taken over space and time increases, the magnitude of possible sampling error decreases. Just how small that possible error should be depends on the nature of any decision that needs to be made. Economic considerations play an important role in determining how much sampling will take place. If the instrumentation involved is expensive, or if highly trained people are required for its operation, the observing network that can be afforded may be sparse. If sampling observations are few and far between, the isolines (see Glossary) interpolated between the data points may be drawn far from their true positions. If the frequency of sampling is low compared to the frequency of temporal changes actually taking place, erroneous conclusions about what is going on may result. If the interest in data collection is sporadic, with long periods elapsing between episodes of activity, inferences about time trends may be on shaky ground.

Maps of Acid Rain: How Helpful? I have described above some of the maps which address the areal distribution of acid rain. The patterns presented suggest that acid rain is distributed fairly generally over wide areas, with gradual transitions from lower values of acid to extensive centers of higher acidity. Do these maps deserve our unquestioning acceptance as valid depictions of actual circumstances?

Let's consider how such maps are constructed. The maps are begun by first plotting discrete values of acidity at each location where observations have been made. Next, isolines of acidity are drawn which are supposed to connect all the points having a particular level of acid-rain experience. Where two observing stations have had differing experience, one or more isolines can be drawn between them, by interpolating intermediate values. The sparser the observing network is, the smoother the analyst can draw the isolines of acidity. There is nothing that can compare with the absence of observed data to encourage the production of a nicely smoothed pattern.

Unfortunately, such smoothing may present a very misleading picture of the variation of acid rain over a region. The acidity of rainfall, at any point, is the combined result of the nature and amount of the rainfall, and the concentration of acid-forming pollution in the air through which the rain falls. The simplest way for a region to experience uniformly distributed acid rain would be for both the rainfall and pollution to be uniform over the region. While such circumstances are conceivable, nonuniformity in the areal distribution of rainfall and pollution is much more likely. That still doesn't preclude the possibility of uniform distribution of acid rainfall. It is conceivable that the areas of lesser rainfall could coincide with the areas of more intense pollution, and the areas of greater rainfall could experience less-polluted air is conceivable, but not very likely. It is much more reasonable to expect variations in rainfall and pollution to reinforce or cancel each other randomly to produce a non-uniform distribution of acid rain.

Experience has shown that, for individual storms precipitation patterns based on very dense networks are much more convoluted and complex than are the patterns obtained by analyzing a sparser set of data for the same storm. This is particularly true where the rainfall results from intense thunderstorms. It is not unusual, under such circumstances, for two stations only ten miles apart to experience rainfall amounts that differ by factors of ten or more. Where the occurrence of such thunderstorms is influenced by topography, in contrast to random placement over level terrain, long-term differences in precipitation usually result. Two stations a few miles apart, which have high ground between them, can experience widely differing rainfall amounts over long periods of record.

The influence of topography on precipitation is not limited to thunderstorm situations. In the complete absence of the convection displayed by thunderstorms, the flow of moist air over a topographic barrier (like a mountain range) will usually produce heavier precipitation on the windward side of the barrier than on the downwind side. Any isoline of precipitation that crosses a mountain barrier without marked deviation deserves to be viewed with scepticism.

The distribution of pollution over a wide area downwind from a source can also be expected to be something less than uniform. Although it is convenient to model diffusion by assuming that the downwind plume covers an ever-widening area within which complete mixing of the polluted air occurs, the reality of diffusing plumes is somewhat different. Experiments employing instrumented aircraft to track the trajectories of traceable substances reveal that diffusion of tracers does not always conform to the convenient classical models. Depending on the wind and the stability of the atmosphere, it is possible for tracers to remain quite concentrated over long distances from the initial release point. If tracers can behave this way, it is reasonable to expect that ordinary pollution doesn't always diffuse uniformly either.

It is interesting to note that, as the observing networks over North America have increased in density, the patterns of acid rain have become more complex, with more individual centers of high pH, and the isopleths losing some of the sweeping smoothness seen in earlier maps.

"So what?" you may be thinking. "What difference does it make whether the pattern is smooth or complicated as long as the general features are similar? Why not get on with reducing the concentration of acid deposition and stop worrying about whether lines on maps are drawn smooth or kinky?"

Those are fair questions. What reason do I have for devoting so much attention to the question of how representative of reality are patterns of acid rain drawn from the sparse data of the past? I am concerned that we not be misled. Assumption, of an unreal generality of circumstances, could lead to the unwarranted acceptance of proposed universal solutions. The study of science teaches the inadvisability of taking anything for granted. A pertinent object lesson can be learned from the following anecdote.

In 1980 William M. Lewis, Jr. and Michael C. Grant, both faculty members at the University of Colorado, published an article in *Science* entitled "Acid Precipitation in the Western United States." I missed the article when it was first published. I had cancelled my subscription to *Science* a few months earlier in an ill-advised move. It was occasioned by my assumption of impending poverty due to my retirement. It wasn't until mid-1984 that I learned of the article while doing some reading about acid rain.

I thought it was an interesting coincidence that people named Lewis and Grant had an interest in acid rain. A long-time friend of mine is named Lewis O. Grant. He is a professor of atmospheric science at Colorado State University. He has a well-deserved international reputation for his work on modifying precipitation in the western United States. I was anxious to share with my good friend my enjoyment of my recent discovery of an interesting coincidence of names and interests. At our next meeting, I inquired of him if he were aware of the paper and the names of its authors. I was ill-prepared for the explosion that followed. "Aware of it! You bet I'm aware of it! I have been repeatedly chastised by people who think I wrote it."

He went on to describe the aftermath of the article's publication. In the article, the authors concluded that the acid precipitation observed in one watershed on the eastern slope of the Colorado Rockies was evidence of widespread transport of acid pollution from the west coast. The possibility that the acid pollution had its origin in the nearby, heavily-polluted Denver area was rejected on the basis that upslope flows from the southeast are sporadic and not as common as flows from the northwest. Knowledgeable meteorologists took strong exception to the conclusion reached by the two authors.

Fascinated by the controversy, John C. Vimont, a graduate student under the tutelage of Professor Lewis O. Grant, abandoned his research already underway and undertook a new study, aimed at finding out just what was going on in the way of acid precipitation in the Rocky Mountains of Colorado. After familiarizing himself with the pertinent scientific literature, he selected ten sampling sites, many of which were near mountain passes in Colorado. Some of these were near known sources of acidic pollutants. Some others were expected to be clean, and some were in the uncertain category. His sampling procedure involved skiing in to the site, digging a deep pit in the snow and taking up to 21 one-quart samples in clean polyethelene freezer boxes, which were then sealed in Zip-lock bags and taken back to his laboratory. The samples were preserved, frozen, until they could be analyzed for pH and conductivity.

At the Wolf Creek Pass site, about 95 miles northeast of the Four Corners Power Plant in northwestern New Mexico, the samples showed pH values ranging from 4.6 to 6.9, with a median value of 5.1. The Rabbit Ears Pass site, due east of coal-burning plants at Hayden and Craig, Colorado had pH values ranging from 4.7 to 5.7

with a median value of 5.0. At the Long Lake site, which was near the eastern slope site used by Lewis and Grant, he found an acidic pH profile ranging from a low of 4.73 to a high of 5.49 with a median value of 5.18. He attributed the acidity to automobile emissions, since there were no power plants in the vicinity. At McClure Pass, the pH ranged from 4.8 to 6.8, with a median value of 5.4. At Guanella Pass, the pH range was from 5.0 to 6.7, with a median value of 5.4.

Vimont concluded that long-range transport was not a dominant contributor to low pH values found in winter precipitation in the Colorado Rockies, nor is it likely to become so in the near future. But the results published by Lewis and Grant continue to be used to support the contention that the western half of the United States is on the verge of joining the eastern half as an area seriously impacted by acid pollution.

Let's strive to keep our minds open while we consider some more geography pertinent to the overall consideration of acid rain.

Two Kinds of Geography: Keys to Understanding As suggested earlier in this chapter, if we are to understand the impacts of acid rain, we need to combine the geography of acid rain with the geography of sensitivity to acid rain. What impact acid rain will have when it reaches the Earth is dependent on the buffering capacity the rain encounters. The amount of alkalinity contained in an ecosystem can make a big difference in determining what the effect of acid rain will be.

Large areas of North American are covered by soils that derive from sedimentary rocks rich in calcium carbonate. They are high in alkalinity and can be expected to buffer, or neutralize, large amounts of acid rain. Other large areas have soils that derive from igneous or metamorphic rocks and are comparatively low in alkalinity with little buffering capacity. As can be seen from Figure 3 (page 78), the coastal part of British Columbia, most of Washington, Oregon, Idaho, northern California, and the northwestern part of Nevada comprise an area with low-buffering capacity. The Appalachian and Adirondack Mountain regions and most of eastern Canada also have low-buffering capacity. Between the far western states and the far eastern areas lies an almost continuous area of low sensitivity to acid rain. Although some granitic areas in the highlands of Colorado have a higher potential for sensitivity than do the surrounding areas.

Surface waters across the continent differ in their buffering capacity in a manner analogous to that of soils. If you live in an area where it is necessary to have a water softener because of large concentrations of calcium carbonate in the water, you are probably not going to be hearing as much about local damage due to acid rain as do the folks whose water is naturally soft. *Hard* water is alkaline. *Soft* water is acid. As in the case of their soils, the waters of the northwestern and northeastern United States have relatively little calcium carbonate content with which to neutralize acid rain.

Does it follow then that the northwestern and the northeastern United States should be expected to have similar problems with acid rain? Not really. While their sensitivity to acid rain may be quite similar, their exposure to acid rain is quite different. The geography of emission of pollutants and the geography of acid deposition resulting from those pollutants are by no means uniform distributions.

We looked previously at the estimates of natural and man-made emissions that have been made and noted the wide range between the estimates made by different investigators. You may recall that, on a global basis, the inputs of sulfur to the atmosphere due to natural processes may range from low of 13 percent to a high of 35 percent. But a quite different picture comes into focus if we turn our attention to the eastern part of North America. There man-made emissions constitute 93 percent of the total sulfur input to the atmosphere. This disparity of estimates of relative contribution creates the basis for some diametrically opposed opinions. By focusing on the data for northeastern United States, an environmental activist can feel justified in stating that natural sources make a small contribution to acid rain. By considering the global estimates, people who are opposed to enactment of stringent controls, can feel justified in stating that the problem of acid rain is not going to be entirely solved by reducing man-made emissions. Which interpretation of the available data do you prefer?

Let's consider again, with a different emphasis, some of the emission data previously discussed. In 1980 the 31 states that lie east of the 95th meridian (that's the north-south line that crosses the Lake of the Woods in north-central Minnesota, then passes a few miles west of Kansas City and a few miles east of Houston) emitted an estimated 19,823,000 metric tons of sulfur dioxide out of a total of 24 million metric tons for the entire United States. A metric ton, which you may recall can also be called a tonne, is about 1.1 times the 2000 pound short ton, to which you may be more accustomed. So a metric ton is about 2200 pounds. Nine eastern states contributed 12,545,000 metric tons, or 52 percent of the total for the country. Ohio led the list with 2,401,000 metric tons. Next came Pennsylvania with 1,835,000, Indiana with 1,822,000, Illinois with 1,334,000, Missouri with 1,180,000, Kentucky with 1,017,000, Florida with 993,000, West Virginia with 987,000 and Tennessee with 977,000.

These impressively large numbers are difficult to relate to in the abstract. Let's see if they can be given a little more meaning in everyday terms. Ohio has an area of 41,222 square miles, and a population of something over 10,600,000. Ohio's 2,401,000 metric tons of sulfur-related emissions turns out to be about 200 pounds for every acre in the state or nearly 500 pounds for every person in the state. That is a lot of fumes per family.

States lying west of the 95th meridian contributed about 4,200,000 metric tons. These emissions were not uniformly distributed either. They ranged from the Texas contribution of 1,158,000 metric tons down to Alaska's 17,000 metric tons.

The lowest contribution of sulfur dioxide from any state was Vermont's 6,200 metric tons.

Now let's turn our attention again to emissions of the oxides of nitrogen. As is true in the case of sulfur, the emission of oxides of nitrogen by natural processes is an important part of the total input to the atmosphere. Estimates of the comparative ratio of natural to man-made emissions of oxides of nitrogen range from 5:1 to 1:1 for the earth as a whole. If we limit our attention to the United States, we see a picture similar to that for sulfur dioxide. Again the 31 eastern states contribute heavily. In 1980 they were responsible for 12,728,000 metric tons out of a total United States emission of 19,293,000 metric tons. The western states of Texas (2,308,000 metric tons) and California (1,111,000 metric tons) came in first and second in this dubious race, with the nine eastern states, that contributed so heavily to the sulfur dioxide input, again contributing heavily. Their combined input of 6,057,000 metric tons was 31 percent of the nation's total.

We have given our attention to the geographic distributions of pH sensitivity to acid rain, as well as sulfur dioxide and nitrogen oxides emissions. Are we ready now to stop studying geography and get down to the business of considering what we can do about acid rain? Not quite yet.

There is just a little more geography to be considered. Our examination of the geography of pH told us where the concentration of hydrogen ions in rainfall was high and where it was low, but it didn't address the matter of how much hydrogen ion was being deposited where. We also have a quantitative idea about where the chemicals that turn into sulfuric and nitric acid start out, but we haven't yet gotten quantitative about how much nitrate ion or sulfate ion gets deposited where.

It isn't as easy to generate impressive statistics about deposition as it is about emission. There are voluminous records that permit the making of credible calculations of amounts and locations of emissions. When we turn our attention to the transfer of pollutants back out of the air onto the earth, we are in a considerably less certain circumstance. On occasion, we can see visible pollution plumes returning to earth downwind from short smokestacks. It doesn't overtax the imagination to consider that some of the pollutants we can't see also return to earth without being scavenged by the purging action of rain or snow. As was discussed earlier, we know it is possible to establish sampling networks that use sophisticated instrumentation to take near-surface samples of polluted air. The data collected make possible inferences about the deposition of various ions.

From such sampling networks, it has been determined that dry deposition of pollutants usually occurs comparatively closer to emission sources than does the wet deposition we call acid rain. We have noted earlier that the longer the polluting oxides of sulfur and nitrogen reside in the atmosphere, the greater the chances for further oxidation to convert them to their more acidic forms. Involvement with precipitation also becomes more likely the longer the resident time of the oxides in the atmosphere.

Estimates of the quantitative deposition of hydrogen ions, the stuff that makes acid acid, have been made. The unit of measurement used in these estimates is milligrams per square meter. It may help to know that a milligram per square meter is equivalent to 5.5 pounds per square mile.

If I tell you that in 1980 Seattle received 10 milligrams of hydrogen ion per square meter, does it help to convert that to 55 pounds per square mile? Can you visualize yourself spreading 55 pounds of chemical fertilizer over an area of a square mile? In 1980 practically all of the area between Seattle and Kansas City, Missouri, received less than 10 milligrams of hydrogen ions per square meter. From the longitude of Kansas City eastward over the United States and Canada the deposition increased. Indiana, Ohio, Pennsylvania and New York received 60 milligrams per square meter or 330 pounds per square mile. Such high deposition isn't surprising, if we recall the major contribution to emission tonnage those states made the same year.

The 1980 geographic distributions of sulfate deposition and nitrate deposition are shown in Figures 4 and 5 (pages 79 and 80), respectively. As in the case of hydrogen ion deposition, the 31 eastern states are shown to be the recipients of the heaviest deposition. Ohio and its near neighbors again stand out. Because sulfate and nitrate ions are much heavier than hydrogen ions, the quantities of sulfate and nitrate are much more impressive. Sulfate deposition over much of Ohio equaled or exceeded 4,000 milligrams per square meter, or 22,000 pounds per square mile. That equals about 10 metric tons for each of Ohio's 41,222 square miles. When you consider that Ohio emitted 2,401,100 metric tons of sulfur dioxide in 1980, it become apparent that a generous portion of Ohio's emissions are coming back to earth elsewhere.

Elsewhere may include places like Vermont. In 1980 Vermont emitted 6,200 metric tons of sulfur dioxide and 22,400 metric tons of oxides of nitrogen. Deposition of hydrogen, sulfate and nitrate ions over Vermont, that same year, appears to have totaled approximately 4,500 milligrams per square meter, or 24,750 pounds per square mile. Vermont's total area is 9,609 square miles. If each of those square miles received the 24,750 pounds of deposition mentioned above, for a total of 108,101 metric tons, Vermont could have hypothetically acquired 79,500 metric tons that were donated by its upwind neighbors. It is understandable why the people of Vermont might view this generosity with severely, restrained enthusiasm.

Who Are The Actors in the Acid Rain Melodrama?

The controversial drama surrounding acid rain is being played out on an extensive stage that crosses national boundaries and spans continents and oceans. The cast of characters is huge. Many of the players have voluntarily sought their roles in the play. Others have been dragged on stage kicking and screaming. A number of special-interest groups are included in the cast.

I have named each of the next five chapters for a group of emotionally involved actors which I have identified as: The Environmental Groups, The Coal Mining Groups, The Electric Power Groups, The Scientific Community, and The Government Agencies.

Don't let the fact that I have divided the vast cast into only five groups mislead you into expecting that only five attitudes will emerge about the nature of the acid rain problem and what should be done to solve it. There are, as you might expect, significant differences of opinion within the designated groups as well as among them.

My intent is to present for your understanding as accurate a representation as possible of the attitudes that exist within the various special-interest groups. To minimize the introduction of unrecognized personal bias, I have elected to make extensive use of words exactly as they have come from the mouths and typewriters of official spokespersons (ugh!) for the various groups. The numerous quotations presented are reproduced as faithfully as the editing process will permit. I have striven to be fair to all in deciding what to present and what to leave out. I recognize that the selection process offers an insidious opportunity for introducing bias, either conscious or otherwise. But it is not my goal to persuade you to favor a particular attitude. That choice, if you make one, is entirely up to you. My hope is that we can discover and understand each group's motivations for being in the play and what each is striving to accomplish and avoid.

It isn't usual book-writing practice to present a few paragraphs of text and call it a chapter. Although I experience an enjoyable feeling of accomplishment when I finish reading a chapter in any book, I am fairly confident that presenting chapters of a page or two (just to encourage a feeling of accomplishment in you) would qualify as going a little too far. A chapter like this one isn't a new record in brevity in my experience, however. I can recall reading a book in which the entire text of one chapter consisted of the words, "Get rid of it."

This chapter is as it is because I couldn't figure out a more even-handed and effective way to introduce the chapters that follow. Thank you for bearing with me.

The Environmental Groups

The awakening of the public consciousness to the folly of tolerating abuse of the environment we all share has spawned a multitude of environmentally-oriented organizations. Each of these has its own agenda and area of special emphasis, but concern about acid rain seems to be a common bond. It would be difficult, and not particularly productive, to attempt to list each organization that has taken a position on acid rain. That list might fill a sizeable book by itself. Examination of a few of the more outspoken positions should suffice for our purposes. Some environmental groups have been most active in lobbying for enactment, as soon as possible, of legislation which would enforce significant additional reduction of the emissions that contribute to the formation of acid rain. Others have dedicated sizeable amounts of money and personnel to the study of acid-rain issues with subsequent publication of their findings and positions. While there is a range of opinion within the environmentally-concerned community about what should be done to reduce the impact of acid rain, the center of gravity of opinion appears to be positioned in favor of application of presently available pollution-reduction technology. I have not encountered within the environmental community, acceptance of the Reagan administration position that waiting for additional knowledge about acid rain is advisable before taking corrective action. On the other hand, one doesn't have to hunt very hard for evidence of outspoken rejection of that policy.

Four well-known environmental groups have written me recently, soliciting support for their programs. Their letters give some insight into the emphasis each is placing on acid rain.

The Environmental Defense Fund is an organization which leaves little doubt where it stands on the question of acid rain. An undated four-page letter signed by William Y. Brown, executive director, solicited my membership in the Environmental Defense Fund, requested a generous contribution, and urged my supportive vote on a National Acid Rain Initiative Ballot. The letter began with a boxed paragraph that stated:

"The administration is mounting a cynical campaign to trivialize the acid rain crisis. You'll hear them refer to it exclusively as a problem of saving fish in Northeast lakes. Yet scientists have demonstrated acid rain's irreversible damage not only to lakes but also to soil. Forests are in decline all over the East and acid rain is the major suspect. Scientists have shown that acid rain leaches toxic chemicals into drinking water. They are investigating damage to human health from sulfuric acid in the air. By completing the enclosed National Acid Rain Ballot, you will help the Environmental Defense Fund resolve this issue now. Can we stand another month of inaction on acid rain?"

The letter went on:

"Dear Friend:

"The alarming scientific facts about acid rain are disappearing in Washington's political smog!

"Inside the White House and Congress, lobbying by utility companies has out-weighed scientific fact and common sense. This backroom maneuvering has crippled the move toward a strong acid rain law!

"Your vote on the enclosed ballot can help break the logjam on acid rain."Your accompanying contribution to the Environmental Defense Fund can put a strong acid rain law on the books . . . a law that would reduce by half America's sulfur emissions and the devastating acid rain they cause!

"Here at the Environmental Defense Fund, we know that millions of Americans are outraged by the administration's stalling on acid rain.

"We know, because the Environmental Defense Fund has been a leader in bringing the truth about acid rain to the American people. Even as the White House stalls, evidence accumulates of new dangers from acid rain.

"EDF recently published a report firmly establishing that the scientific knowledge behind acid rain is comprehensive enough to assure that a 50 percent reduction in sulfur emissions will protect the environment.

"Though many Americans know acid rain as a threat to fishing, scientists are now finding that acid rain wipes out whole lake ecosystems and may do irreversible damage to soil and to timber stands.

"Moreover, some water supplies are suspected or proven to be contaminated with toxic metals leached by acid rain.

"And in major cities, suspended sulfuric acid particles — one of the 'demons of acid rain' — may be the most dangerous part of air pollution.

"See the enclosed fact sheet for more details on the vast damage now being done by acid rain!

"President Reagan made a big show of accepting the need for action on acid rain. He made a big show of instructing his (then) new EPA administrator, William Ruckelshaus, to formulate recommendations to Congress, where momentum is building for an acid rain bill.

"But when business lobbyists tightened the screws, the White House announced that recommendations by EPA and by its own select scientific panel on acid rain would be postponed — indefinitely.

"Do you want political wrangling in the White House and Congress to stall our efforts to stop acid rain?

"If not, I urge you to sign and return the enclosed Acid Rain Initiative Ballot today!

"If possible, please include a contribution to the Environmental Defense Fund, to continue our leadership in the fight against acid rain.

"The Environmental Defense Fund has led the way in the rigorous scientific analysis of facts like these:

"'The acid rain problem is not limited to the northeastern United States and neighboring Canada.'

"The Environmental Defense Fund's Colorado office has compiled data demonstrating that acid rain is beginning to affect high-altitude mountain lakes in the Rockies. Widespread damage in the Northeast foreshadows a nationwide problem to come, unless we act promptly and strongly.

"Acid rain can be lessened by reducing emissions from coal-fired plants.

"The Environmental Defense Fund's physicist, Dr. Michael Oppenheimer, has proved that restrictions on sulfur-dioxide emissions will be effective in reducing acid rain. This conclusion has been adopted by the National Academy of Sciences.

"Congressional leaders, spurred by this new scientific evidence, are ready to enact an acid rain law. The Environmental Defense Fund has led the way in creating this momentum. We must continue to lead, to make sure that the bill passed is the strongest one possible.

"To lead this campaign, we need your support as a member of the Environmental Defense Fund.

"Right now, the Environmental Defense Fund is actively involved in economic and scientific analysis of several acid rain bills. Our initial studies indicate it is feasible to reduce sulfur emissions by 12,000,000 tons per year by 1993. I'm sure you know that such a proposal must be supported by very accurate documentation. We must be able to defend our figures against a utility lobby that will have many times our budget at its disposal.

"We must not let our hard-earned momentum dissipate while the White House and Congress play politics with this devastating acid pollution. That's why we need your contribution today.

"The administration needs to hear loudly and clearly that millions of Americans are opposed to playing politics with critical environmental issues.

"The Environmental Defense Fund is uniquely qualified to lead the battle for an acid-rain bill because of our long-standing reputation for finding economically sound solutions to environmental problems. Members of Congress and the scientific community know that the Environmental Defense Fund backs up its recommendations with hard scientific research and exhaustive economic analysis of the consequences.

"But to succeed in Congress, our plan needs the public endorsement of citizens like you.

"Will you add your voice to this nationwide cry for action?

"When you sign and return your Acid Rain Initiative Ballot, you put yourself on record for swift and effective action to reduce the 26 million tons of sulfur dioxide that we pour into the atmosphere every year! You put yourself on record for strong legislation that will address the problem.

"When you accompany your ballot with a membership contribution of $20, $25, $50, $100, or more to the Environmental Defense

Fund, you strengthen the campaign to put real scientific facts before Congress and before the people.

"As a member, you will also be eligible to receive periodic updates on our work, including the informative EDF Letter six times per year.

"We need your help today.

"In coming months, we must not only reach millions more people with the facts, but we must also continue to provide members of Congress with the detailed analysis of the acid rain crisis that will allow them to make informed decisions on the measures needed to stop our acid rain losses.

"Please join us today. Cast your vote for stopping acid rain . . . and please join our membership of concerned citizens by making a generous contribution to the Environmental Defense Fund.

Sincerely,
William Y. Brown
Executive Director

"PS: Whether you join EDF or not at this time, make sure you send us your vote on the enclosed National Acid Rain Initiative Ballot."

The above letter conveys clearly how the Environmental Defense Fund views its mission relative to acid rain, and its opinion of the role played by the White House and lobbyists for utility companies.

In following weeks I received letters soliciting my support from the Natural Resources Council, the Sierra Club, and the Solar Lobby. While each organization stressed its own particular environmental concern, the letters had a remarkable similarity. Reproducing them as completely as I have the letter from the Environmental Defense Fund might add up to too much of a good thing. I'll present portions of each of the letters selected to give you a feeling for the nature and intensity of the concerns expressed.

The following paragraphs were part of a letter from John Adams, executive director of the Natural Resources Defense Council.

"Dear Friend,

"For the past several years, you and I have been victims of pollution scams run by some of America's most reputable corporations.

"These companies have used the scams to avoid installing air pollution controls that are required by federal law.

"The result? You and I are being robbed of clean air — one of our most precious and critical possessions.

"Air pollution kills at least 15,000 people every year. It causes chronic illness in millions of others. Not to mention the billions of dollars polluted air costs us in hospitalization, disability payments, damage to crops, lakes, and forests.

"That's why the Natural Resources Defense Council has already blown the whistle on eight of the pollution scams. But we cannot stop the rest alone. We need your help."

In addition to presenting the details of how NRDC had successfully confronted National Steel, Monsanto and General Motors in court over air-pollution related issues, the letter presented strong criticism of how the Environmental Protection Agency is conducting its business. Here are a few examples of that criticism:

"I know, such a deal (EPA's agreeing to accept paving of dirt roads for dust control in lieu of requiring installation of scrubbers on National Steel furnace #2) is almost impossible to believe. Yet, there's more! The Environmental Protection Agency allegedly told National Steel in private meetings that this trade would be 'easy to approve.' So the Court's deadline to halt the pollution from Furnace #2 passed without any action being taken.

"We let EPA know that we were on to Monsanto's ploy. So right now, EPA is reexamining Monsanto's clean-air credit.

"In an annual spot check, EPA discovered that nearly 700,000 General Motors engines failed to meet federal pollution standards for hazardous nitrogen oxides. Nitrogen oxides cause acid rain, as well as lung diseases in children and the elderly.

"But, instead of recalling the cars and protecting the owners as the law specifically requires, GM asked EPA if it could take clean-air credit — by promising to install better-than-required controls on some of the following year's cars. EPA okayed the deal. Naturally GM was only too delighted to avoid a costly recall.

"So we took EPA and General Motors to court. The result: three judges unanimously struck down GM's deal with EPA. And GM is now liable for fines up to $10,000 for every single car it failed to recall.

"Now consider this: Major polluters have swamped EPA with no less than 150 applications for clean-air credits.

"NRDC uncovered three phony credits — and five more just like them — after inspecting only ten credit applications. Imagine what awaits EPA, and us, in the 150 credits we haven't even looked at!

"Why isn't EPA doing more to uncover these frauds? The excuse we received recently from an associate EPA administrator was, 'We're trying to police as best we can, but, well, some people rob banks.'

"We say: EPA's bank is being robbed far too often! If EPA can't catch the robbers, then NRDC will do it for them."

The NRDC is obviously concerned about the effects of pollution on human health and has set itself the task of seeing that polluting industries and the federal government abide by existing pollution-control laws, as opposed to stressing a need for new pollution-control legislation. Although acid rain was mentioned only once in the above letter, NRDC has a strong interest in seeing large-scale control programs mandated by legislation. Here is part of the testimony delivered on behalf of NRDC at the February, 1984, Senate Hearings on Acid Rain:

"I am Richard Ayres, chairman of the National Clean Air Coalition. I am here today to testify on behalf of the Natural Resources Defense Council.

"Mr. Chairman, the acid rain data has been distorted by a mistaken political paradigm. This paradigm holds that acid rain control will benefit only a few lakes and streams, mostly in the Adirondacks. It also holds that all of the cost of the control programs will be in the Midwest but none of the benefits will occur there because no sensitive lakes and streams are found there. Believing this paradigm, many midwestern politicians oppose acid rain control. Others argue that any control programs should be small and should focus on the sources closest to the affected lakes and should not include controls on midwestern sources.

"Well, Mr. Chairman, this paradigm is wrong. First, controls on acid rain-causing pollutants will produce a wide range of human, ecological, and economic benefits. Second, the largest pollution reductions under the leading acid rain program will occur in the Midwest resulting in major benefits there. Third, a 12-million-ton SO_2 reduction program is needed to fully protect lakes and streams and to increase protection for other resources. Fourth, the sources with the largest impact on lakes and streams, on visibility, on materials, and on human exposure are located in the industrialized areas of the Midwest and the Southeast. These sources must be included in a control program if it is to be effective in achieving broad resource protection benefits."

The word "paradigm" didn't trigger instant understanding when I read Mr. Ayres' statement, so I turned to the dictionary for help. I offer you what I learned, par.a.digm (the last syllable can be pronounced "dim" or "dime," whichever suits one's fancy) n. 1. A list of all the inflectional forms of a word taken as an illustrative example of the conjugation or declension to which it belongs. 2. Any example or model. Until I got to the word "model," I was in the dark as to how to recognize a "political paradigm" the next time one came my way. I hope I'm not the only one.

The concerns of the Sierra Club were revealed in an undated six page letter signed by Michael McCloskey, chairman of the Sierra Club. Again I've selected a few paragraphs that reflect the attitude of the writer.

"Dear Friend,

"Believe me . . . There is nothing so dangerous to the environment as a lame duck president. Especially one who doesn't care one whit about environmental protection.

"The president doesn't have to answer to the voters again. The right-wing ideologues and corporate cronies around him know that they have four years and only four years to make it easy for some of America's biggest, richest, most powerful and most dangerous corporations to get their selfish way. In fact, their four-year assault on your future has already begun.

"Timber companies want to radically step up logging operations and timber sales in our national forests. Giant oil and gas conglomerates are pressing — again — for rights to drill on as much public land as possible. The chemical companies want to block aggressive clean-up of abandoned toxic waste dumps. And, despite scandals and enormous surpluses, the coal industry continues to demand new, huge coal lease sales.

"And beyond all this, industry and the far right are also trying to get their way in the back rooms, far from the headlines and public scrutiny . . .

. . . Unlike the early years of the Reagan administration, when environmental abuses were so blatant that the public was keenly aware of the need to fight the economic interests, today those who scorn nature have become FAR MORE SUBTLE.

"They've stayed out of the headlines. Off TV programs. In short, they have taken great pains to avoid the spotlight and the harsh glare of public opinion.

"They know that their best chance is to quietly strip federal agencies of their watchdog function . . . and they are doing it. So who's going to be on guard watching out for the public health and the environment? Who's going to see that the laws are enforced as written, not as polluters wish they had been written?

"The Sierra Club, that's who — America's oldest and most effective environmental lobby."

Mr. McCloskey went on to recount the role he and the Sierra Club's supporters had played in protecting a valuable forest resource from potentially negligent treatment at the hands of the Forest Service.

"When I was a young field representative with the Sierra Club, one of my jobs was to survey roadless areas that the Forest Service might stop protecting. If left undefended, the areas would have been ruined — roaded, logged, and mined.

"Well, I spent hours pouring (sic) over Forest Service maps. Some areas did not demand protection. Others did. Often, I would hike into remote places to evaluate the land first hand.

"One such trip took me to the magnificent Sky Lakes region in southern Oregon.

"I fell in love with this magnificent, untrammeled landscape. Its lakes stretch serenely along the crest of the Cascades south of Crater Lake National Park. Their waters reflect the shifting patterns of towering cumulus clouds. Few knew the Sky Lakes even existed. But I knew at once the Sierra Club had to protect this special place.

"It has been 22 years since I first visited the Sky Lakes. But it is only recently that its 118,000 acres received statutory protection.

"The Sky Lakes Wilderness bill was passed by Congress — and signed into law by the President — only because of the two decades of vigilance by the Sierra Club, our seasoned lobbyists, our network of activists nationwide, our local chapters' continuing concern —

and our loyal members. The public will now receive a dividend whose worth is beyond measure.

"The Sky Lakes story helps me to explain why the Sierra Club really does need your help today to protect and preserve our life-giving environment tomorrow — and for years to come.

"You see, bureaucratic wheels turn ever so slowly. Environmental fights are usually complicated, sometimes tedious, and almost always lengthy. With the Sky Lakes, our battle spanned six administrations and 11 Congresses. So vigilance and tenacity really are important.

"And no other environmental organization — not one — is more vigilant . . . tenacious . . . successful, when it comes to lobbying our lawmakers and leaders and protecting the land we love, the air we breathe, the water we drink, and the wildlife we cherish, than the Sierra Club."

The Sierra Club's attitude was revealed in these paragraphs:

"Clean Air: Utility lobbyists representing the dirtiest power plants and smelters will fight even harder to block acid rain legislation than they did last year. Meanwhile EPA is moving to dismantle regulatory protections under the act; and higher emissions from power plants, trucks, buses, and strip mines are all in the process of being approved by EPA. The Sierra Club is vigorously pursuing a major campaign to get the Clean Air Act amended to clean up acid rain and toxic pollutants, and is fighting EPA's efforts to weaken its regulations under the current law.

"With the help of our friends in Congress . . . we can reinstitute the practice of oversight hearings, established to enable Congress to monitor the workings of the Executive Branch.

"Through our expert lobbyists . . . we can urge our elected officials to launch formal investigations into the most blatant cases of government favoritism.

"Through dedicated and hard-working staff attorneys . . . we can, if necessary, take the government and the corporations to court, literally forcing them to obey laws written specifically to protect America's public lands."

The fourth and final letter that I am about to present for your consideration of attitudes came to me from Dennis Hayes, chairman of the Solar Lobby. Like its predecessors it was undated and addressed me in friendly terms:

"Dear Friend,

"We don't think that President Reagan and his administration really want to despoil our land, assault us with acid rain and toxic wastes, choke us with air pollutants, expose us to unsafe nuclear plants and send our utility bills soaring.

"But that's just what they're doing!

"The problem — the real problem — is that the Reagan administration's fiscal priorities are so structured that the traditional fatcat energy providers — nuclear, coal and oil — continue to receive massive tax subsidies, while the developing renewable energy technologies — wind, solar, and wood — get little or no help from public funds.

"There is no responsible energy analyst in the field today who doubts that the future will have to be powered by renewable energy. These experts recognize that without inexpensive, renewable energy sources, the world will face cold and dark days ahead. The only disagreement is about how soon these dark days will be upon us.

"Solar Lobby's concern is with making the nation and the world become better prepared to plan instead for a bright future."

After urging me to join in supporting their efforts, the letter continued with:

"In the past five years, we have seen this country's commitment to renewable energy sources gutted and then ignored. With astounding short-sightedness, our government continues to dip into the pork barrel to fund the nuclear energy industry lavishly, while slashing the very research and development funds that could make our nation 100 percent energy-independent.

"For inexplicable reasons, the administration has argued that renewable energy, alone among the available energy sources, must develop on its own, with virtually NO HELP in the way of public funding, subsidies, or tax incentives.

"Perhaps that's a persuasive argument — except that at the same time, this administration continues to funnel over $25 billion annually into subsidies for the tired old conventional energy industries!

"The Solar Lobby's first commitment was to achieve a phaseout of all energy subsidies - tax credits, depletion allowances, etc. We feel that our national tradition of independent enterprise should apply to the energy industry just as it does to most of the rest of the economy.

"But as long as the fossil-fuel and nuclear industries continue to receive such huge tax subsidies — as the President's tax reform plan calls for — we are determined to see that renewable energy technologies can compete fairly by sharing in the extension of their tax credits.

"In early April of this year, the Solar Lobby was instrumental in getting a new bill introduced in Congress. This bill, entitled The Renewable Energy and Transition Act, was H.R. 2001 in the House and S. 1220 in the Senate.

"As a transition measure until all energy subsidies have been eliminated, this bill extends renewable energy and conservation tax credits to users of these sources for several years. The passage of this bill has become a crucial part of our work this year, as the existing credits will expire December 31, 1985.

"The unfairness of the distribution of tax credits is quite evident: Renewable sources now provide almost 10 percent of this country's total energy. Yet they receive less than $1 billion in tax incentives. At the same time, the nuclear industries take in $10 billion (in incentives), while producing only 4.3 percent of the nation's energy.

"THESE NUMBERS JUST DON'T MAKE SENSE!

"Why should the nuclear and fossil-fuel lobbyists be able to swarm all over Capitol Hill and take away this unwarranted bounty? Because they have been around longer, and have enormous funding resources behind them!

"Yet the long-run consequences of this short-run use of power could be disastrous . . . we all watched Three Mile Island with horror a few years ago . . . we've seen the results - both economically and socially - of shortages of petroleum . . . and strip-mining of coal ruins the useful development of millions of acres of land for generations.

"Renewable energy sources are the way of the future — possibly the only way!

"Yet the electric utilities and nuclear power industries are advocating the construction of more than 400 major centralized power plants over the next 15 years. The price tag? $1 trillion dollars . . . ($1,000,000,000,000)!!! And you can bet that we taxpayers are going to spring for the vast part of that, one way or the other, either through taxes or through higher utility bills!

"If we are not successful in getting the Renewable Energy and Conservation Transition Act passed this year, it could threaten the very existence of the emerging renewable energy technologies.

"That is why the work of Solar Lobby is more critical than ever. We must move away from short-term traditional solutions to face the complex energy problems head on. We just can't duck the future — it's not going to go away.

"America is now at an energy crossroads. If you and I do not act, we as a nation could be swept down a path of increasing dependence on dwindling energy resources and imported oil. The environmental, economic, and national-security consequences could be devastating."

The letter went on to urge me to join in support of the Solar Lobby's membership. It then reaffirmed the Solar Lobby's position regarding renewable energy technologies:

"We are dedicated to ensuring that renewable energy technologies — solar, wind, geothermal, biomass (including ethanol), hydropower, and ocean thermal — have an equal chance of competing with the more traditional and heavily subsidized forms of energy.

"It will be an extremely tough uphill fight. And the responsible energy path will probably be abandoned in the unhappy event that we are unable to counteract the massive political pressures that can be brought by the major energy corporations."

The letter concluded with a description of the benefits I would receive from becoming a member.

Let's look analytically at the information from these four groups. There is some remarkable similarity. The tone of the letters from all four is sincere. I was impressed by the fact that in each of the letters I received I was greeted as a dear friend, informed of a conspiracy against my best interests, and urged to act promptly to support the good fight that was being waged on my behalf. So similar were the techniques of giving emphasis by underlining, additional indentation of some paragraphs, frequent use of three periods and two hyphens as punctuation, and the use of numerous one-sentence paragraphs that I began to wonder whether all four letters were prepared by the same person, or if all four authors had attended the same workshop on persuasive letter writing.

Acid rain is mentioned in each of the letters, with emphasis that ranges from intense to casual. Each of the organizations is seen by its spokesman as providing leadership in a crucial fight against powerful and corrupt forces that are conspiring to inflict more acid rain on an unsuspecting public in order to gain selfish ends. The suggested strategies for winning the fight involve court action by dedicated lawyers, lobbying for more favorable legislation than now exists, and/or more stringent enforcement of existing controls.

The Reagan administration, much of the Congress, EPA, and government, in general, are considered to be less-than-worthy and perhaps even corrupt. Adversarial confrontation is offered as the way out of the particular crisis that each organization seeks to highlight. There seems to be conviction that power, not reason, will determine the outcome of the acid rain controversy.

Many other environmental groups have been active in addressing the acid rain problem. For example, an organization, headquartered in Concord, New Hampshire, held "A Citizens' Conference To Stop Acid Rain." Listed as sponsors and cosponsors were: Friends of the Earth Foundation, New Hampshire Citizens' Task Force on Acid Rain, Acid Rain Foundation, Appalachian Mountain Club, Appalachian Mountain Club New Hampshire Chapter, Audubon Society of New Hampshire, Defenders of Wildlife, Massachusetts Audubon Society, National Clean Air Coalition, National Wildlife Federation, Natural Resources Defense Council, New Hampshire Natural Resources Forum, Sierra Club, Society for the Protection of New Hampshire Forests and Vermont Clean Air Coalition.

The conference produced the following document which was placed in the record of the February, 1984, Senate hearings:

"CITIZENS' PLATFORM

"Air pollution and associated acid rain are national problems which are causing extensive damage to our environment. Without immediate action to stop acid rain, this damage will continue with severe consequences to the natural resources, public health and economy of our nation.

"Solutions to the acid rain problem must be initiated by the federal government. Congress has tried but failed to pass a law that would stop acid rain. President Reagan has failed to provide leadership in solving the problem.

"The citizens of the United States urgently call upon the President and Congress to establish, early this year, an Acid Rain Control Program which provides for the following:

"1. A commitment to reduce sulfur dioxide emissions nationwide by 50 percent by 1990 toward reducing wet sulfate deposition to less than 18 pounds/acre/year (20 kilograms/hectare/year) in moderately sensitive areas and eight pounds/acre/ year (nine kilograms/ hectare/ year) in extremely sensitive areas

"2. Significant interim reductions in sulfur dioxide emissions

"3. Further reductions in nitrogen oxides emissions by 1990

"4. Acid rain control accomplished without extensive economic disruption. Proven and environmentally sound technologies to control acid rain are available now. Control techniques that both preserve existing jobs and create new ones can and should be applied.

"5. Measures to protect sensitive but still healthy ecosystems to prevent degradation from increases in acid pollution

"6. Establishment with the Canadian Government of a joint United States/Canada Acid Rain Control Program to achieve these objectives"

The National Wildlife Federation made its position clear at the same 1984 Senate hearings. The Federation is the nation's largest conservation organization, with over 4 million members. It was represented by Benjamin Dysart, president and chairman of the board. Included in the testimony were the following statement:

"We are now, at National Wildlife Federation, just completing a brand new survey of 1,027 United States acid deposition researchers. The respondents to date have indicated their overwhelming support, based on the record, based on the evidence, for an aggressive acid rain control program. Only 14 percent of our respondents believed that more research or monitoring was needed before further controls should be undertaken. Four out of five of those scientists responding considered the risk sufficiently great as to necessitate immediate and decisive steps to curtail emissions that cause acid rain. This seems to afford little support for the logic of delay embraced by the administration."

I think by now you should have a pretty accurate picture of where environmental organizations stand on the subject of acid rain. Let's move on now to some of the other actors in the melodrama.

The Coal Mining Groups

The coal mining industry in the United States has a very strong interest in the subject of acid rain. Coal, for use in the utility market, is mined in 22 of the 48 contiguous states of the United States. There are significant regional differences in the sulfur content of the nation's coal. These differences work against the development of a uniform, industry-wide attitude about what should be done to mitigate the impacts of acid rain, but there does appear to be an industry-wide consensus that the early enactment of control legislation advocated by environmental groups would be ill-advised. It is not often that coal-mine owners and unions representing coal miners see eye to eye on a subject of concern to both groups, but unanimity does appear to exist where acid rain is concerned. There is intense concern on the part of both management and labor that disastrous economic disruption could result from enactment of presently proposed acid-rain-control legislation.

Several coal-mining associations made their positions clear in testimony presented to the February, 1984, Senate hearings on acid rain. Let's look at the positions presented.

The Alliance for Clean Energy represents the interests of the nation's low-sulfur coal producers. Its position was presented by William T. McCormick, Jr., president, American Natural Resources Co. ACE believes that mandatory scrubber legislation would not be as cost-effective as legislation that permitted freedom of choice between scrubbers and fuel switching. Mr. McCormick made seven points in support of the ACE position:

1) There is as much low-sulfur coal in the eastern part of the United States as there is in the western part, so the scrubber-non-scrubber issue is not one of East versus West.

2) In most cases converting to use of low-sulfur coal would be less expensive than installing scrubbers.

3) Many states have done a good job of cleaning up the environment and should not be made to pay for states that haven't.

4) Cleaning up the environment can be accomplished more quickly by switching to low-sulfur coal than by installing scrubbers.

5) Job loss, due to fuel switching, is an issue only in Ohio and Illinois. Congress could enact cost-effective assistance programs that would help affected people to relocate and adjust.

6) Mandatory scrubbing would lock-in existing technology with its sludge problems.

7) Proposed legislation would limit growth in those states which have done a good job of cleaning up their environment.

Carl E. Bagge, president, National Coal Association testified, "The nation's coal industry is united in its opposition to this legislation." (S.768). He characterized the nation's air-quality management philosophy as successful during the thirteen years that the Clean Air Act had been in existence and urged that its workable framework not be tightened by new legislation. He labeled the acid rain provisions of the proposed legislation an "environmental neutron bomb" which would leave the Clean Air Act's structure in place but destroy its strength. He offered what he considered to be glaring examples of how the acid rain debate had been plagued by dealing with perceptions rather than realities. These were:

1) The perception that the long-distance transport theory of sulfur dioxide emissions is proven and universally accepted, whereas the reality is that the matter is still under research.

2) The perception that acid rain is the cause of widespread ecological damage and may be linked to human health problems, whereas the reality is that laboratory experiments have produced ambiguous results and no credible evidence exists that acid rain is involved in human health problems.

3) The perception that thousands upon thousands of lakes can no longer support fish and other aquatic life, whereas, according to the U.S. Fish and Wildlife Service, there are some 200 acidified lakes in the country all of them in the Northeast, chiefly in the Adirondacks, and situated at the higher elevations.

4) The perception that acid rain is increasing, whereas the reality is that no trends are evident based on existing information.

5) The perception that acid rain is the dominant influence in the acidification of lakes, whereas the reality is that the available evidence suggests that acidification of lakes is influenced more by the inability of the lake's surrounding soils to buffer naturally-occurring acids in the soils and vegetation.

6) The perception that existing clean air laws are inadequate to lower sulfur dioxide emissions from coal plants, whereas the reality sulfur dioxide emissions are falling steadily even as coal consumption continues to go up.

Mr. Bagge cited estimates that put the total capital and operational costs of the legislation at $100 billion, which he considered to be a "crapshoot with the consumers' money," with the odds weighted against success. In contrast to the environmental groups' position on the President's acid-rain policies, Mr. Bagge voiced his support and applause for Reagan, "Who courageously, we believe, is proposing direct, effective action to mitigate damages to lakes from acidification. The President's plan maintains the integrity of the Clean Air Act and its purposes and air quality regulations while expanding, considerably, acid rain research by the federal government."

Mr. Bagge's testimony concluded with:

"Why shouldn't sick lakes be healed at reasonable cost with proven methods? Why are we attacked when we suggest that and why is the administration attacked when it suggests that we heal the sick lakes by proven methods which the Scandinavians have done quite successfully with a minimal cost? Why should these crucial mitigation efforts continue to be reviled by the environmental community as 'band-aid' solutions if we are truly interested in dealing with the realities and not the perceptions of acid rain?

"The coal industry is deeply committed to finding the answers about acid rain's causes and effects that confound the best scientists in the world. Let's go ahead and repair the damage but let's not ask American consumers to spend additional billions of dollars more on a crapshoot before we know what we are doing. This is both unwise and imprudent public policy.

"We hope, and I add we sincerely pray — and we pray about these issues, I do at least, at night — that this Congress rejects this costly course and urge this committee to reject this unwise and imprudent legislation."

William G. Karis, vice president, corporate planning, Consolidation Coal Company, presented a written statement and a brief oral presentation which supported the position that the emission reduction legislation under consideration by the Congress was predicated on concepts that had little scientific support. He pointed out that the analyses of economic impact that had been made to the committee by others had only scratched the surface and ignored significant additional costs associated with closing mines — sealing the mines, removing surface structures, and reclaiming the surface areas disturbed during mining had not been addressed, nor had the ongoing liabilities for pensions, black lung payments, and workers compensation that would be funded from other sources if the mines were closed.

Consolidation Coal Company, which employs more than 17,000 people at 30 surface and underground mines in nine states, Canada, and Australia, is a subsidiary of Du Pont. It co-sponsored, with Peabody Coal Company, research studies by independent research groups to acquire a firm foundation for the company position on acid rain. Environmental Research and Technology, Inc., Systems Applications, Inc., Arthur D. Little Co., as well as Du Pont's Haskell Laboratory were enlisted to study trends in acidification, and carry out modeling of sulfate and nitrate chemistry, and of societal impacts and sulfate air pollution health effects, respectively. Here are some of Mr. Karis' statements about those studies:

"In support of our position, Mr. Chairman, I offer several items for the record. First is a list of recent scientific papers which show that the charge of widespread acid deposition damage in the United States cannot be substantiated by the evidence (Attachment B). Data going back as far as 1910 have recently been assembled which suggest that sulfur deposition throughout the eastern United States has remained more or less constant over the last 70 years. Higher quality data, gathered since the 1960s, show that dramatic reductions in bulk sulfur deposition have occurred during the last twenty years in the northeast. Other studies show that the acidification of lakes and streams in the northeast is an extremely slow process and may be primarily natural in occurrence. Last week, this committee heard EPA Administrator Ruckleshaus mention the possibility that all of the damage to lakes that will happen has already occurred. This hypothesis is consistent with the finding of no changes in lake water chemistry in several intensely-monitored lakes over the last five years.

"Second, I offer a study by Environmental Research and Technology, Inc. (Attachment C). The principal author of this study, Dr. George Hidy, was also one of the authors of the most recent National Academy of Sciences review of acid rain. This study examines historic trends in SO_2 and NO_x emissions in the eastern United States and trends in the deposition of acidifying substances. Among other findings, it reveals that only in the northeast (EPA regions I and II) do sulfur emission and sulfate deposition trends track each other closely. This suggests that, should protection of the Northeast prove necessary, far more control of locally-generated northeastern emissions than would occur under S. 768 will be required. The National Academy of Sciences Review stated that SO_2 emissions were limited to a relatively small zone of influence — on the order of 300 to 600 kilometers. S. 768 focuses too strongly on long range transport. As this committee is well aware, S. 768 employs an emission reduction allocation formula which includes only those sources in a state emitting at a rate exceeding 1.5 pounds SO_2/million British Thermal Units. If further SO_2 emission restrictions are a matter of critical concern, as this bill suggests, then it is not scientifically justifiable to allocate emissions reductions only from sources emitting greater than an arbitrary rate. SO_2 is SO_2 regardless of emission rate.

"Controlling SO_2 on the basis of emission rates would produce a kind of environmental gerrymandering which would subject the Midwest and the South to large emission reductions while virtually ignoring the considerable emissions generated by industrial and non-coal sources in the Northeast.

"To underscore the inequities which would be created by the allocation system in S. 768, I submit a calculation based on published emissions data (Attachment D). Although the tons of pollutants emitted per state may be less in the Northeast, the density of emissions (tons of acid precursor pollution per square mile) is not. Emission densities in the Northeast are comparable to those in the Midwest, further demonstrating the dominant role northeastern emissions may play in northeastern deposition.

"In sum, Mr. Chairman, these data suggest that the immense emission reductions contemplated by this bill are not warranted either by identified ecological damage or by current scientific understanding of source/receptor relationships. The particular method of allocating reductions in S. 768 is simply not supportable from a scientific viewpoint.

"Finally, Mr. Chairman, I would offer for the committee's consideration two other scientific studies. The first is a study by Systems Applications Inc. which will be printed next week. Copies will be submitted to the record shortly thereafter. This study advances the state of scientific understanding of atmospheric chemistry and reopens the question of nonlinearity. It demonstrates that, in sharp contrast to the *NAS Review,* the atmosphere may behave in a strongly non-linear fashion. That is, large reductions in SO_2 emissions might result in much smaller reductions in sulfate deposition.

"The other is a study (performed by Du Pont and Du Pont's Haskell Laboratories for Consol) which lays to rest the charge that excess deaths are occurring because of sulfate concentrations in the atmosphere (Attachment E). The allegation is not supported by the evidence."

Mr. Karis went on to urge the committee to withold judgment until research programs authorized by Congress were completed.

Key Terms: Linearity and Nonlinearity If Mr. Karis' discussion of linearity and nonlinearity left you wondering what he was talking about, this might be a good place to insert some discussion of linearity as it applies to acid rain. The term will come up frequently in the debates over controlling acid deposition. If a debate about linearity versus nonlinearity is to be understandable, the terms *linear* and *nonlinear* should have clearly-defined meanings in your mind.

If your daily use of mathematics doesn't include practice with the finer points of geometry, you may not remember that the word *linear* is used in mathematics to describe a straight line. A relationship between any two variables that can be represented on a graph as a straight line is considered to be a "linear relationship." If a curved line is required to represent the relationship, the relationship is considered to be *nonlinear*.

To carry this just a little further, suppose you wanted to buy a fleet of cars. If the first dealer you contacted quoted you a price of $10,000 per car, regardless of the number you bought, the relationship between fleet number and total cost would be linear. Five cars would cost you half as much as ten and one fourth as much as twenty. The graph of the relationship between fleet number and fleet cost would be a straight line.

If you went to a competitive dealer, who offered to sell you the first car at $10,000 with a progressively increasing discount on each succeeding car, the relationship between fleet number and fleet cost would be nonlinear, and its graph would be a curved line which continually increased in curvature as the number of cars in the fleet increased. Under such an agreement, the cost of a five-car fleet would be somewhat more than half the cost of a ten-car fleet and a lot more than a quarter of the cost of a twenty-car fleet.

To bring things closer to the acid rain control issue, consider an idealized case of a land in which there was only one SO_2 emission source and one acid-sensitive receptor site. If the wind always blew from the source toward the receptor site with a constant velocity, and, if the SO_2 traveled under the influence of a constant coefficient of oxidation, turbulent mixing, and washout by rain, a 50 percent reduction in the amount of emissions from the source could be expected to reduce the acid deposition at the receptor site by a comparable 50 percent. But if one or more of those supposed constants became a variable, the relation between the emissions leaving the source and the acid being deposited at that one sensitive site would change, with a good chance of becoming nonlinear.

If we turn our attention now to the real world, where there are muliple sources and multiple sites and where the wind direction and velocity, turbulent mixing, oxidation, and rainfall are all decidedly variable, just what the outcome of a 50 percent reduction in emissions will be at a particular site is difficult to predict. Over long periods of time it is possible for highly-variable individual events to have average effects that resemble those that would occur if each event were identical.

In this way, the long-term, long-range relationship between emissions reduction and acid deposition reduction could appear to be linear even though the individual events operated in a variable and nonlinear mode. It would depend on how much nonlinearity was masked by the averaging process.

Averages can be tricky. There are desert sites where the average rainfall for a summer month may be as much as half an inch, but if that average results from a five-inch rain once every 10 years, with nine years of absolute drouth intervening, you could get awfully thirsty waiting for the average rain to occur. The average pH in a lake may be a value usually considered harmless to fish, say 5.0. But if that average results from an intense but brief burst of very high acidity snowmelt followed by a return to months of harmless acidity levels, there may not be many survivors around to enjoy the average condition.

The linearity versus nonlinearity debate pits the people who want to move ahead now on stronger emissions control legislation against those who aren't convinced that reducing emissions by 50 percent will reduce acid deposition by anywhere near that percentage. If the supply of effective oxidizing substances turns out to be the limiting factor in the conversion of SO_2 to sulfuric acid, a 50 percent reduction in emissions could result in disappointingly small changes in acid deposition.

Back to the Coal-Mining Industry Let's return now to our discussion of Mr. Karis' testimony. The assertion that the study by Du Pont lays to rest the charge that excess deaths are occurring because of sulfate concentrations seems just a bit wishful. A report prepared by Brookhaven National Laboratories for the United States Office of Technology Assessment included an estimate of 51,000 "excess deaths" in 1978 in the U.S. and Canada due to sulfate pollutants. The Du Pont study did a quite thorough job of discrediting the methodology employed in arriving at that estimate, but it isn't likely that the subject has been laid to rest. There aren't many acid-rain issues that have been laid to rest so completely that "Yes, but . . . "s can't be found, if the stakes are high enough.

Additional testimony, by a number of people representing associations of coal interests, gave support to the "Don't rush to legislate" position. Joining in backing a go-slow-on-legislation policy was the Mining and Reclamation Council of America, an association of over 200 coal producing companies and 32 state and regional coal associations. The council represents over 3000 coal operators and coal industry suppliers.

Mr. Neal S. Tostenson, president of the Ohio Mining and Reclamation Association took on the press, Canada, and the League of Women voters in his testimony. His positions were made very clear: "I am president of the Ohio Mining and Reclamation Association, a coal trade association in southeastern Ohio. As a farmer and landowner and resident of that part of the state of Ohio, I stand here today in support of President Reagan's position; and we in Ohio feel it took real courage with the press the way it has been on this issue to stand up and take the position he has. We feel it is a responsible position." Mr. Tostenson told the committee that he was a registered Democrat, but that didn't affect his support of President Reagan's position on acid rain.

Mr. Tostenson was equally outspoken in his explanation of Canada's interest in seeing the United States reduce emissions by 50 percent. "I am not going to go into the scientific debate on this issue but how I see it affects Ohio. We have had continuing forays into Ohio by the Canadians and I think, number one, when you look at what the electrical industry is doing in Canada, with the construction of three new power plants in Ontario by the federal government up there, with an excess power capacity, it is very obvious why they want a 50-percent reduction in the United States. They want to capture power being generated in Ohio which unfortunately is the largest coal-consuming state in the country."

He went on to attack previous testimony by a representative of the League of Women Voters.

"And on top of this, in closing I would like to say that there has been a lot of rhetoric on this issue. The representative from the League of Women Voters talks about damage to corn crops, yet my hometown newspaper in southeast Ohio says tests show crops thrive by acid. We didn't do this study, it was done out at the University of Illinois. I wonder where all of the truth is in this whole issue. Our biggest concern is not for the grandparents and the kids being able to go fishing, it is for the parents to have a job and work and raise those children with a decent environment.

"Thank you. It is a very emotional issue in Ohio and we appreciate your consideration, Mr. Chairman."

Spokesmen for the coal industry were not united, however, in opposition to the acid-rain legislation then being considered by Congress. A marked difference between the eastern coal interests' opinion and western opinion surface in the testimony of Harry L. Storey. He is director of Industry and Legislative Affairs, Anaconda Minerals Co. He appeared on behalf of the Western Regional Council, a coalition of 46 companies active in the eight Rocky Mountain States. He expressed a preference for the approaches taken in S. 768 and urged the committee to adhere to its concepts. He opposed spreading the cost of emissions reductions to include the West, and urged that legislation not reward the last to clean up for their delay.

Mr. Storey took issue with those concerned about protecting jobs in high-sulfur coal mines when he testified: "Some legislative proposals have also included provisions mandating the use of control technology. Again we agree with the source flexibility provided in S. 768 for emission reductions. Mandatory scrubbing has nothing to do with the environmental problem of acid rain but instead with preserving midwestern high-sulfur coal mining jobs. Coupling forced scrubbing, to preserve jobs, with a national cost-sharing program for purposes of political coalitions obscures the environmental goal of acid rain legislation. It makes the nation's cost unnecessarily high, particularly in this period of economic recovery and a high federal deficit.

"Proponents of protecting high-sulfur coal mining jobs claim there would be severe regional dislocation without mandated scrubbing. We believe that the miner displacement issue is an overemphasized consideration in the acid rain debate. Studies indicate that if utilities were to select nonscrubbing options for emission reductions, there would be some shifts in high-sulfur versus low-sulfur coal mining employment and location. But there will be overall increases in coal mine employment of approximately 120,000 jobs over the next 15 years."

The foregoing discussion of coal industry positions on acid rain should suffice to establish the reality of some markedly different opinions, both within the coal industry and between that industry and environmental groups. Do you agree that controversy exists? Are you ready to move on and get to know some of the other actors in the drama?

11.

The Electric Power Groups

By this time you are probably as aware as anyone one needs to be that the generation of most of the nation's electric power is intimately associated with combustion. The burning of coal, oil, natural gas, or even waste paper plays a role in providing us both huge amounts of desired electric energy and large amounts of undesired acid rain. There are means of generating electricity that do not involve combustion, such as nuclear reactors, hydroelectric power dams, wind turbines, and other solar applications. These *clean* approaches to generating electric power, which currently are responsible for an important minor fraction of the total energy supply, have environmental impacts all their own, but don't result in emission of acid precursors. It is increasingly true, however, that many utility companies which use the *clean* approach to electric generation do so in combination with combustion-related approaches.

It should come as no surprise that any proposed enactment of legislation designed to limit acid-precursor emissions receives the immediate interested attention of most of the electric utility industry and many of their major customers. But like their close associates, the coal-mining interests, the electric utility industry is not of one mind when it comes to acid rain legislation. This is to be expected. The industry is somewhat heterogeneous. Some electric utilities are stockholder-owned private enterprises, intended to turn a profit. Others are publicly-owned, intended to serve their citizen-owners at minimum cost compatible with reliable service. Some generating plants serve a single customer, others serve millions. Representatives of this broad spectrum of utility interests showed up at the hearings conducted by the U.S. Senate in February, 1984. Let's look at their various positions.

Tennessee Valley Authority: The Nation's Largest Producer of Electricity The Tennessee Valley Authority is both a corporate agency and an instrumentality of the United States government. Let's discuss it here as an electric utility. Later on we'll examine TVA's role in acid-rain mitigation when we look at what the government is doing about acid rain.

TVA proclaims itself to be the nation's largest producer of electricity. It is one of the nation's largest consumers of coal, which, unfortunately, makes it one of the nation's largest emitters of acid-rain precursors. As a federally-owned electric utility, it sees its role as one of leadership in seeking solutions to the problems facing the nation's electric utility industry.

TVA's testimony at the February, 1984, Senate hearings on acid rain was an outstanding example of independent thought. TVA is not a government agency in the usual sense, but it looks a lot like a government agency to a casual observer. One might expect the leadership of even a quasi-governmental agency to reflect, at least publicly, concurrence with the current president's policies. Not so with Charles H. Dean, Jr., chairman, board of directors, Tennessee Valley Authority. Here is an interesting portion of his statement:

"TVA is not in accord with the program of the President. Our position represents the opinion of the TVA board. Simply put, our posiion on acid rain is that a reduction in acid precursors is essential in eastern North America and that federal legislation is necessary to accomplish this. Reductions should be required of all significant emitters of SO_2, both utilities and other industries. These SO_2 reductions should be allocated to the states proportionally to their total SO_2 emissions for the 1980 base year. States should have flexibility in allocating their required emissions reductions.

"TVA believes in the principle that the polluter should pay, and we practice what we preach. The costs of further reduction should be borne by the polluters and thus passed on to consumers. Maximum flexibility should be given to emitters to select the most cost-effective way to reduce their emissions. If acid rain legislation is structured in this way, we estimate the increased cost to TVA ratepayers could be about 4 to 6 percent for our share of a 12-million-ton national reduction. We stand willing to do our fair share in any cleanup effort.

"Acid rain is too often thought of as a regional problem, confined to the northeastern United States and eastern Canada. However we have rainfall in the Tennessee Valley which is as acidic as that found anywhere in North America. A monitoring program, which began in 1971, determined that on an average annual basis our rainfall is in the pH 4.1 to 4.4 range — typical of the values for New England, and we get much more rainfall than New England

"While we have no direct evidence of of a link between acid deposition and impacts to resources in our region, several observations over the last several years could be related to acid deposition. The printed statement gives information on these observations and on the TVA acid rain research program."

Comments from Some Other Utilities Dr. William B. Harrison, senior vice president, Southern Company Services Inc., spoke on behalf of the Edison Electric Institute. His testimony presented a quite different position than that of TVA, and he was not at all bashful about challenging statements by the TVA representative. Here is what he had to say:

"Mr. Chairman, I am very pleased to represent the Edison Electric Institute which, as you know, is an association of investor-owned utilities. It is especially pleasing because I have had the opportunity to hear testimony of the TVA representatives. I want to bring to your attention that I represent a number of utilities who are opposed to legislation for acid rain control at this time, and I would like to quickly summarize for you the reason for that opposition.

"I have submitted for the record and I will attempt to synthesize that quickly and add other comments derived from my observations at the hearing this morning.

"First of all we oppose the legislation because the objective is not clear. It seems to me that, as we talk about 8-million-ton reduction or 10-million-ton reduction of SO_2 emissions, we need to relate that to some environmental objective that will be achieved after having implemented that reduction. It is not clear at all to me what that objective is.

"We hear words this morning about emergencies that exist. If we look at the most credible data by the National Academy last summer, on the trends in SO_2 or SO_4 deposition or acidic deposition in the

Northeast, we cite, for example, the Hubbard Brook data which show that in the period 1965 through 1981, the sulfate deposition was steadily going down. The nitrate deposition was going up, and this raises a question right up front. Why this preoccupation with SO_2 (which is a precursor for sulfates) when the nitrates are relatively being ignored? Also, you will find in that same data that the acidity levels being measured are also going down. Where is the evidence of an impending crisis in a sudden and drastic change of conditions that must elicit an emergency response and immediate legislation without a clear understanding of the facts?

"It should also be stated that, as we look at the great uncertainty between causes and effects of acid rain, we should examine what might be achieved as the result of the implementation of a 10-million-ton or 8-million-ton reduction. We find that at best it can represent a change of pH of the order of 0.2 or 0.3 of a unit.

"We heard earlier today from the representative from the TVA that the pH measured in the TVA district ranges from 4.1 to 4.4. So what we are talking about is an effective change of pH, on the basis of the more stringent emission-reduction plan, which is still the same order of magnitude of the normal fluctuation of what we have today. So it is perfectly clear that the perception of the acid rain issue has a big gap between the cause and the effect that you are trying to achieve.

"Now let us also ask the question of what will be the consequences if this legislation is enacted, even though we are not quite sure what we will accomplish? I heard the TVA statements about cost of implementation in their system. Let me point out to you that TVA's assumption that the other utilities are not taking these estimates as seriously as they is simply not correct. In the Southern Electric System, we have taken S. 768 and examined our facilities plant by plant to see what would be the most cost-effective strategy for implementing the provisions of that bill, whether it is shifting from high-sulfur to low-sulfur coal or installation of scrubbers. I can assure you that it has been a reasoned and careful approach.

"Also, I can assure you that we start from a level of greater compliance than TVA. You may recall the statement that TVA only achieved compliance with the existing environmental regulations as of last year. The Southern Electric System, which burns between 30 and 35 million tons of coal per year, was in compliance with these laws in the mid-seventies and it is a significant difference from point of departure that we have from the TVA system, as we attempt to implement the provisions of S. 768.

"Also, you heard the statements that TVA is bringing on a number of nuclear facilities now in construction during this time-frame which obviously shifts the burden from coal to uranium, another explanation for why TVA costs for compliance are lower than ours. For the Southern Electric System, the least cost option for compliance is going to amount to about $850 million per year for our customers; and we have to ask you and ourselves what will be the benefit derived from this significant increase in cost? That amounts to an 11.3 percent increase on a 5-year levelized basis or a 13.6 percent increase for the first year cost. These estimates are expressed in 1982 dollars.

"Yes, these are different numbers from what you heard from TVA, but it is irrational to say that the TVA numbers are a benchmark for the whole industry when each one of our companies has its own mix of coal versus nuclear or its own expectation for growth in the next decade or its own starting point for the baseline of 1980 emissions.

"Well, the other thing I wish to add is that, though I am speaking for others opposed to legislation at this time, this is not to say that there is no problem; it is to say that we don't know exactly what the problem is or how to fix it. I speak from what I have judged to be a responsible position in this context. The Electric Power Research Institute and others in the electric utility business are committing or have committed more resources to an understanding of causes and effects of acid rain than any other party to this debate. It seems to me that an awful lot of emphasis is being made on public relations and misinformation to dramatize the urgency for some legislation when, in fact, a much better purpose for current efforts would be to fully understand what the problem is before we attempt to implement a national strategy to address it.

"Now, regarding the praise that you gave TVA, and I certainly don't want to take anything from that, I would like to point out that others in the electric utility industry are supporting what you saw there, Senator Stafford. In our company we have been principals in advancing the development of five different scrubber systems over the past 10 years. We have been pioneers of solvent refining, which is a way to make a clean boiler fuel from coal prior to combustion. We currently manage the most advanced development project for removing fine dust from high-sulfur coal combustion emissions.

"So there are other players in this beside TVA, and I hope you will take that into account as you evaluate their testimony, which was supporting your bill, and ours, which is opposing the bill, but for what we believe are good and sufficient reasons. I hope that you will give the research effort now underway a chance to work. The Federal Interagency Task Force on Acid Precipitation is now beginning to gather some facts which will go far beyond the Electric Power Research Institute program. So all I am appealing for is time. I think it is in the public interest to be sure we know what we are doing before we commit to what is often called 'the $100 billion experiment."

The American Public Power Association (APPA) was represented at the Senate hearings by Ruth Gonze, assistant legislative director. Her testimony was in support of acid-rain-control legislation and dealt mainly with the question of how to fund the control program. Here's the APPA position, as revealed by Ms. Gonze's testimony:

"APPA is a national trade association of about 1,750 publicly-owned electric utilities throughout the country. About one out of every six consumers is served electricity by a nonprofit public power system.

"The American Public Power Association supports national acid rain control legislation which meets reasonable standards of effectiveness, economy, and equity. As suppliers of electric power, about two-thirds of which is derived from fossil fuel, our members are willing to pay their share. Yet, we also have a responsibility to millions of consumers to assure that costs are fairly apportioned and that an acid rain control program achieves environmental objectives with a minimum of economic disruption.

"We know that this committee appreciates the potential threat that acid rain poses to sensitive ecosystems. While a scientific consensus seems to be emerging that acid rain has to be controlled, the effects of acid precipitation are highly controversial. What is known is that all fossil fuel emissions from both local and distant sources, stationary and mobile sources are involved. There is just as much controversy about what kinds of controls to adopt and how to pay for them. A national program will cost a lot of money.

"APPA believes that a reasonable balance of the public interest in a clean environment, while spending the fewest possible dollars to achieve it and dividing the costs fairly, can be achieved through legislation incorporating the following principles:

"First, the program should be funded through a nationwide tax on sulfur dioxide and nitrogen oxide emissions from all major stationary sources and mobile sources for which an emissions tax is feasible;

"Second, the funds raised should be applied to a least-cost emission reduction program;

"Third, the program should be divided into two phases with implementation of the second phase to be triggered by affirmative congressional action; and

"Fourth, emission reduction goals should be set to account for future growth, which means, in part, stating the real reduction requirements at the outset and rejecting offset requirements for new emissions.

"To take that in more detail, let me start with emission taxes, the only scheme which assures that the polluter pays because polluters pay in exact proportion to their contribution to the problem. The tax should be nationwide because acid precipitation is a national problem and it needs a national solution.

"We all know that a lot of the cleanup will be done in the Midwest, which, without a national financing scheme, would suffer economic disruption unacceptable to the nation as a whole. Not only residential electric consumers are involved, not only direct electric consumers are involved, but energy-intensive industries located in the Midwest, including steel, aluminum, autos, and chemicals are involved. The higher their rate increases are, the harder their recovery from recession will be and the more job losses they will suffer.

"Look at what an emission tax does.

"It credits past cleanup. States like Michigan and Minnesota which have made large emission cuts, pay less because they emit less.

"It gives incentives for future cleanup. Sources reduce emissions without any further federal mandate simply to avoid the tax.

"It is regionally equitable. States with low emissions, like many in the West, pay only their fair share.

"It is administratively workable. Administrative difficulties have been raised as an argument against emissions taxes. We think that issue is a red herring. For sources which do not continually monitor emissions, calculations can be made based on fuel sulfur content fairly easily. In any case, taxes can be fixed for ranges of emissions levels, just as we do for personal income taxes, and that will give us defensible tax liabilities without undue administrative burdens.

"Let me add here that we oppose funding mechanisms in some proposals that have been based on kilowatt-hour taxes or other irrelevant units of measurement. The problem is emissions, and the solution should be a tax on emissions.

"Our second recommendation is that we use the money to fund cost-effective emission-reduction measures. The cost savings for a least-cost approach have been conservatively estimated at 25 percent. Such measures specifically include fuel switching, fuels pretreatment and scrubber systems. We know that fuel switching is politically controversial and relatively uneconomic. But, even if fuel switching is legislatively limited, a least-cost standard is valid. Its cost-effectiveness is lessened, but not lost.

"Even assuming that large unemployment impacts from fuel switching would occur (which are not acceptable), such impacts should, for example, be examined carefully to minimize extra costs, by taking into consideration methods such as those suggested today by the Alliance for Clean Energy.

"Another way in which least-cost principles may have to be abridged is in directing controls to particular source areas in order to help a particular sensitive receptor area. We support such limitations on the application of least-cost principles, if and when such determinations about source/receptor relationships can be made.

"The third point is that an emissions reduction program should have two phases, given the scientific uncertainty surrounding both the problem and the solution, the large cost of any control program, and the likelihood that we will know more in the future than we know now. A phased program assures us that midcourse corrections can be made if we need them.

"Fourth, emission reduction goals must adequately account for future growth. That means that offset requirements should be rejected by the Congress. Offsets understate the real reductions which are required. The new capacity has a double whammy. It first pays for control technologies to meet new source performance standards, and then it pays for offsets from existing sources for the emissions that remain. (I'll interrupt Ms. Gonze's testimony to explain what she means by her remark about offsets. Suppose an electric utility wants to install additional generating capacity at a location where they have an existing power plant. Suppose, further, that the new plant will emit 10 tons of sulfur dioxide per year, and that the existing plant emits 30 tons per year. In order to prevent further degradation of the environment, the utility would be required to install some means of reducing the emissions of the older plant by 10 tons per year, offsetting the air-pollution to be caused by the new plant. Does that clear the air about offsets? I hope it does. I'll return you now to Ms. Gonze.) Those offsets will be costly and scarce. We urge that the total emission reduction required be incorporated upfront in the program's emissions reduction requirement.

"Mr. Chairman, APPA is the only national electric utility organization to embrace a comprehensive program for dealing with acid rain. We hope the committees will review the policy report which is attached to our testimony in detail. We are willing to take responsibility for the costs and requirements to bring acid rain under control in direct proportion to our responsibility for the problem. We believe our proposals point the way to a meaningful consensus in dealing with one of the most difficult environmental issues of our time."

Although APPA's position was the consensus of many publicly owned electric utilities, it didn't speak for all of them. Evern Wall, president and chief executive officer, El Paso Electric Company, offered quite different testimony on behalf of WEST Associates, a group that looks after the interests of some western publicly-owned as well as investor-owned electric utilities. Here's his position statement and the advice he offered as transcribed into the record of the hearings. (I insert that qualification to explain that, in quoting this and earlier testimony, I have reproduced the statement as it was printed in the published record, even though it is sometimes apparent that the word heard by the stenotypist and the word spoken by the witness are only distantly related. If your grammar teacher taught you to have a measure of agreement between the subject and the predicate, don't hold violations of that principle against me or the witness. Someone may have coughed in the hearing room at exactly the wrong moment. I am aware that putting "(sic)" after some erroneous use of the English language can be used to call attention to the boner, but there is a limit to the number of (sic)s I am willing to impose on you.)

"I am Evern Wall, president of WEST Associates and president and chief executive officer of the El Paso Electric Co., which is an investor-owned utility in Texas.

"WEST is a research and information group of 21 publicly-owned and investor-owned electric utilities serving about 19 million customers in eight western and southwestern states. WEST believes that there are important regional differences. The western customer is already paying a stiff price for clean air. We think that these things should be considered in any acid rain discussion.

"I would like to take just a few moments to highlight five of the differences and then offer a number of principles which WEST Associates believe should guide any acid rain legislation.

"First, the 17 states (sic), WEST (sic) have (sic) (probably meant to read: the 17-state West has) far fewer total emission sources. The sources are much less than those in the East. The western SO_2 emission represents only 7 percent of the sulfur dioxide emission from all the coal-fired generation. The West has less than one-fifth of the coal-fired electric power producing generation stations in this country versus 81 percent in the East. Additionally, the West coal is far cleaner, with an average of one-third the sulfur content of eastern coal; specifically about 0.64 sulfur average in the West versus a conservative 2 percent in the East.

"In addition to that, the western states have very strong regulations on emission standards, much stronger than the national requirements. Despite the low-sulfur coal, the West already cleans up more than four times the percentage of coal-fired generation than does the East, specifically 31 percent of the coal generation is struck (he probably said "scrubbed") versus only 7 percent in the East.

"Electric utility customers in the West are permitted to pay billions of dollars to reduce powerplant emission without help from other regions. Up to 30 percent of electric bills in some western states is directly attributable to power plant pollution controls. To give you an idea of the West commitment to clean up its emissions, customers of the 21 WEST member companies have thus far been committed to pay an investment of approximately $2.4 billion for emission controls on our power plants alone.

"I am submitting, for the record, two WEST Associates maps which use EPA data to illustrate the striking difference in sulfur dioxide emission density between the East and the West. The first map depicts the 1980 SO_2 emissions and shows that peak emission density in the East range (sic) from 6 to 20 times those densities in the West. The second map projects 1995 SO_2 densities after a reduction of 10 million tons in 31 eastern states.

"The maps show that peak emissions in the East remained dramatically higher than those in the West by as much as four times in some areas. Despite these regional differences, various acid rain legislative proposals in the Senate and the House seek to have western utility customers pay additional amounts for pollution-control equipment in other areas; some bills propose a tax of 1 mill per kilowatt-hour on most of the electricity generated in the East and the West. This could amount to a transfer of nearly $700 million annually from the West, a particularly unfair and discriminatory proposal, considering that all of the top 60 SO_2 power plants which have been identified are owned or are east of the Mississippi River.

"Given this situation, WEST Associates strongly object to cost - sharing proposals which will unfairly burden western consumers who now pay a premium for clean air. We in the West have already paid. We are paying, we will continue to pay our fair share for clean air.

"Now I recognize this committee is considering provisions in S. 768. That bill does not include the cost-sharing mechanism or a number of the other objectionable provisions which are contained in H.R. 3400. Regarding additional WEST acid rain principles that should guide the legislation, we believe that more research and demonstration is required. We ought to first spend millions on research before risking the expenditure of billions of dollars on a hopeful control program.

"We believe that if the control efforts are prescribed, they should be based on research findings and should be applied where demonstrated, significant problems exist. We believe that least-cost methods for emission reductions such as fuel switching and coal washing should be carefully considered. Mandating particular control technology such as scrubbers, which are the highest cost option, does not represent sound public policy. Finally, we believe unique differences (in regions of the country) must be considered."

Electricity's Biggest Consumers: Their Views

Before we pass on to look at other groups of actors, I'll provide just one more position statement having to do with electricity. This one doesn't come from people who produce and market electricity. That group's various viewpoints have already been fully reported. What hasn't been covered yet is the position of the really big consumers of electricity. They have quite an economic stake in how the debate over acid rain turns out. Let's look at what concerns them.

"My name is Jay B. Kennedy and I represent a group of industrial firms gathered together in an organization we call ELCON, the Electric Consumers Resource Council. Our interest in acid rain is not because we are sellers of any particular fuels for utilities or any other commercial interest in that particular sense. Our firms produce a variety of products: automobiles, steel, aluminum, fibers, chemicals, even a brewery is one of our members. Their interest in the subject of acid rain legislation is that they buy huge amounts of electricity. Our members, 16 of them, purchase approximately one-twentieth of all the electricity marketed in the United States, so electricity is to us a very important subject.

"Industrial electricity consumers are concerned about the environment. We expect to pay our fair share of any necessary program. However, we are forced to deal with the facts of the market place. During these times of increasing competition in world and domestic markets, we must be certain that any additional cost imposed on U.S. industry generates a benefit at least equal to that cost. This is really the thrust of our testimony, Mr. Chairman.

"We do not oppose any of the bills under consideration nor do we support them. Our concern is that we have seen no evidence what benefits will be derived at any level of SO_2 reduction. It is really a pretty basic question from our point of view.

"There are many problems in the country that need to be addressed. The question is which ones to address and how much of our resources to devote to the particular problems. In other words, how much is it worth? It is not sufficient to say that there is a problem that must be addressed. We recognize that; we admit there is an acid rain problem. Anyone will admit that. The question is how much of a problem and how much do we spend to offset it.

"We estimate the cost to the industry to be a 20 percent rise in electric rates on a state-average basis as a result of the 10-million-ton reduction, and as much as 50 percent increase in rate on particular utility systems. These costs will place United States firms at a disadvantage. To give you some idea of the impact of these costs, for some of our firms electricity represents 70 percent of operating expense. A mill increase in rates here and a mill there is no small sum when you are talking about the quantities of electricity I'm referring to.

"We are not commenting on the method of collecting funds to support a particular program. The important point at present, from our view, is to determine the benefits from various levels of SO_2 reduction and then establish the one we are willing to buy. Later we can consider the best method to collect the dollars to fund that program, and we would be happy to address that problem at the appropriate time.

"We are somewhat concerned that there (sic) (these?) certain factors have been neglected in all the discussions on acid-rain options and alternatives. There is a serious question as to the impact acid rain legislation might have on the demand for and the price of OPEC oil. Certainly, utilities would be encouraged to continue burning oil when they have the capacity to do so rather than spend huge sums on new (coal fired) units or plant modifications. This is of particular concern, I think, given the fact that the Department of Energy, for some years now, has been heavily involved in oil blackout; trying to encourage utilities to get off of oil and onto coal. This doesn't mean that we should not have acid-rain legislation. However, an increased dependence on OPEC oil, combined with a lack of enthusiasm for nuclear units, might jeopardize the electricity supply in the United States in the near future.

"You have heard substantial comment by ELCON and others as to the dollar cost of an emissions control program. The important issue, we feel, is that the real cost to the United States and its standard of living is tens of billions of dollars' worth of resources used to control acid rain with no assurance of an equivalent real benefit. Those resources have alternative uses in the private and public sector for schools, medical care, roads, and so forth. If used to control acid rain, then, by definition, they are not available for other real income purposes. We are willing to participate in the settlement of this issue; however, we feel someone has an obligation to give us some idea of the kind of benefits we can expect so we can decide which program is the best to adopt."

In a written statement that accompanied Mr. Kennedy's oral testimony on behalf of ELCON the following appeared:

"ELCON has reviewed the statement of EPA Administrator Ruckelshaus presented before this committee on February 2, 1984. On that basis, we support the position of the Reagan administration which calls for increased and accelerated research of the acid rain phenomenon, increased research and development for improved control technology, and liming of affected lakes to mitigate the effects of acidity while research continues."

After considering the above testimony by people intimately involved in the generation, marketing, and intensive use of electricity, what can be said about an electric industry position on acid rain? Is there an electric industry position on acid rain? It is clear that there is no single position about further control legislation that characterizes the thinking of the whole industry. The publicly-owned portion of the industry appears to favor early passage and implementation of acid-rain-control legislation. The investor-owned portion appears to support the position that more needs to be learned about the nature of the problem before further control legislation is enacted and the large investments involved in possible solutions are undertaken.

Industry spokesmen made it clear that they do consider acid rain to be a problem. Their differences appear to be focused on issues of urgency versus non-urgency, extent of economic impact, and the level of knowledge required to undergird a sensible solution.

Although there are wide differences of opinion about how much needs to be learned about acid rain before corrective action is taken, no one is outspokenly against the idea of continuing the learning process. Let's look now at the sector of our society that is being looked to for that additional learning.

12.

The Scientific Community

As we have noted earlier acid rain has been a matter under study in the scientic community for a long time. In view of this it might seem reasonable to ask whether there is a consensus among scientists on the subject of what should be done about acid rain? The answer that best fits the evidence I have examined is an emphatic negative. The absence of a scientific consensus is a predictable state of affairs. Scientists are encouraged, from the beginning of scientific training, to think independently, to take nothing for granted, and to be sceptical of published research results until the work has been independently validated. Much of the research pertaining to acid rain is too recent to have passed the test of independent validation, so it isn't surprising that a genuine consensus has yet to develop.

The scientific community involved in acid rain-research covers a broad spectrum of disciplines and a broad range of employment circumstances. There are acid-rain researchers who work for universities, private research firms, government agencies, and environmental groups. These differing employment circumstance may well influence the positions individual scientists take on the urgency of reducing acid rain. When scientists break into the public press they don't always confine themselves to discussing scientific issues.

One of several scientists employed by environmental groups is Dr. Michael Oppenheimer, a physicist who works as a senior scientist with the Environmental Defense Fund in New York. He and his frequent co-author, Robert Yunke, an attorney also employed by the Environmental Defense Fund in their Boulder, Colorado office, have published a number of articles on acid rain. Some recent newspaper articles suggest that they have been engaged in a detached but interesting debate with Dr. Donald Stedman, an atmospheric chemist employed in the Chemistry Department of the University of Denver. The debate was carried out on the pages of the *Rocky Mountain News*.

On Friday, March 1, 1985, the "Commentary" section of the *Rocky Mountain News* carried an article by Dr. Oppenheimer which was headlined "Acid rain is coming west to Rockies." Here is what the article had to say:

"Acid-rain legislation died last spring when Congress split along regional lines: the Northeast, with its sensitive lakes, against the Middle West, with its coal-burning power plants, with other states wondering why they should worry about someone else's problem. This year's debate promises to be different: recent studies have shown the Rocky Mountains to be threatened with the same devastation that has poisoned Appalachian Mountain ecosystems.

"The singular physical characteristics that lend such beauty to the West also make it vulnerable to acid rain. High mountain watersheds, with their thin soils, rocky outcroppings and limited flora, lack the chemical components that would counteract the sulfuric and nitric acid pollutants that fall in acid rains and snows.

"A 1982 study of the Sierra Nevada Mountains, by a team from the University of California at Santa Barbara, concluded that most alpine lakes are extremely sensitive to acid rain. Alpine lakes in Colorado's Rockies, Wyoming's Wind River Range and Washington's Cascades share this low resistance to acid rain. A recent study by the Environmental Defense Fund showed that similar lakes in Scandinavia began losing fish and plant life after rainfall became about as acid as it is now in the West. In recent years, rainfall in Mesa Verde, Rocky Mountain, Yellowstone and other national parks has been as polluted as rain in Scandinavia and parts of the eastern United States are suffering acid damage.

"The first signs of biological damage may be appearing. Salamanders, among the most acid-sensitive creatures, have ceased reproducing in a few high-mountain Colorado lakes that receive an "acid shock" during the spring thaw. Fogs and clouds as acidic as lemon juice may be contributing to the damage observed in pine trees in the mountains of southern California.

"Acid rain in the West arises from the same man-made pollutants that are its source in the East: oxides of sulfur and nitrogen from factories, power plants and automobiles. However, copper smelters are a major source of sulfur oxides in the West, emitting about two thirds of the total. Two Arizona smelters alone, emitting without any controls, contribute 550,000 tons of sulfur dioxide annually, more than one-third of the total in the Rocky Mountain states.

"The pollution, already at critical levels, could worsen. Dozens of new power plants and synthetic fuels plants, emitting hundreds of thousands of tons of oxides of sulfur and nitrogen, are currently on the drawing boards. A mammoth uncontrolled source of sulfur dioxide, more than 500,000 tons a year, will be added just 60 miles south of the border, in Nacozari, Mexico, by 1986. These new sources will send the acidity marker through the roof even if American copper smelters are brought under control.

"We need federal action to protect our natural resources from irreversible damage without deterring economic growth. Any such plan must establish regional limits, on emissions from currently uncontrolled sources, and assure adequate controls on all new sources. Much can be accomplished with stricter enforcement of existing regulations, but we must ultimately strengthen the Clean Air Act.

"The plan should also include provisions to bring the emissions of the Nacozari smelter under control. However, it will be difficult for the administration to accomplish this goal given its current position on acid rain. When President Reagan meets with Brian Mulroney next month, the Canadian prime minister will undoubtedly remind Mr. Reagan that acid rain is one American export that Canadians could do without. The president will almost surely repeat his administration's refrain: We don't know enough to act on acid rain. This would seem to bar negotiations with the Mexicans.

"A more prudent course is available. The administration should acknowledge the entreaties of the National Academy of Science and its own Office of Science and Technology Policy, both of which have called for reductions in acid emissions. Then it should drop its opposition to the strengthening of the Clean Air Act, while negotiating with Canada and Mexico to reduce transboundary air pollution.

"The clock is running on our priceless but fragile forests and waters."

Now let's take a look at how Donald H. Stedman, Ph.D, an atmospheric chemist employed in the Chemistry Department of the University of Denver discussed the issue of acid rain in the West. In an article headlined "Western acid rain reports are greatly exaggerated," published on the "Speak Out/Letters" page of the Friday, May 17, 1985, issue of the *Rocky Mountain News* . Dr. Stedman wrote:

"After a conference in Gunnison (Colorado) on acid rain, a scientist interviewed by a radio reporter said that rain just one little pH unit lower, could spell real trouble.

"It is true that rain of pH 5 is falling in the mountains of Colorado and that rain of pH 4 is potentially damaging. It is not true that one pH unit is 'little;' pH is a logarithmic scale such that each pH unit is a factor of 10.Thus, 10 times more acid needs to be present for the pH to drop from five to four.

"A recent report by the World Resources Institute claims to be a comprehensive regional look at acid rain in the West. In fact, it is a review of the scarce scientific literature on the subject, mostly written by scientists whose salaries depend on acid rain being enough of a problem to justify research dollars.

"The wording of the report is appropriately cautious and ambivalent. The report states that acid rain may be a growing menace, environmental damage has not yet been observed, and monitoring has shown that streams have become less alkaline. Curiously, their conclusions are on much firmer ground.

"They state that actions to control emissions are now warranted because of 'clear evidence' of acidic deposition, and the attorney for the Environmental Defense Fund has speculated that the problem of acid rain in the West may have political implications.

"What problem? Bulk deposition in eastern and western Colorado has an average pH of 6 and above, because of blowing dust from the characteristically-alkaline soils of the arid West. There is less dust in the high mountains, hence pH drops to five, but the pH of rain in the cleanest areas of the world is naturally between 4.7 and 5.3.

"Dry deposition of sulfur dioxide, nitrogen oxides and particulate matters is certainly an important fate for these compounds; but its importance to the generally alkaline ecosystem is unclear. There are fruit growers who never had worms in apple orchards near the railroad lines until the railroads switched from coal to diesel. Diesel emits much less sulfur dioxide; apparently, dry deposition or occasional fumigation provided a good pest control.

"Certainly, there are potentially vulnerable lakes in granitic areas of the high mountains. Certainly, there are regions around local sources (urban areas and smelters) in which environmental damage has taken place.

"There is little doubt that sulfate (from coal burning and smelters) contributes to regionally-reduced visibility, together with wood-smoke and mobile source emissions. Where, however, is the 'acid-rain problem'?

"It is certainly not to be found in 'one little pH unit' that has the same value as the difference between a 40-year-old and a 4-year-old!"

What appears to be a response to Donald Stedman's letter from Michael Oppenheimer and Bob Yunke was not long in coming. On Monday, June 10, 1985, the *Rocky Mountain News* published their article headlined "Acid rain is coming to the Rockies":

"Some argue that the pH of rain and snow in Colorado is not acidic enough to do harm to our generally-alkaline ecosystem. But this statement very much misses the point: that while the deserts and plains are protected from acid damage by generally-alkaline soils, Colorado's high country lakes are not.

"The high country of the Rockies cradles more than 7000 lakes. Many lie on granitic bedrock, surrounded by the shear walls of glacial cirques, above the protecting mantle of forest. Exposed to winds carrying pollutants a thousand miles or more, these lakes have little, if any, natural ability to neutralize acids. Many are so vulnerable to acid pollution that with 10 times less acid, they could suffer as much damage as some lakes that have already been acidified in the Northeast.

"Last spring, the first acidified lakes were found in the Rockies. Lakes adjacent to the Snowmass Wilderness were found to have a pH of 4.9 for a month during snowmelt. Snow traps acid pollution for seven to nine months, then releases it into lakes over a short period. During that period, the lake became 70 times more acidic than it normally is.

"The death of a lake is the final event in a sequence of changes in lake chemistry. Before the acidity of a lake increases dramatically, the ability to neutralize acid, i.e., buffering capacity, is being exhausted. If declines in buffering capacity continue, some lakes could be acidified, threatening the survival of trout and other aquatic species.

"Short-term acidification occurs when the acid entering the lake exceeds its buffering capacity, and is a warning signal that a lake is on its way to being permanently acidified. Because of the difficulties of access, only a handfull of high-country lakes are being studied intensively enough to detect short-term acidification episodes. But there is every reason to believe that if it is occurring at lakes where researchers are looking; it is likely to be happening at hundreds of other lakes as well.

"In 1983 and 1984 biologists found populations of trout and salamanders in high-country lakes that have failed to reproduce. The eggs and young of these species are known to be highly sensitive to the acidification of their habitat. Experience in the Adirondacks tells us that the failure of these species to reproduce is one of the early symptoms of acidification. Since egg hatch often occurs during snowmelt, the increased acidity during snowmelt in the Rockies is thought to explain the failure of salamanders to reproduce.

"Native trout have also failed to reproduce in high lakes that are part of Boulder's drinking water supply. We don't know if this is caused by acid rain, but the isolated location of these lakes suggests atmospheric inputs may be a cause.

"Current levels of acid pollution are already causing the early stages of acidification. Fortunately, we have not yet found dead lakes in the Rockies. Given what is happening to the high country and expected increases in the regional levels of acid pollution in the next 10 to 20 years, acid lakes may not be long in coming.

"Both the pH of rain and snow in the high country, and the amount of sulfur pollution entering the lakes is near or above the levels that have caused acidification of mountain lakes in Scandinavia. Acid-pollution levels in Colorado are expected to increase substantially as new coal-fired power plants throughout the West, a new smelter in Mexico, and synfuels projects in Colorado and Utah are built. Do we need to wait until we have destroyed some mountain lakes before we heed the evidence from Scandinavia that our poorly-buffered lakes are already at the limit of what they can tolerate?

"Given what we have learned about acid rain from other parts of the globe, we have the opportunity to prevent the devastation that has occurred in other regions. Prevention does not mean preventing growth. It does mean ending the legal exemption for copper smelters and requiring them to clean up their emissions, as other sources have been required to do. It also means installing the the best available pollution controls on new sources. Acid lakes need not be the price of growth in the West, but they will be if we fail to head nature's warning signals."

Let's spend a few moments considering the above three newspaper articles. Let's see if we can determine what the controversy between the opposing authors is all about?

It seems clear that Michael Oppenheimer's aim was to alert the readers of the *Rocky Mountain News* to what he perceived to be a developing threat to fragile and priceless natural resources in the Rocky Mountain region. He also appeared to be trying to influence the readers to support efforts aimed at changing the Reagan administration's policies on acid rain. His use of the present tense in the word "emitting" to describe power plants and synthetic fuels plants that "are currently on the drawing boards" is certainly questionable, but it does not provide much basis for doubting the sincerity of his concern about what is happening to the Rocky Mountain region's environment.

Donald Stedman's perception of the situation appears to have been quite different. He recognized the vulnerability to acidification of lakes in granitic areas, and that environmental damage has taken place in some regions, yet felt justified in asking "Where, however, is the acid-rain problem?" He reported what can be considered a desirable effect of sulfate pollution on apple orchards. He suggests that salary-preserving motivations are responsible for some scientists' attitudes about the seriousness of acid rain.

What seems to be at the root of the controversy is widely differing value systems. A tenfold change in acidity, a mountain lake devoid of fish, a worm-free apple are either significant or insignificant developments depending on the values espoused by the person making the assessment. There are no absolute standards of intrinsic merit.

Dr. Stedman's perception, that some scientists are deliberately overstating the importance of the problem in order to ensure generous funding for their ongoing research efforts, has been voiced by others in the scientific community. This charge has some validity. The history of research support in the United States contains examples of violent swings in funding levels. Obtaining stable research support for a particular line of investigation is certainly made easier if the matter under investigation can be related to some generally perceived ongoing crisis. Competition for scarce research dollars has been known to motivate very unscientific behavior on the part of scientists whose careers are threatened by funding cutbacks.

It would be unfair, however, to suggest that selfish pursuit of research funding motivates all that is happening in acid rain research. There are well-supported scientists who have turned their attention to acid rain in the sincere belief that its problems deserves their attention, even if their previous research must suffer as a result. There are also scientists who have little or no interest in acid rain who feel seriously threatened by the intense interest being focused on acid rain.

Linearity: A Particular Point of Dispute Sincere interest in acid rain certainly does not imply a pursuit of knowledge that is characterized by calm discussion of issues, free of emotion-ridden controversy. One of the most bitter controversies had to do with the question of linearity in the relationship between emissions and deposition. Here is how that controversy was reported by Kennedy Maise in *The Energy Daily,* Volume 11, Number 179, Friday, September 16, 1983:

NATIONAL LABS DEBUNK WORK ON ACID RAIN BY THE NATIONAL ACADEMY OF SCIENCES

"A group of scientists from the Department of Energy's national laboratories have panned the recent National Academy of Sciences report on acid rain. The scientists from the National Laboratory Consortium take particular exception to the NAS study's key conclusion of linearity: that reducing what goes up a smokestack will result in an almost equal reduction in what comes down as acid rain.

"The National Lab group performed the review of the NAS study at the request of Rep. Don Fuqua (D-Fla.) chairman of the House Science and Technology Committee, and Reps. James Scheurer (D-N.Y.), and Marilyn Lloyd (D-Tenn.), subcommittee chairmen. Bernard Manowitz of Brookhaven National Lab, chairman of the consortium, wrote to the legislators that the reviewers 'disagreed almost uniformly with the methods used to reach this conclusion [of linearity] and with the conclusion itself.'

"Manowitz outlined two major areas where the scientists from Brookhaven, Argonne National Laboratory, Oak Ridge National Laboratory, and Battelle Pacific Northwest Laboratory take issue with the Academy.

"The first is the linearity conclusion. Manowitz noted that several of the labs found that the data the academy used to justify its conclusion 'show spacial patterns in the same direction and of the same magnitude that are used to justify a nonlinear relationship in Europe.' Also, the NAS focused on such large geographic areas and such long averaging periods that it obscured 'a wealth of detail that is pertinent to the mechanisms of acid deposition. A closer look at final spatial scales is particularly important in regard to and discussion of linearity,' Manowitz wrote.

"The scientists from the national labs were also critical of the Academy's reliance on data from Hubbard Brook, New Hampshire in reaching their conclusion. 'Detailed statistical reanalysis of Hubbard Brook data, using multiple regression analysis, to account for meteorological variability over the period of record as well as emission estimates for every year, find substantially less than 1:1 proportionality between sulfate deposition and sulfur oxide emissions,' wrote Manowitz. 'This lack of proportionality suggests a nonlinear relationship.'

"Brookhaven's Fred Lipfert was particularly critical of the NAS study's reliance on large geographic areas. He said the academy obscured the fact that in source regions sulfur deposition seems to be less than nitrogen, while it rises in remote regions. Lipfert said this may reflect 'a saturation phenomenon' in source regions, which he calls 'a significant non-linearity.'

"S.E. Lindberg of Oak Ridge National Lab focused on the European situation, where the data seems to demonstrate nonlinearity. Lindberg criticized the academy for not looking at this data. 'The European data is far more extensive in both space and time than the single Hubbard Brook set on which so much emphasis has been placed,' he wrote.

"Scientists from the Pacific Northwest Lab also took issue with the Hubbard Brook data, noting that 'it is unfortunate that the committee was forced to place so much weight on the data from a single deposition monitoring site. We agree that the Hubbard Brook data are the best of more than five years duration, but the site is located outside the region of highest recent acidic deposition, and a single site's data — however high in quality — cannot serve to characterize a region, particularly if the measurements involve strong dependence on meteorological variations.'

"In addition to sending the report to Congress, Manowitz sent copies to Frank Press, chairman of the National Research Council, the arm of the academy that organized the study, and to Jack Calvert, who headed the academy committee that produced the report.

"The critique from the national labs is timely, as Environmental Protection Agency Administrator William Ruckelshaus is set to unveil his policy views on acid rain soon. Ruckelshaus had a full briefing on the NAS report, at a round-table discussion led by Press and including most of the scientists who worked on the report."

The Manowitz review and the publicity given it by *The Energy Daily* had repercussions that were not long in surfacing. The issue of *The Energy Daily* for Wednesday, September 28, 1983, carried the following:

SCIENTISTS COLLIDE OVER ACID RAIN FINDINGS

"Earlier this summer, the National Academy of Science's National Research Council published the results of several years' study of acid deposition. Briefly, the National Research Council committee of scientists (led by Jack Calvert, senior scientist at the National Center for Atmospheric Research) concluded that what goes up must come down — that there is an approximate 1:1 linearity between emissions of sulfur dioxide and acid rainfall. The results shocked the electric utility industry, which has been resisting proposed legislation to control sulfur oxide emissions, particularly when the National Research Council's general conclusions were shortly corroborated by a group of scientists assembled under the direction of the White House Office of Science and Technology Policy.

"Several weeks ago, there emerged the first rebuttal of the National Research Council's work, prepared by a group drawn from some of the Energy Department's national laboratories and chaired by Bernard Manowitz of Brookhaven National Lab. The Manowitz group attacked the National Research Council's conclusion about linearity, and criticized the council for relying too heavily on data from a single site in Hubbard Brook, N.H. The Manowitz study was adopted by the electric utility industry with undisguised glee.

"The Manowitz review of the National Research Council work sent Jack Calvert and his colleagues into a fury. 'The Manowitz review is seriously flawed scientifically,' Calvert told *The Energy Daily*. 'Manowitz and friends have presented a most unscientific, unprofessional, and erroneous critique of our efforts.' In the rebuttal to Manowitz published below, Calvert observes acidly that 'scientific issues cannot be influenced by legal or legislative actions or by pressures from business, conservation groups, or other special interest groups, including that headed by Manowitz . . . . One must question the motivation for [the Manowitz] review.'"

The article went on to publish the following, co-authored by Jack Calvert and Alan Lazrus, senior scientists at the National Center For Atmospheric Research, located at Boulder, Colorado:

"Recently *The Energy Daily* published an article on an informal review of our recent National Research Council report on acid deposition. The so-called 'review', which was headlined as 'debunking' our report, was prepared under the guidance of Bernard Manowitz (Brookhaven National Laboratory) by selected representatives of three national laboratories supported by the Department of Energy: Brookhaven, Battelle Pacific Northwest and Argonne. This 'review' was sent to the National Academy of Sciences, to me, to various members of the Interagency Task Force on Acid Rain and others. My friends in industry and government tell me that the report was widely circulated to the leadership and research arms of the power industry and related industrial operations throughout the United States and within the extensive communications pipeline of the administrative and legislative staffs of the federal and state governments. The original report has been sanitized and presented to Representatives Fuqua, Scheuer, and Lloyd, with additional comments from a group at Oak Ridge National Laboratory. This has been or will be introduced into the *Congressional Record.* Our more extensive comments will appear also in the record of the recent hearing of the two subcommittees of the House Committee on Science and Technology (September 13, 1983).

"*The Energy Daily* is not well suited to scientific debate. In the long run, scientific issues cannot be influenced by legal or legislative actions or by pressures from business, conservation groups, or other special interest groups, including that headed by Manowitz. The scientific world does not accept blindly the stated opinions of any scientist or group of scientists, including the National Research Council committee on acid deposition, without extensive testing and checking of the ideas proposed. Fortunately for science, the unresolved issues will be decided after extensive research and suitable discussions in the referred scientific literature. However, I feel that the Manowitz group and its informal 'review' cannot be disregarded by me, since their 'review' has been presented to a wide and important audience as a 'scientific' response which disputes some key aspects of the National Research Council acid rain report. Although it is difficult to sort out the science from the rhetoric in some of these 'reviews,' we will focus on what we judge to be the most important scientific questions which have been raised.

"First, the use of Hubbard Brook data by the National Research Council acid deposition committee and our conclusions derived from them have been questioned. Fred Lipfert (Brookhaven) has attempted to treat these and other unpublished data using a multiple linear regression analysis of 'adjusted' data. He concluded that there is no 1:1 correspondence between sulfur oxide emissions and sulfate deposition at Hubbard Brook. However, his conclusions must be rejected since his methods of data treatment and his arguments are flawed, scientifically. The detailed analysis of the errors in his treatment have been submitted as part of the record of the Congressional Hearing on Acid Rain (September 13, 1983). It suffices for present purposes to indicate that he has made two serious errors which invalidate the treatment. He made an inappropriate choice of variables in the multiple linear regression analysis; and he 'corrects' the observed data using a long-range transport model and assumptions about the source regions based on 'local' winds (measured 100 miles from Hubbard Brook on the coast of Maine) which are definitely incorrect. Given the lack of reliable models to predict accurately the source regions for the receptor site of Hubbard Brook, it is not scientifically sound to attempt the treatments of emissions and sulfate concentration at remote sites given by Lipfert.

"The conclusion of the National Research Council committee: that a large decrease in sulfate deposition at Hubbard Brook corresponded, in time, with a large decrease in sulfur dioxide emissions in the Northeast, is as definitive a statement as was permitted by the data. Certainly the attempt to be more quantitative made by Lipfert is obviously flawed scientifically, and must be rejected. His treatment of the sulfate-to-nitrate ratios, which appears in the revised version of the Manowitz group 'review, suffers from many of the same problems, and the results are of highly questionable quality.

"Reviewer 'E' of the original Manowitz 'review' (now identified as W.G.N. Slinn, M.T. Dana, and/or R.C. Easton of Battelle Pacific Northwest Labs) questioned the near constancy of the SO_4/NO_3 ratios observed over wide areas of eastern North America in the annual averaged deposition data. The comments of reviewer 'E' show such an extraordinary degree of rancorous disdain and distortion that one should not honor them with a response. However, our analysis of his comments (placed in the written material for the *Congressional Record)* shows no scientific basis for his claims. Instead, a serious distortion of the observations is evident.

"Our conclusion, that reliability for present long range transport and transformation models is low in relating specific sources with receptor sites, has been questioned by one of the Manowitz 'review' group (Jack Shannon of Argonne). The objection is surprising since our view seems to be the consensus of the National Research Council committee on acid deposition, the Interagency Task Force on Acid Rain (of which the Manowitz group is some undefined part), and the Acid Rain Peer Review Panel appointed by the President's science advisor; it is also supported by other members of the Manowitz group.

"Models are used by all scientists today, and, certainly, definitive uses have been and will continue to be made of them. Our caution relates to their inappropriate use. If long-range modeling, involving the attribution of specific sources to specific receptor sites, is used today, and of course it is now used by some for this purpose, then the modelers should provide the user with realistic estimates of the magnitude of the large uncertainty associated with the results so that these can be incorporated into the control strategy planning. Such a practice is not suggested to frustrate a control plan development, if one is deemed desirable at this time, but it is necessary to provide the sense of realism that is demanded in the formulation of a sulfur oxide emission control strategy, in view of the very high costs associated with the various control strategy options.

"Those who are interested in our more detailed response to this so-called review may find it in the *Congressional Record.* Certainly the conclusions of the National Research Council committee on acid deposition are necessarily very limited in nature, and indeed, they must and will be checked by extensive further experimentation. Our conclusions represent the best judgment of a group of highly-qualified and diversified scientists, and we certainly would not alter or compromise these conclusions on the basis of this most unusual 'review' by the Manowitz group. One must question the motivation for such a 'review.'"

It is not unusual for scientists to differ with each other over the adequacy of an analysis or the interpretation given to a set of data. It is unusual, however, for these differences of opinion to be debated in the public press as this one was. It is clear that severely aroused emotions entered into this debate. I contacted Jack Calvert at the National Center For Atmospheric Research to learn if there had been any resolution of the controversy in the more than two years that had elapsed since the above-quoted articles appeared in print. He generously offered to send me a copy of his statement about the controversy that appeared in the *Congressional Record,* saying his position had not changed from what was presented in that document. He told me of a letter sent to Representative Scheuer from the Brookhaven contingent, which he remembered as modifying that group's original position somewhat, but was unable to provide a copy of the letter. He suggested that, if my interest warranted it, I should check with the folks at Brookhaven.

That is what I did. My letter to Bernard Manowitz at Brookhaven National Laboratory, dated January 2,1986, explained my interest and asked if he could provide a copy of the correspondence that Jack Calvert had mentioned, along with any remarks that might be warranted to update his position on the controversy. Because I expected a one or two page letter in reply, I sent along a stamped, self-addressed envelope, hoping to minimize Dr. Manowitz' trouble in replying. Was I ever naive! On January 15, 1986 a large, well-filled manila envelope arrived in the afternoon mail. The metered first-class postage came to $2.40. Evidently the Postal Service rose to the challenge of finding me without delay. Only two days elapsed between the sending and the receiving.

Dr. Manowitz' reply was prompt, courteous, and very helpful. Included in the packet of information he sent, were: 1) a copy of his statement to the Senate Committee on Environment and Public Works of November 2, 1983, which contained his response to the Scheuer Committee that Dr. Calvert had mentioned; 2) a copy a letter from Representatives Dingell and Lloyd to Dr. Chris Bernabo, director of the Interagency Task Force on Acid Precipitation, dated

October 25, 1983, requesting his assistance in resolving the conflict; and 3) a copy of his March 22, 1984, testimony before the House Subcommittee on Health and the Environment, which included the text of Dr. Bernabo's response to the request for his help. It puts the controversy in a different light than you might have seen in the two articles that appeared in *The Energy Daily*. Here is Dr. Manowitz' lucid and well-reasoned three-page statement in its entirety:

"My name is Bernard Manowitz. I am chairman of the Department of Applied Science at Brookhaven National Laboratory. I am also the chairman of the National Laboratory Consortium consisting of Argonne National Laboratory, Brookhaven National Laboratory, Oak Ridge National Laboratory, and Pacific Northwest Laboratory of Battelle. This consortium has a congressionally mandated role in the National Acid Precipitation Assessment Program.

"My presentation today represents the views of the National Laboratory Consortium and is not the official position of the Interagency Task Force on Acid Precipitation.

"On August 4, 1983, I was requested by the House Committee on Science and Technology to conduct a review of a National Academy of Sciences study entitled 'Acid Deposition: Atmospheric Processes in Eastern North America.' On August 30, 1983 I submitted a response to the House Committee in behalf of the National Laboratory Consortium. That response and further comment on the committee report were presented to the Senate Committee on Environment and Public Works on November 2, 1983, and are part of the records of that hearing. Dr. Chris Bernabo, the executive director of the Interagency Task Force on Acid Precipitation, has recently written the following statement on the relationship between the Calvert Committee (NAS) report and the National Laboratories' critique:

'The criticisms of the recent NAS report expressed by the group of scientists at national laboratories appear to be more a matter of emphasis than of fundamental differences in sources of data or in interpretation.

'Both the National laboratories' critique and the NAS report agree that, in general, the detailed processes involved in acid deposition are inherently nonlinear. The NAS committee expressly set out to determine the the extent of the nonlinearities. It found that sufficient data for the analysis were available only for assessing relationships between long-term (annual) average values of emissions and deposition integrated over large spatial scales. Several lines of evidence and theoretical calculations suggest that if nonlinearities exist between annual average emissions and deposition over large areas, they are not dominant. The NAS report phrased its conclusion as "there is no strong evidence that the relationship is nonlinear" because the data are not sufficient to prove the relationship is linear. The data can only be used to assess the strength of the nonlinearity.

'The NAS report points out that short-term (episodes) are very complex and may indeed involve non-linearities. Nonlinearities clearly arise, for example, in short-term meteorology and may be important for chemical processes taking place in clouds in winter. When the individual episodes are summed or averaged over the year, however, the nonlinearities appear to balance out, or, in the case of the cloud processes in winter, apparently do not contribute much to annual totals.

'Both the NAS report and the national laboratory scientists agree that further research on atmospheric processes is crucial to advancing our knowledge of the phenomenon of acid deposition. If we are to improve our ability to construct computer-based models useful for predicting the consequences of alternative emission control strategies, we need to study the detailed processes that occur on short temporal and spatial scales, where nonlinearities can be expected. Only by building up this area of understanding can we have confidence that the models accurately reflect what is happening in nature and that reliable projection of the specific consequences of targeted emission reductions can be made.

'The NAS report asserts that current models are not sufficiently tested to be relied on for quantitative evaluations of targeted control strategies. This conclusion is, of course, a matter of judgment. Dr. Calvert, chairman of the NAS committee, has suggested in congressional testimony that current models can make, and have been used to make broad-based qualitative comparisons that have provided useful contributions to the policy debate.

'The seeming conflict between the NAS committee report and the comments of the National Laboratory Consortium's scientists is more apparent than real, resting mainly on different approaches.'

"I have reviewed the statement, as has Dr. Calvert, and I agree that it represents an accurate and reasonable description of the situation.

"Let me then address what I perceive to be an interpretation by the non-technical community of the NAS committee statements. I fear that some are interpreting the term 'linearity' as that acidic deposition will be proportional to SO_2 emissions regardless of the location of either the deposition or the emissions. This is not what the Calvert committee has said. My interpretation of the Calvert committee report statement is that if there were to be a uniform reduction of SO_2 emissions over a large area, that is, for example, the same percent in SO_2 emissions for every state east of the Mississippi, then there would be a corresponding proportional annual reduction in deposition everywhere within that large area.

"On the other hand, the position of the scientific community, as I understand it, is that deposition on any given sensitive area is nowhere near proportional to emissions from any source area, but rather varies over orders of magnitude depending upon the prevailing wind direction and source-receptor distance. It follows that a control strategy which is not based on source-receptor transfer considerations is highly unlikely to be as effective as one which is.

"Whether the source-receptor relation is linear or non-linear, a key question would be: 'How far away from a source, in a long-term-average sense, does the deposition, both wet and dry, of the emitted material and its transformation products take place?' Of course, deposition takes place at a distribution of distances from a source, some near, some further along, some still further, and some at long distances. Nonetheless, it is meaningful to ask what is the average distance between source and receptor. I am sure that you can appreciate the fact that the answer to this question can greatly affect the development of an effective control strategy. Very different strategies would be contemplated if this average distance were say 50 miles, 150, 500, or 1500 miles. Unfortunately, in my judgment, the current state of understanding does not permit a very precise answer to be given to this question. Indeed I would say that you could find highly-respected scientists who, if pressed, would venture opinions, based on their best judgment, that would be rather broadly distributed over the above range. Such a range of answers is a measure of the present degree of uncertainty in the atmospheric science community of the answers to this question.

"If the process is, indeed, nonlinear, i.e., if the deposition depends upon the concentration of pollutant, and thus a change in emission from a source S of N percent does not result in a change in deposition (from S) of N percent at a receptor location (or region), then the formulation of control strategies is even more difficult. Determination of the generalized source-receptor function is the overall problem facing atmospheric scientists engaged in deposition research.

"These questions are priority research subjects of the National Acid Precipitation Program. They are being approached, as suggested by the National Academy Committee, by direct observations in the field. These major field programs are being coordinated by both federal agencies and industrial participants. It is my belief that in several years these studies will provide basic phenomenological evidence with sufficient reliability to substantially improve control strategy options.

"I recognize, however, that it is sometimes necessary for legislative bodies to act on some hypothesis even when it is not firmly supported by scientific evidence.

"In this case, I believe that the nation would best be served by using the approach of the OSTP (Neirenberg) Committee, i.e., provide for a reduction in sulfur emissions that is least disruptive and most cost-effective, acknowledging the uncertainty in where and when deposition changes will occur. Should such legislation be enacted, I would hope that the legislation provide for a mid-term correction so that the results of the research programs now being undertaken can be factored effectively into modified legislation."

How Did the Controversy Get Overblown? After reviewing the information just presented, do you wonder what led to the aroused emotions in the first place? Were some preexisting antipathies at work? Was the wording chosen by some reviewers to express their disagreement with the conclusions of the National Academy of Science committee the cause of the problem? Was the review objectionable because it seemed to evidence an unflattering lack of trust in the work of the NAS committee? Was there some hidden agenda operating on the part of the reviewers?

I checked back with Jack Calvert, seeking to learn the answers to these questions. He was very generous with his time and gave me quite a bit of additional background information.

Dr. Calvert called my attention to the extremely critical remarks of Reviewer "E," couched in very colorful language, that were included in the documents he had sent me earlier. These remarks were given wide circulation in written form, before any opportunity for rebuttal was accorded the NAS committee.

The reviewing process, as usually applied to scientific articles or reports, is intended to be carried out meticulously and critically. It is intended to call to question any statement that the reviewer does not consider fully justified. Any interpretation of data that the reviewer considers to be faulty is expected to be challenged. Scientists submit reports of their work to refereed journals of high repute, expecting that their work will be critically reviewed before it is published. Scientific journals request well-qualified scientists to perform reviews as a means of obtaining expert advice about the article's suitability for publication. It is usual practice for the journal to provide a copy of the reviewer's remarks to the author, without identifying the reviewer by name.

In preparing his review, the reviewer is expected to confine himself to matters of science. There is, in the United States, an unwritten code of behavior that precludes crossing the boundary between acceptable and unacceptable criticism. Denigration of the author as a person, or questioning his motives is usually considered to be unacceptable, at least in written form. There is not a universally-applied standard of courtesy, however. Some scientists, who were trained abroad, have evidently been encouraged to be brutally frank in expressing their evaluations.

I happen to be personally acquainted with Reviewer "E." I have always considered him to be a highly-qualified scientist and a pleasant person to be around. But I have never found myself the target of his criticism. His role model, when it comes to criticism, may be a world-famous British scientist whom I once observed stand up at an international meeting and tell the author of a just-presented paper, "You ought to be ashamed of yourself for wasting the time of this august body by presenting such garbage. Your paper is absolute nonsense." Scientists who have studied under this man, exhibit two qualities in common. They are, themselves, outstanding in their chosen field and, their critical comments are frank to the point of sometimes being crushing.

Reading Reviewer "E's" comments about the NAS commmittee's report reveals several things about the psychological climate in which the review was prepared:

1) Reviewer "E" was not pleased with having to spend his weekend preparing the review for which he received no payment.

2) He was unhappy with the composition of the NAS committee.

He saw the committee as too heavily populated by chemists and chemical engineers, with no meteorologists who were expert in modeling long-range transport of pollutants.

3) His confidence in the quality of his own judgment was unmarked by doubt, but he was prepared to conclude that the committee's collective judgment was frequently faulty.

4) Reviewer "E" was unhappy with society for releasing huge quantities of pollution, without considering the consequences beforehand, and then expecting scientists to help solve the problem without providing the support for keeping trained scientists adequately employed as scientists, instead of as taxi drivers.

Many a review has been drafted in an extremely critical mood, but usually, after a cooling-down period, the objections are rephrased to preserve the dignity of the critized people. That didn't happen in this case, and as a result, the flames of controversy were fanned. This affair became much more than a petty quarrel between rival groups of scientists. Its fallout extended to the deliberations of Congress, and may yet be affecting progress toward decisions about acid rain.

Understanding Really Does Take Time In most of the arguments over acid rain that involve scientific issues, inadequate data sets and uncertainty about the details of natural processes play a role in intensifying controversy. The time required to reduce such uncertainties to acceptable levels is measured in years or even decades. You may have already encountered an overly-cynical perception about the behavior of research scientists. According to this idea, scientists are willing to study, at a leisurely pace, any given problem for as long as the funding allocated to the problem lasts. There is considered to be little regard for the importance of finding timely answers. But before you accept as valid the charge that scientists are dragging out their acid-rain studies to preserve their financial well-being, consider the previously mentioned survey of 1027 U.S. acid-deposition researchers, conducted by the National Wildlife Federation. It showed that four out of five of the responding scientists were in favor of immediate and decisive steps to curtail emissions. Only 14 percent favored more research before further controls be undertaken. Apparently something beside selfish financial gain had to be operating. Much of the support for acid-rain research is justified on the basis that additional knowledge is required before emissions control can be approached wisely. Early application of stronger emissions control measures would very likely result in a decreased level of support for further research. Why would such a high percentage of the scientists involved in acid-rain research support a policy that could turn out to be career threatening? What was really on their minds?

The January, 1986, issue of *The Environmental Forum* contained an article that bears on this matter. Under a headline that read:

SO ENDETH THE SCIENTIFIC DISPUTE OVER ACID RAIN? NOT HARDLY

"Declare victory and pull out. The notion is attractive to a lot of people. But the problem is that it often just does not work. In this case, six scientists calling themselves the 'Ad Hoc Committee on Acid Rain: Science and Policy' declared an end to the scientific uncertainty surrounding passage of a federal acid rain control program. Poof! Gone. Or is it? The scientists, who included some of the biggest names in the field of acid precipitation research, said they had examined six major governmental studies in an effort to answer 17 major scientific questions. 'Substantial consensus exists on sources of acid deposition, on certain types of damage caused by deposition, and on likely effects of reducing the emissions responsible for the acidity,' they concluded in a joint statement. In an undated letter to 'Those Concerned with Resolving the Acid Rain Issue,' they said: 'We are convinced that the scientific community now understands at least qualitatively, and in some cases quantitatively, the sequence of physical and chemical steps that lead from emission of oxides of sulfur and nitrogen in North America to eventual changes in widespread ecosystems.' They said the governmental reports 'establish a strong consensus that reducing the emissions of a large number of air pollutants, most notably sulfur dioxide, would benefit biological systems in North America significantly.' Maybe, but to many it appeared that the scientists' confidence was exceeded only by their arrogance in professing to speak for all of science. Judging by utilities', midwestern states', and high-sulfur coal interests' responses, the six scientists may be ready to declare victory and pull out; the debate doubtless will continue without them. In any event, few doubt that the political debate could persist even in the absence of scientific uncertainties, at least for the time being."

Let's move on now to see what is going on in yet another special-interest group: governmental agencies whose mandates involve them in the acid-rain issue.

The Government Agencies

There is, in our nation, an interesting notion that the operation of the executive branch of the federal government should be guided by some well-conceived logic. According to this notion, progress toward the attainment of national goals should proceed at a steady pace, under the enlightened guidance of our elected chief executive, the president of the United States.

The reality seems to be somewhat different. Even on those occasions when the various departments and independent agencies of the executive branch do their level best to implement the policies handed down from on high, many day-to-day governmental activities are carried out under the influence of conflicting points of view. Policies are not always handed down unambiguously, and may be subject to revisions which do not take all the consequences of policy change into account. Even when there is no intentional ambiguity, differences in interpretation can still operate. Each agency has its own unique viewpoint, rooted in tradition, and many have a body of influential constituents drawn from among the tax-paying public. Some agencies are outwardly oriented and operate as if their intended purpose is to help solve the problems of the tax-paying public to the best of the agency's ability. Other agencies are inwardly oriented and operate defensively, with an attitude that suggests that the tax-paying public is the problem.

This diversity of viewpoint exists both among and within departments. The not-surprising result is a high probability of less-than-perfect harmony. Sometimes the disharmony is so intense that it takes on the appearance of open warfare.

With these circumstances in mind, you may be wondering why anyone would consider lumping all of the government agencies that are involved with acid rain into a single special-interest group. My aim is to promote understanding of what the government is doing about acid rain and how it is going about the task that has been assigned to it by external forces.

How Different Agencies Have Become Involved When a complex technical problem, such as acid rain, develops enough importance that it can no longer be ignored by the federal government, high-level deliberations begin on what should be done to solve the problem. The initial push for a solution may come from a member of Congress, whose interests encompass the subject matter area in which the problem lies.

The first step may be telephone calls to responsible officials in the departments having charters related to the problem area. The purpose of these calls is to sense how each department reacts to legislation that assigned responsibility and funding for tackling the problem.

An enthusiastic response from any department is apt to be followed by rapid drafting of proposed legislation. Shortly thereafter, congressional hearings are called. These are aimed at learning how the problem and the attack proposed in the draft legislation are evaluated by knowledgeable experts and public groups whose special interests pertain to the problem.

At this point destructive warfare can break out among departments of the executive branch, in spite of the best efforts of the Office of Management and Budget to create the impression that someone is really in charge. Competition to land the new assignment can be intense, with each department pulling out all stops to put the competence of its staff and the aptness of its charter in the most favorable light. Each may try to prove that it already has underway a well-thought-out program aimed at solving the problem, and that all that is really needed is expanded funding to speed the arrival of the final solution.

Eventually the warfare subsides. Then the realities begin to operate. No one department employs all the skilled people needed to construct a suitable solution. The required skills may reside in employees of other departments or in groups completely outside of government. It becomes apparent to all concerned that it is time for a measure of cooperation to replace at least some of the original intense competition.

The tried and true governmental mechanism for substituting

cooperation for competition is the formation of an interagency task force. Such a task force can provide the opportunity for each interested department to bring to bear the skills it has to offer while keeping an eye on what the competition is up to. The federal effort, to pin down what is happening with acid-rain and what isn't happening that needs to happen, is going forward under just such an interagency task force.

The Interagency Task Force on Acid Precipitation was established by Congress as part of the Acid Precipitation Act of 1980. (If you are really a glutton, that act was Title VII of the Energy Security Act, P.L. 96-294. Those final numbers indicate that the 96th Congress had enacted 293 public laws before it got around to passing this one.) The Task Force is responsible for conducting the National Acid Precipitation Assessment Program. NAPAP has the goal "to develop and progressively improve upon the analytical tools necessary to understand processes critical to the acid precipitation issue."

The task force is required by law to issue to the president and Congress an annual report of progress made in the National Acid Precipitation Assessment Program. Their third report, the one covering progress made during 1984, was released to the public in the fall of 1985. If that doesn't seem as timely as you might expect in this age of electronic publishing, you should appreciate that it takes a lot of time and effort to write, coordinate, and produce a comprehensive government document in a form suitable for presentation to the president and Congress.

On the fly page, one is notified that the report was prepared by the Interagency Task Force on Acid Precipitation. The rest of the page is given over to a display of the official seals of the cooperating agencies that make up the task force, and, in addition, a listing of the names of those agencies in large type, just in case a reader's eyesight isn't up to extracting the information from the the artistically-designed seals.

There are twelve seals in all, but three are much larger than the other nine. The seals of the Department of Agriculture, the National Oceanic and Atmospheric Administration and the Environmental Protection Agency are each about the size of a silver dollar. The remaining nine are dime-sized and read from left to right: Council on Environmental Quality, Department of Commerce, Department of Energy, Department of Interior, Department of Health and Human Services, Department of State, National Science Foundation, National

Aeronautics and Space Administration, and the Tennessee Valley Authority.

The task force is jointly chaired by NOAA, EPA, USDA, DOE, DOI and CEQ. In view of this sextuple co-chairing, it isn't immediately obvious why the first three rate dollar-size seals but the fourth, fifth and sixth must be content with dime-size seals. The remaining six small seals belong to the "other participating and nonfunding Federal agencies."

The level of funding provided by each agency doesn't correlate well with seal size either. For the 1984 fiscal year, the president requested $27.5 million for the acid deposition research program, but Congress, in its collective wisdom, granted $35.3 million. Following the example set by a Congress interested in acid rain research, the president requested $55.5 million for 1985 and $85 million for 1986. Congress provided $64.9 million for expenditure in 1985, and the 1986 figure is $81.9 million. EPA's share in 1984 was about 58 percent which would certainly seem to entitle EPA to display a large version of its seal. But both large-sealed USDA and NOAA contributed about 8 percent of the total while small-sealed DOE and DOI contributed 11.2 percent and 14.5 percent.

The not-exactly-earth-shaking matter of the allocation of seal sizes was about to join many other unresolved mysteries of government which have intrigued me over the years, when it occurred to me to check the *1983 Annual Report.* When I did, the mystery of the seals dissolved and oozed away. In 1983, the Joint Chairs Council of the Task Force consisted of three people, the representatives of EPA, NOAA, and USDA. The three large seals and 9 small seals made somewhat better sense for that state of affairs. Evidently, in 1984, when the Joint Chairs Council was increased to five by the addition of representatives from the DOE and DOI, the seal size distribution was not revised to agree with the new power hierarchy. CEQ became the sixth co-chair in 1985. What once deserved to be called, in the words of the King of Siam, "a puzzlement" now achieves the status of a non-problem. Just what would be wrong with all of the seals being the same size isn't entirely obvious.

The task force also includes four presidential appointees and the representatives of Argonne, Brookhaven, Oak Ridge, and Pacific Northwest National Laboratories. No seals at all are displayed for them, but the national laboratories can take some measure of comfort from their intimate association with the properly-if-minimally-sealed

DOE. Enough about seals already!

The annual report lists the main responsibilities of the task force as:

"Overseeing and implementing the long-term comprehensive interagency research program;

"Issuing an annual report to the President and Congress on the status of science and research progress;

"Issuing assessments to distill and synthesize the information developed in a format useful for decision-makers;

"Maintaining an inventory of all federally-sponsored acid deposition research projects;

"Developing and updating the Operating Research Plan of the National Program;

"Developing an annual interagency budget for the Federal program;

"Ensuring that research projects are technically sound, credible, and relevant through peer and program reviews by the scientific community; and,

"Encouraging productive interaction between the Federal, private sector, academic, State and local government, and international acid precipitation research programs."

There are ten categories within the research effort. The emphasis placed on each, by the people responsible for distributing the $35.3 million in funds allocated to the National Acid Precipitation Assessment Program in 1984, can be judged by the percentage of total expenditures figures shown in parentheses in the following list of ten categories of activity: Natural Sources (2.4 per cent), Man-made Sources (5.9 percent), Atmospheric Processes (17.6 percent), Deposition Monitoring (17.9 percent), Aquatic Effects (31.7 percent),Terrestrial Effects (13.0 percent), Effects on Materials and Cultural Resources (4.2 percent), Control Technologies (0.0 percent), Assessments (7.9 percent), and International Activities (0.0 percent). The annual report includes descriptive paragraphs about what was accomplished in each category of activity. The fact that (0.0 percent) appears after Control Technologies and International Activities does not mean that no government funding was available to carry out those activities. It means only that no NAPAP funds were expended in those categories. Actually EPA has other funds to spend on the development of Control Technologies that are part of a broad interest in clean air.

There were international activities in connection with NAPAP, even if the budget figures don't show expenditures in that category. The report mentions a meeting held in May, 1984, with the Canadian Research and Monitoring Committee, to discuss ongoing research cooperation in a number of fields and to propose additional subjects for joint research. Approximately thirty projects, including air pollution research, deposition monitoring and effects research, are jointly coordinated by people from NAPAP and RMCC. It is nice to be reminded that we and the Canadians are talking to, rather than shouting at, each other about acid rain. There have been too many newspaper articles that give a contrary impression.

There was also a meeting with people from the Federal Republic of Germany regarding a program of research cooperation. Projects already underway in the United States and in Germany will be coordinated as a result of this meeting and further joint efforts are intended. It is good to learn that the "not invented here" syndrome that requires the solution to every problem to be made in the U.S.A. is not dominating the acid-rain research picture completely.

Determining Which Government Agency Is Doing What In preparation for discussing with you what the federal government is doing about acid rain, I got the idea that you might be interested in learning how each of the agencies represented on the task force saw its role in the acid-rain drama. To obtain first-hand information on this aspect of things, I wrote to each of agencies, telling them what I was up to and asking for a clear statement of the goals, present programs and expected duration of its acid-rain efforts. I sent out 17 letters in all, since some departments have more than one agency involved with acid rain. I think you'll find what happened next interesting.

The first result of my well-intentioned survey didn't have much to do with acid rain, but did provide some interesting insight into the present service attitude of the U.S. Postal Service. Years ago, as legend has it, a letter addressed

Wood
John
Mass.

was promptly and properly delivered to John Underwood, Andover,

Massachusetts. It would appear that times have changed. My letter to the U.S. Forest Service, mailed November 15, 1985, to the address for that agency listed in a recently-published directory of federal agencies, was back on my desk by November 19, 1985. On the face of the envelope was a red stamped message. A hand with the index finger scoldingly extended, pointed toward the return address and bore the message: Returned to Sender. Below the hand in bold capital letters was the message:

NOT DELIVERABLE
AS ADDRESSED —
UNABLE TO FORWARD

My letter was sent by first class mail and included a beautiful 22-cent stamp showing Old Glory waving over the Capitol Building in Washington, D.C. My mistaken notion has been that a letter sent by First Class Mail leads a kind of charmed life until it is finally delivered into the hands of its addressee by one of those dedicated people who, according to Postal Service propaganda, let "neither rain, nor snow, nor dark of night" stay them from their appointed rounds.

To find out why my letter was not forwardable to wherever the United States Forest Service is hiding from the U.S. Postal Service, I called the Information Office of the local Post Office. I was told, "Those big companies are very careless about providing us forwarding addresses. To teach them a lesson we quit forwarding their mail after two years." It isn't clear to me what the U.S.Forest Service learned from this incident, but I learned a lot. I pass it on to you with the best of intentions.

By calling a local office of the U.S. Forest Service, I was able to obtain the current address of their Washington, D.C. office. I readdressed my letter of inquiry and succeeded in making contact before the post office figured out a new reason for teaching the Forest Service a lesson.

The reply I received from the Forest Service was prompt and courteous. It enclosed information that answered my questions fully. It turns out that the Forest Service manages a large atmospheric deposition research program as part of the National Acid Precipitation Assessment Program. Forest Service research is conducted in support of three NAPAP task groups: Deposition Monitoring, Aquatic Effects, and Terrestrial Effects. The Forest Service represents the U.S. Department of Agriculture as the lead agency for the Terrestrial Effects Task Group.

Forest Service Research units maintain and operate eleven wet deposition monitoring stations throughout the United States. These stations are part of the National Atmospheric Deposition Network. Research in support of the Aquatic Effects Task Group is conducted by five work units at various experimental watersheds, including the Marcell, Fernow, and Hubbard Brook Experimental Forests, and the Coweeta Hydrologic Laboratory. These studies involve long-term monitoring of deposition inputs, estimation of chemical budgets, and looks at the processes that influence the chemistry of the water that makes its way to the groundwater, streams, and lakes. These same studies benefit the Terrestrial Effects Task Group as they seek to determine how terrestrial ecosystems affect acquatic ecosystems.

Most of the rest of the Forest Service acid-rain research concerns effects on forests. This question is being attacked cooperatively with EPA and members of the forest industry. The Forest Service and EPA are joint managers of the program which will involve multi-disciplinary, multi-institutional research cooperatives, chosen on a competitive basis to study each of the forest types in the nation. The original request for proposals to study the spruce/fir forests in the northeast and southeast brought in 50 proposals. It would appear that it won't lack of interest on the part of the research community.

The second return on my survey of goals, programs, and intentions was not as productive as the first, although the Postal Service did succeed in discovering where the National Science Foundation is located in Washington, D.C. A member of NSF's Public Affairs Group replied promptly as follows:

"This is in reply to your recent request for information or material. The National Science Foundation does not maintain large stocks of material on scientific or other subjects for distribution to the public. I regret to inform you that we do not have available the type of information you seek.

"The National Science Foundation is an independent agency of the federal government, devoted chiefly to the support of basic research and of projects for the improvement of science education. The foundation's programs are generally administered by the nation's colleges, universities, and other research and educational institutions."

The postscript informed me that the National Academy of Sciences, 2101 Constitution Avenue, NW, Washington, DC 20418, recently issued a publication on this subject (acid rain).

As pleased as I was that my letter had actually reached the agency, I can't say that the reply told me much I'd be thrilled to pass on to you. In fact I was more-than-somewhat miffed by the reply. For the past 30 years I have known, as you may have, what the National Science Foundation is and how it goes about its assigned task of supporting research. I have: 1) enjoyed the experience of receiving and/ or administering millions of dollars worth of NSF research grants; 2) provided, at NSF's request, peer review of numerous research proposals submitted by other scientists; and 3) served as a member of a NSF Advisory Committee. It was disappointing to have my request so casually dismissed, without even so much as a hint as to why the NSF logo appears on the flypage of the *NAPAP Annual Report*.

In view of the above quoted non-reply to my letter to NSF, you may have joined me in wondering why NSF is mentioned on the flypage of the *NAPAP Annual Reports*. I found a possible clue in a section of the report entitled Program Management Activities, where we are told that peer reviews of research projects were conducted to evaluate the adequacy and comprehensiveness of the National Program.

If there is anything the National Science Foundation knows how do to well, it is how to obtain peer reviews of research proposals at minimum cost. Many of the experts you would want to turn to for advice on the adequacy of a proposed research project are themselves indebted to the National Science Foundation for past support of their own research. Turning down a request to provide a review might cause severely adverse future developments, so a vast array of knowledgeable academic scientists stand ready to contribute their time and judgment to the reviewing process without cost to the NSF.

Do the words peer review convey a clear message to your inquiring mind? Perhaps more discussion will help. Peer review involves seeking advice about the merits of a research proposal which has been submitted to a potential sponsor by an ambitious scientist or group of scientists. A panel of highly-qualified but personally-disinterested scientists, usually three in number, provides the advice. Each member of the panel submits a presumably independent judgment of the proposal. This includes recommendations to the potential sponsor about whether or not the proposal deserves to be supported.

The peer review process is often represented as an even-handed way of discovering the intrinsic merit of a research proposal. Sometimes it really is.

There are, however, a few aspects of the process that deserve to be looked at at least sceptically, if not cynically. The manager of a particular NSF research program area, for example, doesn't have to be in his job very long before he has a good working knowledge of which reviewers are apt to lean to the optimistic side and which to the pessimistic side in their appraisals of other scientist's research proposals. This knowledge provides the opportunity for the manager to stack the deck in favor of or against a proposal, by choosing a review panel with tendencies favorable to his point of view.

There are other influences which operate against dispassionate reviewing. Can you put yourself in the shoes of a well-established science professor who has been asked to review two competing research proposals? One of the proposals has been submitted to NSF by a recently graduated Ph.D., who had the good judgment to do his graduate work under the supervision of the reviewer himself. The other proposal is also from a recently-graduated Ph.D., but this one was so ill-advised as to have done his work under the reviewer's long-time rival, with whom there has been a consistent record of strong differences of opinion over matters of science. Which of the two proposals do you think would receive the fine-tooth-comb treatment and which would be graded with a forgiving attitude? Isn't that an ideal situation for the practice of impartial objectivity?

My idea that NSF might play an important role in satisfying NAPAP's need for peer review of research proposals turned out to be a poor guess, but it won't hurt anything for you to know how the plusses and minuses of the peer review process. Now that you are well acquainted with the ins and outs of the process, let's leave it and return to the survey saga.

When several weeks had passed with several agencies still unheard from, I placed a call to Dr. J. Laurence Kulp, director of research for NAPAP. I told him of my interest in learning what NSF, and four other as yet unresponsive agencies, did to merit mention on the title page of the *NAPAP Annual Report*. He told me that: the Council on Environmental Quality served as a sixth co-chair of NAPAP; the Department of Health and Human Services was interested in indirect effects of acid rain; the Department of State provided liaison with foreign governments; and the National Aeronautics and Space Administration provided instrumented aircraft for sampling the atmosphere as well as satellite data about global pollution for use in calibrating atmospheric models. But he was apparently reluctant to address my question as it concerned NSF. When I suggested the possibility of peer-review function, he indicated that people at NSF could, conceivably, be contacted for that purpose, but that NAPAP was quite able to handle its peer review needs on its own.

Because I was reluctant to admit to you that I couldn't find out what role NSF plays in NAPAP, I decided to make a second attempt at contacting the agency directly. On February 11, 1986, I wrote to the official who had answered my November 15, 1985, letter and asked that a second effort be made to find someone in NSF who would be able to clear up the mystery of how NSF finds itself included on the title page of NAPAP's annual report. Perseverance paid off. A very informative four-page letter, written by W. Franklin Harris, deputy director of the division of Biotic Systems and Resources reached me in mid-March. He informed me about the background of NSF's involvement with NAPAP and provided extensive detail about the acid-rain-related research that NSF has sponsored over the years.

It turns out that NSF became involved in the support of acid-rain research long before NAPAP was created. NSF supported the first modern documentation of acid rain in the United States. Data on rainfall pH, collected at Hubbard Brook, New Hampshire, beginning in 1961 has provided the basis for many research studies. In 1979, NSF participated in the drafting of the Federal Acid Precipitation Assessment Plan. This plan provided some of the foundation on which NAPAP was built after the passage of the Energy Security Act of 1980. The people who put NAPAP together included all the federal agencies that had a resource management mission. They also included NASA, HHS, and NSF. NSF was included because of its unique charter to support the conduct of basic research at colleges and universities. An early decision by the Office of Management and Budget put NSF, NASA and HHS into a different budget category than the agencies that had resource management or acid-rain mitigation responsibilities. Although NSF has no defined mission specifically focused on acid rain, much of the research it supports at colleges and universities is acid-rain related. In 1985, there were 56 such awards of support totalling over $1 million.

The third reply to my survey came from the Department of Energy and was a joy to receive. It actually provided answers to my questions! It read:

"Thank you for the opportunity to provide background information for your forthcoming book on acid rain. The Energy Department's principal related areas of involvement are two-fold:

"1) Interagency Task Force on Acid Precipitation — The Department participates in the federally sponsored National Acid Precipitation Assessment Program, a 10-year effort (now in its fifth year) to better understand processes critical to the acid precipitation issue. In addition to serving on several of the Task Force's working groups, the Department heads the Manmade Sources working group. The entire task force effort is described in the *Annual Report to the President and Congress — 1984*.

"2) Coal-Related Technology Development — The Department also maintains an ongoing research and development program. A major focus of this program is the development of new coal utilization technologies that offer improved pollutant reduction potential. Projects include the development of new coal preparation technologies, more effective or less expensive fuel gas/gas stream cleanup concepts, and several clean burning coal combustion techniques.These projects are described in the two pamphlets I have enclosed. Together, these technology development efforts received just over $58 million in research funding in fiscal 1985.

"Should you have any additional questions, please do not hesitate to contact us."

I'll report to you on the contents of the two pamphlets entitled *Advanced Coal Systems* and *New Technologies For Burning Coal* when we look at what can be done to reduce acid-forming pollution in a later chapter.

My letter to the Department of Interior also received a lot of thoughtful attention. It was first forwarded to the United States Geological Survey. The USGS provided a very complete description of their acid rain program. The six elements of the Geological Survey's Acid Precipitation Program are:

"1. Atmospheric-deposition monitoring: Coordination and operation of selected sites in National Trend Network. Lead agency for Deposition Monitoring Task Group.

"2. Identification of waters sensitive to acid deposition: Provided a large fraction of the data used to produce sensitivity map for the United States.

"3. Monitoring of sensitive water bodies: Measuring deposition loadings and water quality at 14 lakes and streams across the United States.

"4. Defining geochemical processes by which acid deposition affects water quality: Developing chemical budgets in seven diverse watersheds across the United States as a means of understanding processes.

"5. Measuring effects of acid deposition on building stones: Catching and measuring material removed by rain from building stones at four locations in the eastern United States. Destructive and nondestructive measurement of changes in building stone samples due to acid deposition.

"6. Identification of cultural resources at risk: Land-use maps are being used to estimate resources at risk in materials-effects area."

In addition to the description of the USGS acid-deposition program, I received the following very informative technical reports which you may want to learn more about:

Trend Analysis of Weekly Acid Rain Data — 1978-83. U.S. Geological Survey Water Resources Investigations Report 85-4211 "Chemical Composition of Bulk Precipitation in the North-Central and Northeastern United States, December, 1980, Through February 1981." Geological Survey Circular 874.

Evidence for Acid-Precipitation-Induced Trends in Stream Chemistry at Hydrologic Bench-Mark Stations. Geological Survey Circular 910.

Design of the National Trends Network for Monitoring the Chemistry of Atmospheric Precipitation. U.S. Geological Survey Circular 964.

Temporal Trends in the Acidity of Precipitation and Surface Waters of New York. United States Geological Survey Water-Supply Paper 2188.

Also provided by the USGS were a *Water Fact Sheet* and several informative press releases. These announced the publication of an annotated acid rain bibliography with 1660 entries, information on recent research reviews that revealed that the acidity of precipitation in the Northeast has changed little in recent years, but appears to be increasing locally in other areas.

To cap off their outstanding demonstration of responsive public service, the USGS asked the Fish and Wildlife Service, the National

Park Service and the Bureau of Land Management to provide additional materials that might be of use.

The Fish and Wildlife Service sent me Fish and Wildlife Leaflet 1, a nine-page pamphlet with the title *Acid Rain: Effects on Fish and Wildlife*. The pamphlet provides several pages of general information on acid rain in addition to a discussion of effects on fish and wildlife. Their letter of transmittal also notified me that my inquiry was being forwarded to Kearneysville, West Virginia, to the attention of the scientist who has supervised much of the Service's research on the impacts of acid rain on fish and wildlife resources.

In due course I received a reprint of an article entitled "The Federal Plan for Mitigation of Acid Precipitation Effects in the United States: Opportunities for Basic and Applied Research" that appeared in the January-February, 1984, issue of *Fisheries*. The paper discusses the strategies further research could make available for mitigating damages to aquatic ecosystems. Liming, the approach that has received the most attention in the press, is not the only treatment to be considered. Others include: creation of favorable micro-habitats for selected life stages, application of other acid-neutralizing materials beside lime, application of materials called "ligands" which serve to detoxify aluminum in the water, development of resistant fish strains, and stimulation of biologically-produced alkalinity.

As this is being written, no word has yet arrived from the National Park Service or the Bureau of Land Management.

Two Department of Commerce agencies submitted replies. These came from the National Oceanic and Atmospheric Administration and the National Bureau of Standards.

The reply from NOAA was as follows:

"In response to your letter requesting more information about acid rain, I am enclosing the recent *Annual Report of the National Acid Precipitation Assessment Program*. I hope the report will be helpful in answering your questions. If you need more information, I suggest that you contact NAPAP directly."

Needless to say, I was thrilled to receive my fourth copy of the *NAPAP Annual Report*. I immediately followed NOAA's instructions to look at the report for the answers to my questions. What I was able to glean from the report was that NOAA's administrator is a member of the six-person Joint Chairs Council; NOAA's share of the 1984 funding was 8 percent of $35.3 million; NOAA stands alone in studying or funding the study of Natural Sources; NOAA shares involvement in Atmospheric Processes with EPA and DOE; and NOAA plays a role in Deposition Monitoring along with seven other federal agencies.

For two months I thought that anyone who wanted to know more about NOAA's acid-rain goals and intentions was limited to contacting NAPAP directly. Then late in January, 1986, I received a second and much friendlier response to my request for information. It came from Dr. John M. Miller. He is deputy director of NOAA's Air Resources Laboratory and has been actively involved in NOAA'S acid rain program. He sent along the following publications you might want to know about:

1. *An Analysis and Assessment of U.S.-WMO Regional Precipitation Chemistry Measurements (1972-1982)* by R.S. Artz and J.M. Miller, NOAA Technical Memorandum ERL ARL-135, February, 1985.

2. *An Assessment of Precipitation Chemistry Measurements from the Global Trends Network and Its Predecessors (1972-1982)* by Uri Dayan, John M. Miller, Alan M. Yoshinaga and Donald W. Nelson NOAA Technical Memorandum ERL ARL-136, April, 1985.

3. *Geophysical Monitoring for Climatic Change No. 12 — Summary Report 1983,* Joyce M. Harris and Everett C. Nickerson, Editors, Boulder, Colorado, December, 1984.

4. *Weatherwise* , October, 1984, Vol.37, No.5 which contains some excellent articles on acid rain.

The National Bureau of Standards evidenced a receptive attitude concerning requests for information about their acid-rain involvement. Here is their reply:

"I'm enclosing some materials that will give you an idea of some of the research we are doing in acid rain here at NBS. This is not, however, representative of all the acid rain work we are doing. Some of the projects are in their infancy and no printed materials are available yet. For example, one project is just getting off the ground that will attempt to investigate the molecular particles that are suspected of rising into the atmosphere and creating the acid part of acid rain. Unfortunately, it is much too early to put anything in writing about this work.

"Another resource I can offer you early in 1986 is a copy of an in-house publication called the *NBS Journal of Research.* A near - future issue will be devoted entirely to rainwater research, I'm told. Please notify me if you'd like a copy of this journal.

"If the materials I'm sending prompt further questions, please don't hesitate to call me. I'll try to answer your questions, or I'll put you in touch with one of our scientists."

Isn't that reply heartwarming? Before mailing the letter its author had called me long-distance to apologize for the long time it was taking for him to collect the material he was sending me. It surely made my day to talk to so dedicated a public servant. Along with the letter came a packet of reports and reprints that were quite responsive to my request for information about what NBS was doing. The following list of titles should give you a good idea of NBS' past involvement in acid rain:

Evaluation of Methods Used for Determination of Acidity in 'Acid Rain' Samples. by G. Marinenko and W.F.Koch. NBSIR 85-114, March, 1985.

Simulated Precipitation Reference Materials, III. by E.R. Deardorff, T.C. Rains, and W.F. Koch. NBSIR 79-1953, April 1980. Issued September, 1980.

Simulated Precipitation Reference Materials, IV. by W.F. Koch, G. Marinenko, and W.J. Stolz. NBSIR 82-2581, June 1982. Issued October, 1982.

Simulated Rainwater. NBS Research Material 8409.

Simulated Rainwater. Standard Reference Material 2694.

Simulated Precipitation Reference Materials: Measurement of pH and Acidity. by William F. Koch and George Marinenko. Authorized Reprint from Special Technical Publication 823 Copyright American Society for Testing and Materials. 1984.

A Critical Review of Measurement Practices for the Determination of pH and Acidity of Atmospheric Precipitation. by G. Marinenko and W.F. Koch Environment International, Vol. 10, pp.315-319, 1984.

The reply to my letter received from the Tennessee Valley Authority was also generous:

"Thank you for your November 15 letter concerning acid rain. Your task of producing a book on this subject will, no doubt, involve a major effort on your part. We are happy to assist in a small way by submitting the information that you requested.

"The Tennessee Valley Authority has vast experience in the reduction of utility SO_2 emissions, and we have been interested in the acid rain issue for the past several years. In December, 1983, TVA completed one of the largest SO_2 emission reduction programs ever undertaken in this nation. This cleanup program reduced TVA's SO_2 emissions from their peak level of 2.35 million tons during 1977 to 1.0 million tons during 1984 — a reduction of more than 50 percent. This SO_2 emission reduction was carried out as TVA's responsibility under the Clean Air Act, and it added about 9 percent to the annual cost of TVA electricity. These costs are high; however, we believe they are justified considering the resulting environmental benefits.

"With regard to the acid rain problem, we believe it is a national problem which is related to the total emissions of both SO_2 and NO_x in this country from all sources. For 1980 it has been estimated that national emissions of SO_2 and NO_x were 27 and 21 million tons, respectively. These total emissions have changed only slightly since 1980. We believe that these emissions are still too high and need to be reduced. Therefore, TVA supports the need for national acid-rain legislation to ensure that necessary emission reductions are accomplished equitably.

"I hope that the enclosed will be helpful to you. Best wishes on the large task of writing your book on acid rain. If we can be of further assistance, please contact Larry Montgomery of my staff at (615) 632-6679."

The enclosures with the letter were:

Assessment of Environmental Effects of Acid Deposition.

Statement of Principles for Acid Rain Control Legislation - TVA Views.

Statement of Board of Directors of TVA Before the Committee on Environment and Public Works, U.S. Senate.

The Risk of Ecosystem Impairment - Can We Afford to Wait?

TVA Acid Deposition Effects Research Plan.

TVA has taken a clearly-stated position in the controversy over acid-rain-control legislation. That position is that control legislation is needed now. What sets TVA apart from many other disputants in the controversy is that it avoids taking an "all-or-nothing" position. At the same time that it advocates control legislation, it is carrying out research aimed at assisting in determining if adequate resource protection can be provided by emission control decisions. Here is how TVA sees its research goals:

"The goal of TVA's acid deposition effects research plan is to determine the extent of impacts on the resources of the Tennessee Valley Region, which have occurred or are likely to occur as a result of acid deposition, and to determine the quantitative relationship of the deposition to these impacts. This goal will be addressed through four specific objectives:

"(1) Determine the extent and severity of damages to terrestrial and aquatic ecosystems in the Tennessee Valley Region that may be caused by acid deposition or to which acid deposition may contribute.

"(2) Determine the role of acid deposition in these damages acting alone and in combination with other air pollutants or natural causes.

"(3) Predict likely future impacts and time-frames for these impacts to occur based on understandings of the processes responsible.

"(4) Predict a deposition level that will afford adequate protection for sensitive resources, based on information developed in Objectives 1, 2, and 3."

The estimate of funding requirements to accomplish their four objectives is $10 million over a five-year period. TVA expects sources outside of TVA, such as EPA for example, to provide around 60 percent of the total, but also expects to be investing $1,200,000 of TVA's own funds annually by 1987.

EPA is the major government actor in the acid-rain drama, so I anxiously awaited their reply to my letter. Here is what I received from them in a letter dated December 16, 1985:

"I am enclosing a copy of the statement on Acid Rain EPA administrator Lee M. Thomas presented December 14 before the Senate Environment and Public Works Committee. This testimony will bring you up to date on EPA's current position on acid rain.

"There is much more information available, of course — too much in fact to attempt to gather everything available on the subject and bundle it off to you.

"You may want to get in touch with the National Acid Precipitation Assessment Program, an interagency group that includes all the federal organizations (EPA among them) with responsibilities relevant to acid rain. The group's 1984 annual report is now available and can be obtained from the Director of Research — NAPAP, c/o EOP Publications (Room 2200), 726 Jackson Place, N.W., Washington, DC 20503.

"For further information from EPA you could contact the Office of Program Development (ANR-445), Office of Air and Radiation, U.S. Environmental Protection Agency, Washington, DC 20460. You also may want to contact our regional office in Denver, where there may be materials that would be of interest to you. That office is located in Suite 900, 1860 Lincoln Street. The phone number is (303) 293-1692.

"Good luck with the book."

The current position of EPA on acid rain appears to have changed very little under Administrator Lee M.Thomas from that reported to the Senate by former EPA Administrator Ruckelshaus in 1984. Here is the introductory portion of the statement Mr. Thomas made on December 11, 1985 before the Committee on Environment and Public Works of the United States Senate:

"Mr. Chairman and Members of the Committee:

"I welcome the opportunity to appear before you today to discuss the acid rain problem. Since becoming administrator, I have found this issue to be more complex than almost any other. Last summer I had the opportunity to personally visit areas in New York and Vermont where I viewed the effects of acid precipitation first hand. I hiked up Camels Hump and flew by helicopter over the Adirondack High Country. During that trip I was struck by the aesthetic and ecological value of these areas. That trip helped shape my strong personal sense of the importance and the complexity of the acid rain issue.

"My appearance here marks the fourth time in less than two years that a Congressional committee has invited the administrator of EPA to testify on acid rain. Administrator Ruckelshaus appeared before Congress on three separate occasions in 1984, and each time he described the admininstration's acid rain policy as well as its commitment to finding a solution. I quote from his March, 1984, testimony: 'The impact of acid deposition on the North American Continent is of great concern to this administration . . . When the fundamental scientific uncertainties have been reduced, this administration will craft and support an appropriate set of measures to solve the the acid-rain problem.'

"Since Bill Ruckelshaus made that pledge, we have put forth a major effort to obtain the scientific, analytical, and administrative answers needed to craft that solution. It is this effort that I would like to address in my remarks.

"As a way of providing an overview, I would like to return for a minute to the administration's policy. As Bill Ruckelshaus testified last year, 'There is no question that there is an acid-rain problem in this country.' Nevertheless, he pointed out that an immediate decision on additional controls would be inappropriate. We have made this determination not because we believe that controls are unnecessary or too expensive, but because it is premature and unwise to prescribe emission controls based on our current scientific understanding of the problem.

"In direct support of this policy, we announced and initiated an acid-rain program made up of three parts: accelerated research, ongoing policy analysis, and Federal/State studies of implementation issues. In addition, we have continued to pursue the active implementation of existing provisions of the Clean Air Act which control acid rain precursors. Each activity plays an important part in creating a coherent and comprehensive program."

To implement its policy, EPA supports research in eight of the ten categories of effort carried out under NAPAP, and provided 57.7 percent of NAPAP's total budget in 1984. For example, at the National Center For Atmospheric Research, which ordinarily receives the bulk of its research support from the National Science Foundation, EPA funds the principal acid-rain research effort. It is a three-year project to model acid deposition, and is the largest of its type in the country. It will involve twenty NCAR staff scientists as well as scientists from universities, government laboratories and foreign countries. Its aim is to combine meteorology and chemistry in a model that will be comprehensive.

The Department of State got around to responding to my letter on February 5, 1986, with a form letter that read as follows:

"We appreciate your interest and have enclosed all available material you requested. If we were unable to send all the items, we have tried to substitute similar ones. If appropriate, we have enclosed a

U.S. Government Printing Office order form.

"If we may assist you in the future, please do not hesitate to let us know."

The available material turned out to be two "Current Policies." Current Policy No. 458, a statement by Ambassador Lawrence S. Eagleburger, undersecretary for political affairs, before the Subcommittee on Arms Control, Oceans, International Operations, and Environment, Senate Foreign Relations Committee, on February 24, 1983, is entitled "Yellow Rain: The Arms Control Implications." It dealt with chemical and toxin weapons. Its relevance to acid rain in the United States has eluded me so far, but I'm still trying.

The second document, Current Policy No. 723, was a statement by Richard E. Benedick, deputy assistant secretary for oceans and international environmental and scientific affairs and U.S. representative to the executive body, before the Executive Body for the Convention on Long-Range Transboundary Air Pollution of the Economic Commission for Europe, in Helsinki, Finland, on July 8, 1985. It is entitled "Transboundary Air Pollution." It endorses the objective of reducing air pollution in Europe and North America, summarizes progress made in the United States in reducing SO_2 emissions, reaffirms the need for more scientific data, recognizes the need for international cooperation and promises that the United States will continue to strive for a better environment.

That about wraps up what I have available to report to you about the government attitude and activity concerning acid rain. I had hoped to have more to tell you, but, four months after my letter of November 15, 1985, was mailed out, no direct input from the Council on Environmental Quality, the Department of Health and Human Services and the National Aeronautics and Space Administration had reached me. I decided to settle for the information Dr. Larry Kulp gave me over the telephone.

I don't think the post office was the source of the problem, because none of my letters to these non-responding agencies was returned. Maybe there are more slow readers in the upper echelons of Washington, D.C. than I have been led to suspect. There is also the possibility that my inquiry about involvement in acid rain reached people who want to avoid any further contact with acid-rain troublemakers. They may have had it with the whole subject.

14.

Political and Legislative Aspects of Acid Rain

In our society, the speed with which an issue becomes involved with the political process is a fairly reliable measure of the importance of that issue. Significant matters are very likely to become political matters. Acid rain has rapidly become a very significant political matter. The politics of acid rain are the attempts, made within the context of our social system, to resolve the important controversies surrounding the complex issue. These controversies arise from differing perceptions of the importance of scientific uncertainty, regional differences in resources, climate, and economy, and from differing value systems that depend on individual needs and interests.

We have already looked at quite a bit of input on how the position of the Reagan administration on acid rain has been viewed, over a span of several years, by differing special-interest groups. Expression of those views is an important part of the political process. It is interesting to consider what effect those strongly-expressed views have had on the administration's position on acid rain.

A version of that position appeared on December 11, 1985, in the statement by EPA Administrator Lee M. Thomas before the Senate Committee on Environment and Public Works. Part of that position statement was discussed in Chapter XIII. Reading that statement is not apt to thrill people who are convinced of the need for immediate corrective action, but it does contain signs of movement. The position that completion of a ten-year research program is a necessary precursor to thinking about what comes next, may never have actually been strongly supported in the administration, but some people thought it was. Active implementation of existing provisions of the Clean Air Act was reported by Mr. Thomas. That announcement doesn't seem likely to win over the segment of our society that considers the Clean Air Act to be a grossly-inadequate base from which to accomplish further reduction of emissions, but it does seem to offer promise of a reduction of the number of lawsuits against EPA, based on charges that the provisions of the Clean Air Act are being entirely ignored.

The charge made by some environmentalists that the administration's program of scientific research is being conducted as a smoke screen to rationalize postponement of decisions to act, is difficult to reconcile with the history of acid rain research funding. A research-based smoke screen would seem likely to be characterized by token support at a minimum funding level. The actual funding history has been one of rapid growth. The budget for the National Acid Precipitation Assessment Program has grown steadily from $11.5 million in 1981, to $17.4 million in 1982, $22.7 million in 1983, $35.3 million in 1984, $64.9 million in 1985, and $81.9 million in 1986. This growth of research funding, during a period when great attention was being focused on the importance of reducing the federal deficit, seems almost paradoxical. The effect of congressional interest in acid rain on this record of continuous funding growth should not be overlooked, but the fact that the administration has not seen fit to rule out acceptance of congressional write-ins to the president's budget says something about the administration's interest in early arrival at a valid scientific basis for corrective action.

There is, in addition, evidence of the administration's orientation toward speeding scientific progress and addressing policy issues concurrently with the extensive program of scientific research. After recounting the changes in NAPAP funding, EPA Administrator Thomas went on to say:

"The changes in NAPAP were not limited to increased expenditures. The expansion in NAPAP research was consciously directed into those areas of greater significance to policy resolution. Our intent is not to simply increase scientific understanding of acid rain; rather we want to concentrate on gathering the scientific information necessary to make a decision on the need for additional controls. Identifying the principal scientific uncertainties hindering policy development, and targeting research to reduce those uncertainties, have been two of our major goals over the past two years.

"As a result of our major policy analytic effort in 1983, we gained a much clearer view of what kind of information is most needed to support policy development. For example, we discovered that existing data on the extent and magnitude of acid rain effects on aquatic systems were hampered by changes in methodology, inconsistent quality control, and the lack of a statistically-based sampling design. Data on the extent, magnitude, and cause of damage in forests were largely lacking. As a result, we have placed much greater emphasis on gaining information on aquatic and forest effects. NAPAP planning has responded by greatly expanding research efforts in both of these areas.

"The third major area of change in NAPAP is closely related to the first two. When NAPAP was first organized, it established as its main goal the production, at the end of ten years, of an integrated assessment of the acid rain problem in the United States. Recognizing the need for expeditious policy resolution, it was clear that we could not wait ten years for a definitive analysis of acid rain. We needed answers, even partial answers, much sooner. Consequently, we have designed research projects that would lead to near-term and mid-term incremental improvements in scientific understanding. We have even tried to build short-term results into those important research efforts that are trying to define long-term trends and processes. In short, NAPAP was put on a dual track. Beside being responsible for defining long-term trends, NAPAP was asked to improve scientific understanding more quickly and incrementally.

"While we have attempted to target NAPAP research to policy-related scientific uncertainties, we are also keenly aware of the need to keep NAPAP scientific objectives unaffected by its policy implications. The task is to make sure that the selection of research priorities is responsive to policy needs but that execution of those priorities is carried out as free from policy influences as possible. We have attempted to address this problem directly by clearly separating the responsibilities for policy development from those of scientific research and assessment. The lead responsibility for acid-rain policy development is in EPA's air programs, with the support of other agencies. Responsibility for science assessment and research is the sole responsibility of NAPAP."

The administration's interest in speeding policy development may not be entirely the result of spontaneous combustion within the administration. Heat has frequently been applied by environmental groups and by the Congress. Acid rain has been a subject of considerable congressional interest and activity in both the House and the Senate. Senator Daniel P. Moynihan (D.-N.Y.) was the author of the first acid-rain bill to be submitted to the Senate. Introduced in April, 1979, and made law in 1980, the bill established a federal research program intended to improve understanding of pollution impacts and pollution transport. Senator Moynihan's bill holds a unique position. It is the only acid-rain bill that has become law, unless you consider the Clean Air Act to be an acid-rain bill. This is not that other bills haven't been submitted for consideration. The Waxman-Sikorski bill, HB3400, and Senate Bills 768, 769, 2001, and 2594 are examples of the numerous acid-rain related bills that have been proposed. The emergence of several bills has been attributed to the breakup of the once powerful clean air coalitions into warring regional factions.

H.R.4567, which was dropped into the legislative hopper on April 10, 1986, attempted to address the regional differences. The bill began life with more than 100 House sponsors from both sides of the aisle. Unlike some of its predecessors, it proposed flexibility. It allowed each state to determine how emission standards would be met. The assumption that such flexibility could be made easily acceptable to the interests involved in mining and burning high-sulfur coal had an Alice-in-Wonderland quality.

Congress has received input on acid rain through a variety of channels. Concerned citizens, lobbyists for special-interest groups, and the expert witnesses at hearings have all taken advantage of the opportunity to make their viewpoints known. But it is not entirely a one-way flow. Hearings have also provided members of Congress the opportunity to make their viewpoints known. The Senate hearings on acid rain have included some rather pointed remarks directed at the administration by Senators whose patience with the administration appeared to be wearing thin.

Here is how The Honorable Robert T. Stafford of Vermont opened the February 2, 1984, Senate hearings:

"The Committee on Environment and Public Works will, please, come to order.

"I welcome all of our guests this morning and my colleagues. I want those who are standing in the back of the room to know we made strenuous efforts to get a larger hearing room but weren't able to do it. So we had to make do with the one that belongs to us.

"This is the first appearance of William Ruckelshaus before this committee since his confirmation hearings on May 4 and 5, 1983. On behalf of the committee, I welcome you back, Mr. Administrator.

"Today's hearings will deal with the problem of acid rain. Before we begin, I will share with you a few observations.

"When Bill Ruckelshaus was nominated and confirmed last year, I and some of the members of this committee, hoped that action would result in a change in both the attitude and the policy of this administration on the subject of acid rain.

"We were encouraged at Bill Ruckelshaus' swearing-in ceremony as administrator of the Environmental Protection Agency when the president placed high priority on the development of an acid-rain strategy for the nation.

"By now we know that our hope and encouragement were without genuine foundation. Last year, the administration's policy on acid rain was more research. Today, the administration's policy on acid rain is more research, but at twice the price.

"I am deeply disappointed.

"I am disappointed first because the administration has chosen to continue its unrelenting opposition to any program designed to control acid rain.

"I am disappointed also because there is every evidence that the administration has reaffirmed its policy of inaction for all of the wrong reasons.

"I am disappointed because the administration has chosen to ignore the findings and recommendations of its panel of science advisors as well as the findings of the National Academy of Sciences.

"I am disappointed because the administration appears to be inconsiderate of the pleas of the people and the government of Canada, one of our most loyal foreign friends.

"Finally, I am disappointed because the administration continues to be insensitive to the plight of millions of Americans who live in a region of this great nation that will continue to be victimized by acid rain unless action is taken — and taken soon — to control this pollution.

"It has been reported that narrow forms of economics and of politics played an important role in the decision of this administration to ignore the need for an acid rain control program. Perhaps Mr. Ruckelshaus will be able to offer us sound evidence that it was otherwise.

"I have heard and read enough of the assertions that it would cost $6000 per fish for an acid-rain control program, and that the addition involved in congressional or electoral votes is more important than the scientific facts regarding this form of air pollution.

"There may be some in this room who believe that those strained and contorted interpretations lead to good public policy. I am not among those who believe that.

"I have been involved in politics and in government service at the local, state, and federal levels for virtually my entire adult life. Each of my colleagues on this committee and in the Congress is well aware of the political forces that ebb and flow across our nation.

"But there is far more at stake in this debate than a few pickerel, or a few votes.

"We are talking about our natural and man-made environments and about the health and well-being of the American people.

"We are talking about fish, and trees, and crops and buildings. Most importantly, we are talking about human health.

"I know there are those that wince when I mention this; but it should never be far from our thoughts that this noxious mix of pollutants we are seeking to control does damage to the human body.

"Some researchers estimate that as many as 50,000 Americans die unnecessarily each year because of air pollution. I know those estimates are controversial. And, I also know that there are those who dispute the validity of the studies on which they are based.

"But there are also many who argue that the number of Americans at risk is even higher. There can be no doubt that air pollution causes health damage to millions of Americans and reduces the quality of life for all of us at some time or another.

"Each of us on this committee is well aware of the economic and political forces that are involved here. Indeed, we take those factors into consideration in virtually every thing we do as we go about our chosen career in this art form of politics and self-government.

"My state and my region of the country have much at stake in this debate. I do not deny my acute awareness of that condition. But, my position is not based on parochial concern for my electorate.

"I believe that acid rain exists because dozens of highly-regarded scientists have told this committee that acid rain is real.

"I believe that emissions from polluting smokestacks in the

Midwest contribute to the acid rain that falls in New England and other parts of the Northeast because study after study has demonstrated that is the fact to be true beyond a reasonable doubt.

"I believe that lakes and streams are, without any question, being damaged by acid rain because there is no longer any genuine scientific dispute over that circumstance.

"Scientist after scientist and study after study have all come to the same conclusion.

"There is some evidence that Administrator Ruckelshaus reached his own conclusion that acid rain is real; that acid rain causes damage, and that acid rain controls should be initiated now.

"All indications are that he reached that conclusion after an exhaustive study and review of the facts. That is exactly the way I expected he would make decisions when I voted to confirm his nomination last year. But he, of course, can speak for himself.

"Perhaps his testimony here this morning will enlighten us all on how decisions regarding acid rain controls were reached at EPA and at the White House.

"My high personal regard for Bill Ruckelshaus has not been diminished by recent events.

"But, as a friend and supporter of his, I would be less than honest if I did not express a very serious concern.

"I fear that the administration's most recent decision on acid-rain controls, and the manner in which that decision was reached, may severely damage the prospects that Mr. Ruckelshaus and the EPA will be able to regain the confidence of the American people that was lost just before he became administrator."

Trying to Assess the Implications of Different Approaches In addition to information provided by lobbyists and expert witnesses, Congress has been the recipient of some pretty voluminous documents entirely devoted to acid-rain issues.

On January 9, 1984, Representative Henry A. Waxman, (D.-CA) chairman, Subcommittee on Health and the Environment, of the House of Representatives Committee on Energy and Commerce, sent a letter to the director of the Congressional Research Service requesting that information on acid rain be compiled. His formal request had been preceded by some discussions between his staff and the staff of the Congressional Research Service, so he knew in advance that his request would probably receive favorable consideration and subsequent approval from the director.

The response to that request was remarkable, both in its promptness and in its comprehensiveness. On March 1, 1984, less than two months after the date of Representative Waxman's formal request, Gilbert Gude, director of the Congressional Research Service, forwarded to Mr. Waxman a nearly 1000-page report entitled "Acid Rain — A Survey of Data and Current Analyses." What makes the promptness of this response even more remarkable is that project coordinator, Robert E. Trumbule, specialist in Environmental Policy of the Congressional Research Service, suffered a fatal heart attack on February 4, 1984. The report is a memorial to him.

The first part of the report provided Congress a review of emission sources, atmospheric processes, impacts, mitigation strategies, and the costs and benefits of acid-rain control. The second part reproduced 58 excerpts or entire articles covering the same list of subjects.

The report was published in May, 1984, by the U.S. Government Printing Office.

Another important source of acid rain information available to Congress is the Office of Technology Assessment, an agency of Congress. Transported air pollutants have long been of interest to Congress. As it debated its way through deliberations pertaining to the Clean Air Act and its subsequent reauthorization, Congress had frequently turned to OTA for information. As a result of its long familiarity with pollution issues, OTA was able in June, 1984, to provide Congress with an excellent report entitled "Acid Rain and Transported Pollutants - Implications for Public Policy." The main body of this 323-page report included thoughtful discussions of the policy dilemma facing the country, the risks of damage and the risks of controlling the pollutants of concern, the regional distribution of those risks, the policy options available for congressional action, and a comprehensive review of the complex decisions involved in specifying the details of legislation aimed at reducing emissions.

In addition, the report contained four extensive appendices which offered Congress information on emissions and the costs of controlling them, the effects of transported pollutants, a discussion of the atmospheric processes pertinent to acid rain, and a review of existing domestic and international approaches to controlling emissions.

If your interest in acid rain motivates ownership of a good book on acid rain — beside the one you are reading, of course — I recommend you contact the Superintendent of Documents, U.S. Government Printing Office, Washington, D.C. 20402 and ask for publication OTA-O-204. I think you'll like what you get.

Not to be outdone by the Congressional Research Service and the Congressional Office of Technology Assessment, the General Accounting Office has also reported to the Congress on acid rain. A 185-page report, dated December 11, 1984, entitled "An Analysis of Issues Concerning 'Acid Rain'" was sent from the Comptroller General of the United States to the President of the Senate and the Speaker of the House of Representatives. He also sent copies to the appropriate House and Senate Committees; the secretaries of Commerce, Energy, and State; the administrators of the Environmental Protection Agency and National Oceanic and Atmospheric Administration; the chairman, Council of Environmental Quality; and other interested parties. If you were somehow left out of the foregoing list, you can get up to five copies of the report free of charge by writing the U.S. General Accounting Office, Document Handling and Information Services Facility, P.O. Box 6015, Gaithersburg, Md. 20760, or if you are in a rush, you can call them at (202) 275-6241.

If you have been thinking of the General Accounting Office as a collection of accountants, and wondering what business they have writing about acid rain, it's time to take another look at your federal government. The GAO's charter includes responsibility for checking to see if federal agencies are wasting the taxpayers money by duplicating each other's services. This sometimes involves the GAO in highly technical matters such as acid rain. Evidently it is considered acceptable for the GAO to engage in a bit of duplication in the process of keeping an eye on other potential duplicators.

Not all the governmental activity relevant to acid rain has gone on at the federal level. Many states surpass the federal government when it comes to doing something about pollution control. The state of New York has reduced its sulfur dioxide emissions by about a million tons annually. This represents about a 50 percent reduction. New York enacted an Acid Deposition Control Law in 1984 which is expected to be the forerunner of similar legislation in other states. Individual states have been involved in the acid rain controversies, both in cooperation with the federal government and independently.

When EPA Administrator Lee M. Thomas testified before the Senate Committee on Environment and Public Works in December, 1985, he directed attention to a program his agency carries out in cooperation with individual states. Here is what he had to say on that subject:

"The study of implementation issues is the third major element of our current acid rain program. Implementation issues are the procedural, technical, and administrative barriers that can hinder or prevent the successful implementation of any control program. Seldom have we taken the time to anticipate and study implementation problems before enabling legislation was in place.

"In the past, implementation issues have often been the most critical link between legislation and environmental results. Unfortunately they also tend to receive the least forethought. Recognizing this problem we have chosen to use this time to analyze and develop contingency plans for acid rain implementation. In pursuing implementation issues, we are not presupposing the need for additional controls. But if they are needed, we want to make sure that everyone, including the states, is ready to make them work.

"We have been actively involving state governments in this effort from the very beginning, because they would almost certainly play a large if not dominant role in any potential implementation effort. This cooperative federal/state program has received direct support from Congress in the form of a three million dollar add-on to EPA's 1985 budget for grants to state air programs. These state acid rain grants have now gone to thirty-four states.

"I hope this part of our current acid rain program gives you some indication of this administration's willingness to seriously consider the possibility of adopting new acid rain controls. Together with state governments, we are studying the very complicated programs that will most likely be associated with any major control program. This kind of anticipatory study carries with it real risks for everyone participating. Those states strongly opposed to controls are uncomfortable, because participation in the study implies a form of acceptance that control programs could reasonably be implemented at some point. Those states advocating controls are uncomfortable, because the study implies that new control programs could be very complex and difficult to make work. However, most participants believe that if a control program were to be adopted, it should be managed fairly and effectively. So studying implementation issues now is in everyone's best interest."

The governors of the region composed of the six New England States and New York have taken a cooperative look at acid rain. The "1986 Action Plan for Water Management in the New England/New York Region," put together by the New England Governors' Conference, Inc., includes an action plan for acid rain. During 1986 they hope to implement an acid rain plan that has already been approved by the New England governors and the eastern Canadian premiers. The goal of this plan is the reduction, within the northeastern U.S. — eastern Canada region, of SO2 emissions by 32 percent by 1995. The Action Plan also calls for continued cooperation and collaboration on all matters pertaining to acid rain, including pressing for reauthorization of the Clean Air Act, enactment of a National Acid Rain Control Program, seeking increased assistance to the states from EPA's acid rain research projects, a fair share for the region of NAPAP research, and strengthened enforcement of the Clean Air Act.

Addressing Regional Differences The New England governors hope to improve cooperation with governors from other part of the United States. This is a worthy goal. There are, however, many governors who are concerned about the possibility that their state will be asked to pay for another state's cleanup. Governors in the West have banded together to form the Western Governors Policy Office. Consider the testimony of Scott Matheson, governor, state of Utah, at the 1984 Senate hearings:

"Thank you. Basically I bring the point of view of a western governor who has had the responsibility for a number of years of addressing the problems associated with the reauthorization of the Clean Air Act, and representing an organization of the western states: the Western Governors Policy Office, made up basically of all of the western states.

"I bring that perspective to the committee today. We took a great interest in the Clean Air Act reauthorization, since 1980, actually, and became concerned about the acid rain component, adopting a fairly-detailed position on that last summer, in Bismarck, North Dakota.

"We have come to the conclusion, in our analysis of the acid rain issue, that we agree that we have a problem and we all want to clean it up. But the thing that keeps splitting the governors apart is the fact that we are not really talking about the environmental issue.

"The acid rain discussion has become a raging battle over economics. The question of timing, the question of scale and the structure of the program are really basic economic problems. What we within WESTPO have attempted to do is address the acid rain question from one of an environmental perspective; but in doing so we recognize that the fallout is still economic.

"There is no way you can get away from regional differences. But we have a five-point proposal which we would like to present to the committee.

"First of all, we think that whatever legislation is adopted by the Congress should encourage the most cost-effective method of reducing the acid rain problem. We do not feel it is appropriate to mandate specific technological controls or to prohibit the use of cleaner fuels to achieve the emission reductions.

"Some legislative proposal(s) designed to protect high-sulfur coal jobs and markets, really will distort economic choices and, we think, ultimately will increase the cost. That doesn't mean we are insensitive to the concern about unemployment or dislocations.

"I happen to come from a coal state myself where we have 22 coal mines. Eleven of them are closed. Seven of the remaining have reduced their production to the point where our coal business is really on its back.

"Our consumption and production dropped 35 percent last year. So we advocate legislation which would extend and provide protection for unemployment benefits, job retraining and relocation. Frankly, putting the price tag on that versus the price tag on forcing and mandating scrubbers, it seems to me, is an economic question that has to be addressed very carefully in terms of ultimate legislation.

"Second, we believe that the legislation, once adopted, should rely primarily upon the states to carry out the emission reductions. We would hope that the states could then, after the legislation is adopted, determine how best to meet the standard which the federal legislation decides is in the public interest, including early retirement of sources, energy conservation, coal washing, fuel switching, whatever method each state could most effectively and most economically adopt.

"Third, we think the legislation should not impose nationwide costs while providing only regional benefits. In other words, the governors in my part of the country object to cost-sharing schemes which would basically tax western utility customers to pay for acid rain controls in other regions of the country.

"We have already invested dramatically in clean air in the West; 31 percent of western coal-fired capacity now has scrubbers compared to 7 percent in the East. Utah's investment, for example, in coal technology is very significant. We are in the process of building two major power plants at the present time. One, the Intermountain Power Project, burns less than 1 percent sulfur coal and we are removing 90 percent of that sulfur through scrubbers. The emission rate will be 0.15 pound of sulfur per million Btu's.

"Incidentally, the cost for air-quality controls at that plant is $308 million. The second powerplant out in the Uinta Basin, the Bonanza powerplant, will remove 94 percent of the sulfur and will end with 0.065 pound of sulfur per million Btu's. We spent $155 million on air pollution control there.

"Combined with the two plants Utah Power and Light has built since the scrubber requirements were adopted, we have invested about $1 billion in air-quality controls in my state alone.

"Utahans have been willing to make that investment to clean up the air in our part of the country, but I feel they would object to an additional levy on their electric bills to clean up the air in other states.

"So we feel that nationwide cost-sharing schemes have the perverse effect of punishing those that have already invested in clean air and rewarding those that have lagged behind.

"Fourth, legislation should recognize regional differences in the size and types of emissions, climate, and topography. Congress, we feel, should not impose additional reductions on the West, based on studies in other regions. Western emissions are really low. The 13 western states produce only 4 percent of the nation's utility sulfur emissions. Those combined emissions are less than the individual emissions of 10 midwestern and southern states. But we are concerned about future problems in the West and would hope the committee would support immediate cooperative studies oflong-range transport of pollution in the West.

"Fifth, we think the legislation should minimize emissions from new sources by retaining the best-available-control-technology requirements. BACT has worked well in Utah and our determinations are ususally more stringent than federal new source performance standards.

"I also have two comments about the proposed legislation. The bill that was adopted by the committee last year, Mr. Chairman, Senate bill 768, is largely consistent with the views that WESTPO adopted and which I have summarized here this morning. I hope the committee will resist pressures to distort the acid rain control program, by changing the approach in S. 768.

"I am here to advise the committee that I certainly want to support S.768 and S. 769 with the higher emission removal with a couple of amendments.

"Specifically, in section 187, there is a little ambiguity about whether fuel switching is available. I am hopeful fuel switching would simply be added to section 187. The regional emissions cap in section 183 seems a bit too inflexible. I believe the other provisions, if we were to rely on best-available-control-technology, are preferable to the cap on emissions which have the effect of penalizing growth states and most western states are, of course, in that category.

"Third, although it looks like a sleeper, I am not sure it is intended to be a problem. I would be concerned about section 121, dealing with interstate transport, that establishes new standards for interstate actions and allows litigation from sister states and the citizens of other states under very, very ambiguous circumstances. I think that the risk of litigation is expanded by the language in that section and would ask that it be examined from the perspective of maintaining some control over the rush to the courthouse, which seems to be a poor way to solve the problems associated with acid rain and other interstate pollution problems.

"In addition, to those few amendments, I would suggest, as Governor Sununu (New Hampshire) has suggested to you, a phasing of the emission reductions program, believing that we should get started on some immediate reductions.

"I think that the research is fine and we should continue that. But it seems to me that we have reached the point in the studies where we need to get about our business and the western states are not here to do anything but to be helpful, and we would like to see the committee and the Congress proceed with legislation with all due deliberate speed."

Crossing National as well as State Borders The politics of acid rain are international in scope. National boundaries are no better barriers to air flow than are state boundaries. In the course of a typical year, whatever that is, vast amounts of air are exchanged across our national borders. On many days, air flows into the United States from Canada. Air also flows into Canada from the United States. The same sort of traffic takes place across our border with Mexico. Much of the time this international exchange of air is most welcome. In the heat of summer, cool air from Canada is a godsend. In the cool of winter, warm air from Mexico can mean money in the bank as the gas meter slows its costly whirring.

But when pollution accompanies the air, attitudes change markedly. Good neighbors begin to look askance. The friendly smiles take on a strained quality. The hands extended across the border tend to feature a pointing index finger. The good relations of yesteryear tend to slip away, and people begin to wonder what they ever saw in those inconsiderate slobs across the way. Consideration is soon given to seeking help from that barely-remembered attorney who once mentioned something about specializing in international law.

This is a reasonably close description of what has been going on between the United States and Canada. There have been some rather rancorous exchanges of both words and air across our northern border. Just where the villains live is a matter of point of view. If we restrict our attention to the number of tons of acid-forming pollution that are exchanged each year, it appears that an approximately even swap is occurring. But if we shift our focus from gross tonnages to percentages and where the acid is ending up, the picture changes drastically. The acid sent to Canada each year accounts for between 50 and 60 percent of the acidic deposition that Canada's vulnerable eastern lakes and forests must endure. The acid Canada sends to us is approximately 15 percent of the acidic deposition in the United States, and much of the Canadian export gets deposited in places that are less vulnerable to acid than are the Canadian lakes and forests.

We are still talking about acid rain with each other. That is part of the problem. The Canadians are ready to substitute talk for action, but the well-known position of the Reagan administration is that it is premature to take control actions.

In the *Time Magazine* issue that was appropriately dated April 1, 1985, there appeared extensive coverage of the "Shamrock Summit" held in Quebec City on St. Patrick's Day between Brian Mulroney, Prime Minister of Canada, and Ronald Reagan, President of the United States, who wore a green tie for the occasion. *Time* reported the discussions of acid rain as follows:

"Reagan repaid Mulroney's hospitality in another way by offering the prime minister a sop on acid-rain pollution, which has long been a sore spot in U.S.-Canadian relations. Canadians charge that at least half of the acid rain currently damaging their forests and destroying aquatic life in their lakes is caused by sulfur and nitrogen oxides released into the atmosphere by fossil-fuel-burning plants and smelters in the United States. The Reagan administration has maintained that the evidence against U.S. industry is incomplete.

"Knowing that Mulroney could not go back to Ottawa without at least some concession on acid rain, administration officials came up with a plan to appoint a joint U.S.-Canadian team to examine the issue. The president and the prime minister announced that former Transportation Secretary Drew Lewis and former Ontario Premier William Davis would be named special envoys to seek ways of combatting the problem. Said Mulroney: 'We have broken a three-year deadlock by agreeing to our common concern and shared responsibility to preserve our common environment.' Added Reagan: 'I couldn't be happier about getting this underway and off dead center.' The agreement, however, did not actually commit the Reagan administration to take any action on acid rain."

Later in the report *Time* returned to the subject of acid rain again:

"Though the prime minister said he was pleased with the agreement on acid rain, several papers took issue with his insistance that he had not come away empty-handed. 'The choreographed cheer in Quebec City cannot disguise the fact that the Mulroney government suffered an abject defeat on acid rain,' said Montreal's English-language Gazette. 'All the agreement means is that action on reducing acid rain of U.S. origin is at least a year further off. How many more lakes will be dead by then?'"

By the time ten months of that year of predicted inactivity had passed into history, signs of progress began to appear. The January 20, 1986, issue of *Business Week* carried an article headlined "ACID RAIN: DREW LEWIS TO THE RESCUE". Here is what *Business Week* had to say:

"Drew Lewis is the kind of guy who seems to pull off the impossible. As transportation secretary in the first Reagan administration, he persuaded a reluctant President Reagan to seek a five-cent hike in gasoline tax. Then, as chairman of Warner Amex Cable Communications Inc., Lewis negotiated increases in cable TV charges in cities that had promised to hold down rates.

"These coups won him numerous job offers, including a recent approach for the top job at Union Pacific Corp. But the 54-year-old Lewis' first love is politics. And, as President Reagan's special envoy to Canada on acid rain, he has adroitly fashioned a package that pleases both the Canadians and the White House. 'The most important thing is to identify a problem and set out to solve it,' says Lewis. But, he concedes, finding a way to deal with acid rain was like 'stepping on a balloon.'

"FIVE-YEAR PLAN. Just last fall, Lewis infuriated White House Chief of Staff Donald T. Regan when he told New England governors that 'saying that sulfates don't cause acid rain is like saying smoking doesn't cause cancer.' This time Lewis carefully kept Regan informed every step of the way, and he put together a plan in which the Reagan administration, for the first time, acknowledges that acid rain is a problem.

"Instead of recommending costly pollution controls to curb emissions from coal-burning utilities and industry, Lewis and his Canadian counterpart, William G. Davis, are endorsing an effort to develop technology to burn coal cleanly in the first place. The plan calls for spending $1 billion a year over five years, split 50-50 between government and industry, to develop 'clean coal technology.' Congressional approval for the effort is likely. Congress has already passed such a program but with lower funding: $400 million over three years, with $350 million to be appropriated later. And 28 utilities have agreed to kick in $2.1 billion.

"Backers of the plan argue that new technology can eliminate up to 90 per cent of the pollution that scientists believe is damaging lakes and forests in the northeastern U.S. and Canada. Whatever the method, any move to reduce U.S. emissions will improve relations with Canada."

The *Wall Street Journal* wasn't exactly thrilled by Drew Lewis's performance. Its January 14, 1986, issue contained an editorial headlined: "All Wet on Acid Rain." After recognizing Lewis' ability as an astute deal-cutter, summarizing what acid rain is and what its suspected effects are, and reporting the provisions of the agreement reached by Mr. Lewis and his Canadian counterpart, the editorialist stated:

"Mr. Lewis's tactic in signing on for the initial $5 billion commitment is obvious: try to do more good than harm. He rejected more extreme proposals, such as burning only low-sulfur coal, which would cause tremendous economic dislocation in Eastern coal states, or mandating the retrofit of costly scrubbers on all existing power plants. Some of these plans could eventually cost as much as $200 billion or more.

"In an interview, Mr. Lewis called his report a 'practical solution' that won't totally disrupt the economy. 'It's not another superfund.' By that Mr. Lewis means that the acid rain program won't run forever, spending money no matter how little good it is doing. Somehow, we find it hard to believe that Drew Lewis the politician actually believes this.

"There is good reason to believe that spending $5 billion over the next five years will have no appreciable impact on the environment. Then, environmentalists and the Canadian public will be screaming again for more money. With the U.S. government on record as accepting the the proposition that sulfur emissions are in fact a severe environmental hazard requiring extensive pollution controls, what arguments would remain for not creating an acid-rain fund with its own dedicated tax?

"Nor are we convinced that Messrs. Lewis and Davis have made an 'overwhelming' case for the conventional theory on acid rain. Much recent scientific work has raised serious questions about that hypothesis. This work suggests that natural factors — not merely coal-plant emissions — must be included in any serious explanation for the excess acidity in these lakes and streams. Of particular note are the acids that drain into watersheds from the surrounding soil. Nowhere in their report, however, do the two envoys address the natural-phenomena arguments.

"Last August, for example, the U.S. Environmental Protection Agency released a summary report on acid rain taken from a 1,300 page study conducted by more than 50 scientists. About the acidification of lakes and streams it states: 'Acidic deposition [from precipitation] must contribute to acidification somewhere in the ecosystem. The deposition inputs may be overwhelmed by the natural acidification processes, however, and not cause measurable change.' In other words, man-made acid rain pales by comparison with natural sources.

"The latest report of the National Acid Precipitation Assessment Program, a U.S. federal interagency group, says: 'It has become evident that to fully understand the potential effects of [acidification] on a lake or a stream, chemical processes occurring in the surrounding watershed must be considered. The hydrology, soils, geology, vegetation, and air quality of the watershed are important determinants of the chemical characteristics of surface waters . . . .'

"In summing up this research for a federal court, an EPA official last year said that 'the extent and nature of acid deposition damage to lakes and streams depends largely on chemical and physical interactions between the deposition and the local soil.' He added that 'there is no scientifically credible way to predict the future environmental consequences either of continued present levels of acid deposition, or of reduced levels.'

"Mr. Lewis admits to being a 'layman,' as are we, in an area fraught with scientific complexity and dispute. Trying to arbitrate this nettlesome diplomatic problem, he was willing to acquiesce on the scientific argument in return for cutting down the price tag on new regulation. Such a deal may sound reasonable. There is little likelihood, though, that Mr. Lewis's solution will stop the environmentalists' pressure for unacceptably high spending levels for their acid rain projects. More important, the Lewis-Davis study ignores the prospect that a thorough investigation may soon reveal that the conventional acid rain theory is unsupportable."

The *Wall Street Journal* editorialist seems to view environmentalists and the Canadian public as unreasonable people who would scream for more money regardless of the justification. There surely must be many people who qualify both as environmentalists and regular readers of investment-oriented publications. How do you suppose that editorial struck them? The writer is in the position of quarreling with Lewis, the official envoy of the Reagan administration, while using the Reagan's official position on the status of acid-rain knowledge to support his own case. The expression "hook, line and sinker" comes to mind, not to mention "lock, stock and barrel."

Some further insight into this situation and a somewhat different point of view was provided by an editorial that appeared in the January 15, 1986, issue of the *Rocky Mountain News*. Under a headline: REAGAN HAS ACID RAIN FACTS AND SHOULD DO THE POSSIBLE, the following discussion appeared:

"President Reagan's special representative on acid rain has asked him to take two actions: acknowledge that acid rain produced by coal-burning powerplants and other smokestack industries in the Midwest is a major environmental problem; and approve a $5 billion, five-year program to attack it.

"The issue is of some urgency since Reagan is scheduled to meet in March with the prime minister of Canada. Canada claims that acid rain coming from the United States is damaging its lakes, woodlands and buildings.

"In a move last year to mollify the Canadians, Reagan agreed to a joint study by representatives appointed by himself and Prime Minister Brian Mulroney. The representatives: former U.S. Transportation Secretary Drew Lewis and former Ontario Premier William Davis, submitted their report the other day.

"Up to now, the Reagan administration has taken the position that there is not enough scientific evidence to show that acid rain is creating the problems claimed by the Canadians, and that further study is needed. Lewis has concluded, however, that it is a severe problem and that, 'We can't keep studying this thing to death; we have got to do something about it.'

"Actually Lewis' proposal is relatively modest. He resisted Canadian pressure to set specific goals and timetables for sharply reducing sulfur emissions from Midwest plants.

"To meet the demands of the Canadians, who are supported by U.S. environmental groups, would require unacceptably high expenditures, perhaps as much as $200 billion, to install 'scrubbers' on smokestacks. Another unacceptable alternative would be to switch to low-sulfur coal, which could put tens of thousands of coal miners in Appalachia out of work.

"What Lewis recommended, and his Canadian counterpart reluctantly accepted, was a U.S. expenditure of $5 billion over five years to develop ways to burn coal more cleanly. Half the money would be put up by the federal government and half by coal-using industries.

"The difficulty is that the federal government doesn't have a loose $2.5 billion. The White House and Congress are struggling to reduce a $200 billion-a-year deficit, as mandated by the Gramm-Rudman budget-balancing law inacted in December of 1985.

"The government already is committed, under legislation approved last year, to spend $400 million over a three-year period on development of clean coal-burning technology. In addition, the administration is spending $85 million this year on acid-rain research.

"Reagan's best course may be to concede that acid rain is a problem and to tell Prime Minister Mulroney that we're doing as much about it as we can at this point."

I must confess that I did not share, one belief of the writers of the above two articles, that President Reagan had put acid rain in the "no problem" category. Approving budgets that included many millions of dollars for research on acid rain is not the expected act of a person who considers acid rain not to be a problem. There is a marked difference between believing that more knowledge is needed in order to obtain a solution to a problem and believing that no problem exists.

The situation across our border with Mexico involves more than one form of undesirable traffic, but there does not appear to be quite the same degree of mutual concern about acid rain that exists across the border with Canada. To be sure, Uncle Sam's scolding index finger is pointed southward toward Mexico, as Canada's is pointed at Uncle Sam, but Mexico appears to have other worries that it considers more important than acid rain. When the presidents of Mexico and the United States met briefly in Mexico in late December, 1985, the press reports of the meeting that I saw made no mention of acid-rain discussions.

As we noted earlier, a large Mexican smelter has been constructed just a little south of the border, and it is in a position to ship sulfur emissions northward in considerable quantity. After months of negotiation, a decision has been reached which requires Mexico to install air-pollution controls on this new smelter at Nacozari by 1988. In return, the United States made a commitment to see that controls will be installed at the Phelps Dodge Douglas facility in Arizona. Interim measures aimed at reducing the impact of emissions are called for in the agreement prior to the installation of permanent conrols. But if negotiations are going on about Mexico's investing in a five-year program of pollution abatement research and development, they have escaped my notice. There does appear to be active negotiation about transborder traffic in marijuana, farm labor, and bank loans to cover the interest on earlier bank loans, and it may be some time before acid rain is considered to be a problem worthy of that much attention at high levels of government.

15.

Policy Considerations and Possible Solutions

There have been many suggestions of possible solutions to the acid-rain problem. Some of these suggestions have been offered in such confident tones that the proponents seem to be implying that their favorite solution is the ideal solution. Whether the suggested solutions are even acceptable, let alone ideal, is, as we have seen, the subject of much controversy. Controversy about choosing a solution is very likely if the decision-making process has not included some important preliminary steps. I'll discuss these steps shortly, after I give you a bit of background for my assertion.

How to make good decisions in the face of uncertainty has been a matter of interest to me for a long time. Until recently, I have considered it a process requiring only dedication to logical thought. There are many textbooks on the subject that encourage this interpretation. A few weeks ago, I came across a book in our local library that changed my mind, and may have changed my life. I think it offers a basis for understanding what has gone wrong with the pursuit of answers to the question, "What should be done about acid rain?" It may also offer guidance on how to set things right.

The book is entitled *Make Up Your Mind.** Its author is John D. Arnold. Mr. Arnold heads John D. Arnold ExecuTrak SystemsTM, a firm that provides management-counseling services. His clients have included executives in giant corporations and in government. His approach to decision making is unique, in my opinion.

*John D. Arnold, Make Up Your Mind (New York: AMACOM, a division of American Management Association, 1978)

Feelings: The Missing Element It is Mr. Arnold's belief that the most effective decisions integrate thinking and feelings, and take into account the thinking and feelings of others. His book details a system for decision making that permits the decision maker to balance logic and emotions. The structure for accomplishing this balancing act he calls "The Seven Building Blocks to Better Decisions."

These are the seven steps he advocates:

1. Smoke out the issues
2. State your purpose
3. Set your criteria
4. Establish your priorities
5. Search for solutions
6. Test the alternatives
7. Troubleshoot your decision

The first step, smoking out the issues, is an appropriate choice of words in regard to the acid-rain debate. In a sense, smoke is the principal issue. What smoke contains when it leaves the smokestack, where it goes, how it is changed enroute to its destination, what effects it produces when it gets there, and what can be done to reduce the damage it does, are questions that have received a great deal of attention.

The second step, stating the purpose, has not been done well. There have been too many narrow either/or type choices considered. "Determine whether to install scrubbers or burn low-sulfur coal" or "determine whether to prevent acidification of mountain lakes or lime them after they are acidified" focus attention on narrow choices. If the purpose were stated as, "Determine how to ensure the best environment for future generations," broader consideration would be encouraged.

To set criteria, Mr. Arnold's third recommended step, three questions must be asked and answered in great detail. These questions are: 1) What do you want to achieve?, 2) What do you want to preserve? and 3) What do you want to avoid? Some of the criteria are absolute requirements, others are merely desirable. The preservation of life in all its forms would seem to be an absolute requirement, if there are to be future generations. Achieving a prosperous and competitive economy is highly desirable, as is preserving outdoor recreation that permits enjoyable fishing and camping. Avoiding reductions in standard of living or disruption of the lives of coal miners are examples of other desirable criteria that need to be considered.

After all absolute-requirement criteria are identified, the remaining pertinent criteria can be valued according to their desirability. John Arnold suggests giving the most desirable a score of 10, and then working down the scale of desirability to the criteria that don't carry a lot of weight and rate a value score of one.

Only after the criteria have been identified and evaluated does it make sense to search for alternative solutions. The consideration of solutions before this step is completed can lead to too few alternatives being considered and the stimulation of emotional quarrels between proponents of the various solutions proposed. This is true whether the decision-making purpose is related to a matter of international importance, like acid rain, or to where to spend a family vacation.

The next step involves considering how well each criterion is met by each alternative solution. Again a scale of 10 to one is applied, to rank the alternatives as to how well each meets each criterion, in turn. Multiplying the value score of each criterion by the rank score for each alternative leads eventually to an overall score for each alternative solution. The best solution will become apparent if an honest job of evaluating and ranking has been done.

The final step involves asking, "What could go wrong?" and then building in protection against adverse developments.

How Does This Process Compare To What's Happened Re Acid Rain? If this seems like an overly-involved, complicated approach to making a decision about acid rain, consider what has been happening in the absence of a truly systematic approach. Endless debates, hearings without number, and emotional charges and counter charges have expended the nation's energy and patience, with little to show for the effort.

Few human approaches to problem solving can be expected to be ideal. A number of decisions need to be made about acid rain. Logic will play a role in the making of these decisions, but logic alone will not suffice. Except for a decision to preserve the status quo, implementation of any decisions will require changes, some of them quite drastic. The hopes and dreams of many people are tied to a continuation of the status quo. Their lives are apt to be impacted negatively by what changes lie ahead, even if wise economic policy decisions are made. The acceptability of any proposed solution will depend on the extent that feelings of impacted people are taken into account.

Congress has gotten into the business of searching for solutions to the acid rain problem because the acid-forming pollutants cross state and national boundaries. Of the several options for change available to the Congress, the one that has been discussed with the greatest passion has been mandating the reduction of acid-forming emissions at their source. Whether or not this should be done has been the subject of often rancorous debate. There have been strong disagreements over the adequacy of scientific understanding, over who should be expected to pay the costs involved, over how to balance the needs of the present against those of the future, and which of several diverse value systems should prevail.

Other options available to Congress include: 1) letting the emissions go where they will and then supporting mitigation efforts in the acid-sensitive areas, or 2) postponing action while awaiting the results of research programs, with or without bringing pressure to bear to accelerate the programs, or 3) enacting changes in the Clean Air Act that would make it better suited to the task of reducing transported pollutants.

If Congress were to make the decision to go ahead with mandating greater reduction of emissions, there would be a number of further questions that would have to be answered before that policy decision could be fully implemented. An excellent discussion of these questions can be found in a report entitled "Acid Rain and Transported Pollutants: Implications for Public Policy" which was prepared by the Office of Technology Assessment of the U.S. Congress and published in June, 1984. These questions are the who, what, where, when, why type. Let's look at them as they apply to doing something about acid rain.

The OTA report discussed eight important decisions that must be made by asking the following eight questions:

"Which pollutants should be further controlled?

"How widespread should a control program be?

"What level of pollution control should be required?

"By what time should reductions be required?

"What approach to control should be adopted?

"How should emissions reductions be allocated?

"Who pays the costs of emissions reductions?

"What can be done to mitigate employment and economic effects of a control policy?"

Each of the above questions has more than one possible answer. Some have many. The number of possible options would be the product of the number of answers to each question multiplied together. This would be a very large number. Even if each question had only two answers, the product would be 28 which is 256. Finding the best solution is not going to be a painless process.

The OTA analysis examined three of the many options available. Here is how the three options were seen:

"Option A-1: Mandate small-scale emission reductions.

"A small-scale program would logically focus on further controlling sulfur dioxide emissions, the major man-made acidifying pollutant in the eastern United States, within a 20-to 30-state region producing and receiving the greatest acid deposition. Two million to three million tons of sulfur dioxide emissions could be eliminated from existing sources for under $1 billion annually; 5 million tons per year could be eliminated for about $1 billion to $1.5 billion annually.

"Control programs of this size would offset expected emissions increases of 2 million to 3 million tons per year by the year 2000, holding levels of acid deposition about constant or reducing them slightly below current levels. Such a program could be enacted alone, or as the first phase of larger programs discussed below, making the latter phase contingent on results of ongoing research.

"Option A-2: Mandate large-scale emissions reductions.

"A large-scale program, similar to those proposed during recent sessions of Congress, would reduce sulfur dioxide emissions by 8 million to 12 million tons per year. It could be confined to the eastern United States or applied nationwide and could also include reductions in nitrogen oxides emissions.

"We estimate that such a program would protect all but the most sensitive lakes and streams in many areas receiving high levels of acid deposition. Areas receiving the greatest levels of acidity, however, still might not be completely protected. Risks of damage to forests, crops, materials, and health would also be reduced and visibility would improve.

"The costs of such a program could range from $2 billion to $3 billion per year to $6 billion to $8 billion per year, depending on its size and design. Congress might choose to spread some portion of the costs across a larger group than just those sources required to reduce. A trust fund generated by a tax on electricity or pollutant emissions could be established for this purpose. Congress could also mandate or subsidize the use of control technology to minimize job dislocations associated with switching from high- to low-sulfur coal.

"Option A-3: Specify environmental quality goals or standards.

"Rather than mandating specific emissions reductions, Congress could set environmental protection goals (including economic considerations, if desired) and direct EPA to establish a plan to achieve them. Because the tools needed to establish are not yet available, this approach would not be feasible in the near future. It could, however, be preceded by small-scale, mandated reductions described earlier if Congress desired some emissions reductions within a decade. The compliance date for the remainder of the program might be set for early in the next century, which might allow enough time to develop the necessary modeling techniques, establish the standards, and achieve the required reductions."

Those look like three options having to do with legislating emissions reductions, but notice that within each designated option there are several choices mentioned, so the actual number of options is much larger than three. And, so far, the discussion has focused on the single optional approach of mandating emissions reductions. When other approaches, like liming lakes and streams, changing the research program to speed up guidance to Congress, or modifying the Clean Air Act, are considered, with each of those approaches offering the possibility of going down one or more of several alternate forks in the road, a bewildering array of alternatives presents itself. Does John Arnold's building block approach seem less ponderous?

To avoid going up in smoke, or down in flames, let's focus our attention, for the time being, on the approach that has to do with mandating emissions reductions. Let's pretend that Congress has legislated a policy that mandates emissions reductions, without specifying the precise means of accomplishing those reductions. What means of compliance are available for consideration?

Potential Responses to Action By Congress The possible ways of reducing emissions of oxides of sulfur and nitrogen fall into three categories, which can be used separately or in concert. The first approach is to use fuel that either starts out with low sulfur content or has been treated in some way to remove a portion of its sulfur content. The second approach involves adjusting the combustion process to reduce the production of pollutant gases. The third approach involves burning the fuel with whatever sulfur it contains and then capturing as much of the pollutant gases as feasible, before the gases are emitted to the atmosphere. The technology required to carry out these approaches is not uniformly ready for widespread application. Some approaches have been demonstrated on a laboratory scale, others in pilot plants, some are in commercial use in special circumstances, and some have been in use commercially for decades.

Let's look at the first approach in some detail. We have already considered the substitution of low-sulfur coal for high-sulfur coal and got some exposure to how the miners of high-sulfur coal feel about that approach. We have also touched lightly on the cleaning of coal by grinding and washing to remove the pyritic portion of the sulfur. Someday removal of organic sulfur from coal by chemical means may become a practical reality. It can already be done on a laboratory scale. One method involves treating crushed coal with calcium hydroxide and microwave energy. The sulfur combines with the calcium hydroxide to form water-soluble calcium sulfite which can then be flushed away from the coal by washing. Another approach enlists the aid of sodium hydroxide in combination with calcium hydroxide and heat. As before, the sulfur ends up as part of soluble sulfites.

Coal gasification and coal liquefaction are two ways of producing low-sulfur fuels. Coal gasification was once a common way of providing gas for street lights and cooking stoves in the days before continent-spanning pipelines brought low-cost methane gas from oil and gas well fields to many American towns and cities. Washed and pulverized coal, treated with steam and air or oxygen, produces a product mix of water, hydrogen sulfide gas, methane, carbon monoxide, carbon dioxide, and hydrogen. The hydrogen sulfide gas can be separated from the other gases prior to combustion. In the coal liquefaction approach, the methane, carbon monoxide, and added hydrogen are converted to liquid fuel by catalytic conversion. The undesirable sulfur and nitrogen in the coal end up in removable gases; hydrogen sulfide and ammonia respectively. Some of the cost of treating coal in this way can be offset by favorable transportation costs where pipelines can replace higher-cost rail transport.

Let's look next at another approach to reducing emissions. This one involves changing the conditions of combustion. Changing combustion conditions is a good way of doing something to reduce the formation of oxides of nitrogen. There are two sources of nitrogen that enter into the production of nitrogen oxides. One is the nitrogen contained in the fuel itself. The other source is the atmosphere, which is about four-fifths nitrogen. The temperature at which combustion takes place determines how much of the nitrogen from the air is oxidized to form nitrogen oxides. In uncontrolled burning, formation of as much as 40 percent of the total production nitrogen oxides results from air-supplied nitrogen.

The design and the manner of fueling determines how much nitrogen oxides a coal-fired boiler puts out. By conducting the combustion in stages, with the initial stage fuel-rich and oxygen-poor, fuel-supplied nitrogen — which would be oxidized if more oxygen were present — leaves the boiler as inert nitrogen gas. In subsequent stages, more oxygen from the air is made available to complete the combustion process. It has been reported that new boiler designs of this type can reduce the emissions of nitrogen oxides from bituminous coal by two-thirds.

Sulfur dioxide emissions can also be reduced by altering the combustion process. Injecting finely-divided limestone during combustion can result in the capture of the SO_2 by the limestone. The resulting calcium sulfate is the same inert solid you may know as gypsum or plaster of paris. Seventy percent reductions of SO_2 and NO_x have been achieved in boilers designed to use limestone injection.

A related approach that also uses limestone in the combustion process is called Fluidized Bed Combustion. This involves introducing finely-divided coal into a bed of limestone that is fluidized by jets of air beneath the bed. As before, calcium sulfate is formed which takes about 90 percent of the sulfur with it when it leaves the boiler, on a continuous basis.

The approach to emissions reduction that involves treatment of the flue gases after they have left the combustion chamber and are on the way to the top of the smokestack involves *scrubbing*. Limestone or lime is the key to the capture of sulfur dioxide in scrubbers as it was in the previous approaches. In some scrubbers a water slurry of limestone or lime is sprayed into the flue gases. The SO_2 combines with the lime or limestone to form either calcium sulfite or sulfate. The resulting sludge is not a thing of beauty and poses a disposal problem that is not trivial. When the lime or limestone is mixed with the flue gases without benefit of added water the process is referred to as "dry scrubbing." The calcium sulfate end product is recovered as a dry material which is easier to handle than the wet sludge. There are flue gas treatments for reducing NO_x emissions, but they have not been as widely used as have scrubbers intended to remove SO_2

Scrubbers do work. Much of the insistence that scrubbers provide presently available solutions to the emission reduction needs of the nation is based on the perception that, unlike some other methods of emission control, scrubbing has been proven in widespread commercial practice. Unfortunately, scrubbing is very expensive. According to a study of the costs of implementing the Waxman-Sikorski Bill, which mandated the use of scrubbers, the nation would spend $1 billion per year more using scrubbers than if an approach that maximized cost-effectiveness were employed. Usually the least-cost option involves switching to low-sulfur coals. In addition to their expense scrubbers use up a lot of land to store and dispose of waste products and don't work equally well on all types of coal.

The Viability of Other Energy Sources As you are undoubtedly aware, not everyone is sold on continuing to rely on burning sulfur and nitrogen containing fuels for our energy needs. The Solar Lobby stressed the advisability of subsidizing the development of solar power as an effective way of cutting down on acid-forming emissions. While solar power approaches, including wind power, are indeed free of polluting emissions, their state of development does not offer much hope of near-term relief from the adverse effects of acid rain.

Nuclear power advocates point out its freedom from acidic emissions. But the public perception of the potential radiation hazards of that technology is so negative, following the "incident" at Three Mile Island and in the Soviet Union, that there probably won't be a groundswell toward nuclear power in the near future.

Other energy systems have been given serious consideration. One of these would make use of clean-burning hydrogen, either as a gas or in the form of a metallic hydrides. The principle byproduct of hydrogen combustion is pure water. Hydrogen combustion could be expected to produce some "thermal" NO_x unless the combustion could be carried out in the absence of atmospheric nitrogen. It isn't clear how hydrogen could be produced in large amounts without reliance on either polluting fuels or underdeveloped technology.

Can Clearer Criteria Help the Search for Solutions_______ Like it or not, we are probably going to be burning sulfur and nitrogen containing fuels for a long time to come. We can each make a personal contribution to decreased acidic emissions by ensuring that our use of electric energy and our pollution-causing automobiles is as free of waste as we can make it. The scientific uncertainties that have caused postponement of action is apt to be with us for a long time, and may expand before they begin to contract. It is a characteristic of scientific research that it is undertaken with optimistic appraisals of the simplicity of the problem. Very often the first thing learned is that the problem is more complex than it appeared to be initially.

Consideration of criteria to be met could focus the scientific research effort and provide a basis for judging when sufficient knowledge has been gained to permit a reasonable decision to be made. There is a risk involved in making decisions in the absence of adequate knowledge, but there is also a possibly greater risk in thinking that complete knowledge is an absolute requirement.

Much is being learned as a result of the acid-rain research process that changes the specifications of an adequate solution. The early attitude that rain with a pH below 5.6 proved the involvement of man-made pollution has been generally replaced by recognition that processes that man does not affect in anyway can produce pH values that center around 5.0. Recognition of this fact should serve to change the scope of emission-control requirements. The reliance on pH is being called into question. Recent thinking by chemists has moved away from concentration on pH to a broader consideration of the total chemistry involved. The hydrogen ion is no longer the focus of total attention. The anions are being looked at too — as are the oxidants, ozone, hydrogen peroxide, and nitric acid. The oxidizing action of the latter two may have more to do with observed environmental effects than does their action as acids. Each such advance in scientific knowledge is probably well worth the cost of making it, but that does not mean that each such advance will or should affect the timing of the decision-making process.

Does this mean that nothing more should be done than is already underway? Not by a long shot. There are useful alternatives to the "all or nothing" distorted thinking that has characterized much of the confrontational debate to date. Effective approaches to problem solving are available to society once the game is transformed from an I-win-you-lose power struggle to a mutual effort to ensure that future generations are the real winners. That will happen when the reign of controversy is replaced by the reign of reason.

Appendix A: Glossary for Use in Arguing About Acid Rain

acid — any of a large class of substances whose aqueous solutions are capable of reacting with and dissolving certain metals to form salts, of reacting with bases or alkalies to form salts, or have a sour taste. Acids ionize in solution to give the positive ion of the solvent. If the solvent is water, that positive ion is the hydrogen ion. (I'll define ions a little later in the glossary.)

alkali — an hydroxide or carbonate of the highly reactive metals such as lithium, sodium and potassium, the aqueous solutions of which are bitter, slippery, caustic and basic in reactions with acids. Baking soda, which is sodium bicarbonate, is an example of a mild alkalai. Chemical drain openers, by no means mild, contains sodium hydroxide.

alkaline — having a pH greater than 7.

anthropogenic — you will encounter this impressive polysyllable in the speech and writing of people who consider it a synonym for "man-made." Originally, its meaning had to do with the scientific study of the origin of man, but it has become an adjective for describing man-made impacts on the environment. If you are one of those people who think that the wordy expression "at this point in time" is preferable to "now," you'll love "anthropogenic" as a substitute for "man-made," when discussing sulfur dioxide emissions from stacks.

atmosphere — a mixture of gases and particles that surrounds the earth to an indefinite height. At a height of 18,000 feet, about half the mass of the atmosphere lies above that level and half below. At a height of 50 miles, the atmosphere is barely dense enough to scatter sunlight. Some estimates of the thickness of the atmosphere place the outer boundary at 100 kilometers or 62 miles. The extreme upper limit of the atmosphere is about 18,600 miles above the Earth's surface. At that elevation molecules of gas can no longer be held in orbit by the Earth's gravitational attraction. This largely gaseous envelope, while vast, does not have unlimited storage capacity. Most of the pollutants released into the atmosphere by man are transported and stored in the lowest 2 kilometers or 1.2 miles. There is a limit to how much chemical waste can be "harmlessly" vented into the atmosphere. The gases and particles which make up the atmosphere have one thing in common — they are all chemicals. In the presence of sunlight they do what comes naturally to chemicals. They react with one another to form new chemicals. That is how we get the acid to make rain into acid rain.

base — any of a large class of compounds having a bitter taste, a slippery solution and the ability to react with acids to form salts.

black box — this term, borrowed from electronics, has made its way into discussions of acid rain. Originally, it referred to an electric device with known performance characteristics but unknown constituents or means of operation. Now, it is used to describe the unknown or poorly-understood process by which a known input is converted to an identifiable output.

buffer — a substance capable of maintaining the relative concentrations of hydrogen and hydroxl ions (see definition below) in a solution by neutralizing, within limits, added acids or bases. You will be hearing and reading frequent references to the ability of soil to buffer acid rain.

carbonic acid — what you get when you dissolve carbon dioxide in water, as in seltzer, club soda, or rain. Carbonic acid is a weak acid. It ionizes slightly to give hydrogen ions and either bicarbonate or carbonate ions. It can form salts called bicarbonates and salts called carbonates. Baking soda is the bicarbonate of sodium. Calcium carbonate is widespread in nature, occurring as chalk, limestone, and marble. It also occurs as Tums™. As you may have observed on television, calcium carbonate will react with strong acids to neutralize them. Unfortunately, the calcium carbonate dissolves in the process. This explains why marble statues exposed to acid rain sooner or later end up without noses.

clean air act — an act put on by western Chambers of Commerce when trying to attract industry away from eastern centers of pollution. When capitalized these words refer to legislation passed in 1970 and amended in 1977 to limit the pollution of the nation's air.

coal — a solid used as a fuel, formed from fossilized plants and consisting of amorphous carbon with some organic and inorganic compounds. When those organic and inorganic compounds contain sulfur, as they frequently do, one of the combustion products is sulfur dioxide. Oxides of carbon and nitrogen are also formed when coal is burned. If these three gaseous, acid-forming oxides associate intimately with raindrops, acid rain is very apt to result.

combustion — a chemical change, especially oxidation, accompanied by the production of heat and light. Discussion of the combustion of coal in the context of acid rain is apt to produce much more heat than light.

correlation — a simultaneous increase or decrease in value of two numerically-valued random variables. This is also called positive correlation. If an increase in one variable is accompanied by a decrease in the other, the correlation is considered to be negative. A large coefficient of correlation may be due to a causal relationship between two variables or it may be due to chance. A complex logical chain may link intermediate causes to intermediate effects. Understanding this chain is what much of the research on acid rain effects is all about.

dry deposition — the process by which atmospheric pollutants reach the ground without benefit of the cleansing action of rain. The effects of dry deposition tend to be lumped into the effects of acid rain. The amount of pollution that reaches the ground by dry deposition may very well exceed the amount brought down in acid rain. Nobody knows for sure.

emission — the stuff that comes out of smokestacks and exhaust pipes. It may be visible to the human eye or invisible. Efforts to render emissions invisible were cheered a few years ago as wonderful contributions to environmental quality. Unfortunately, the removal of the visible fly ash had an unforeseen price attached to it. Reduction of the amount of alkaline fly ash available to neutralize acid-forming sulfur dioxide in the vicinity of the stack resulted in increased likelihood of acid rain.

fume — an irritating or disagreeable exhalation. It is also what people tend to do when arguing about acid rain.

government — the administration of public policy within a political unit. Also the the ill-defined group that is being held responsible for solving the acid rain problem or problems.

hydrogen ion — an atom of hydrogen minus its only electron. You can call it a proton. Hydrogen ions are what makes acid acid.

hydroxl ion — the combination of one atom of hydrogen with one atom of oxygen results in the formation of a negatively-charged ion called "hydroxl." Hydroxyl ions are capable of neutralizing acids by combining with the hydrogen ions in the acid. The substance that results from the combination of a hydrogen ion with a hydroxyl ion is water.

hypothesis — a speculation regarding the cause of a phenomenon. It is, at present, an hypothesis that acid rain causes the disease that kills some trees. Experiments to test this hypothesis will eventually provide the basis for either accepting or rejecting the speculation. But careful experimentation can be a long, drawn-out process. Even when the experiments are completed, the results are apt to require careful interpretation. Experiments comparing groups of trees treated with acid rain with groups which have been kept free of acid rain are likely. The final results of the experimentation will be stated in terms of the odds that the observed differences between the treated and untreated groups are due to the operation of random chance. When you start dealing with random chance in science, you start taking risks. You may find yourself thinking that something is so when it really isn't. Or you may bet that some thing isn't so when it really is. People have differing tolerances for taking risks. Some scientists are so anxious to avoid being wrong that they consider a hypothesis rejectable until the odds are a hundred to one that random chance was not responsible for the experimental results. Odds of twenty to one offer other scientists acceptable risks. Farmers invest heavily in the hope that the odds in their favor are as good as 51 to 49. Decisions about what to do about acid rain will inevitably be influenced by the risk-taking proclivities of the decision makers. What the decision maker has to gain and lose will play an important role in determining his decision. When the cost of a wrong decision is not borne by the decision maker, careless decisions become quite likely. People who see no way in which they will be held responsible for the consequences of a wrong decision are apt to be in the forefront of those urging speedy decisions.

ice — the solid form of water substance. Ice taken from ancient glaciers has offered evidence that acid in precipitation is not a recent innovation.
ion — an atom, group of atoms, or a molecule that has acquired a net electric charge by either gaining or giving up one or more electrons. Positively charged ions are called "cations" (pronounced cat ions), because the are attracted to a negative electrode or cathode. "Anions" (pronounced an ions) are attracted to a positive electrode or anode.
isoline — see isopleth.
isopleth — a line of equal or constant value of a given quantity with respect to either space or time. Usually it is a line drawn through points on a chart or graph at which a given quantity has the same numerical value. If the quantity is pressure, the isopleth of equal pressure is called an isobar. If the quantity is temperature, the isopleth is called an isotherm. Lines of equal rainfall are isohyets. Lines of equal elevation can be called isohypses, if you want to be stuffy, but most people settle for calling them contours. The patterns of isopleths on a map or chart are analagous to the contours on topographic maps.
koniscope — an instrument which indicates the presence of dust particles in the atmosphere. When the dust particles are alkaline they can play a role in the reduction of the acidity of rain.
leaching — the process by which soluble constituents are removed from a substance by a percolating liquid. Leaching of aluminum and other metals from the soil is considered to be the mechanism by which acid rain accomplishes some of the undesirable effects being attributed to it.
logarithm — the exponent indicating the power to which a fixed number, called the base, must be raised to produce a given number. This base has nothing to do with the chemical base already defined. Just think of it as a convenient number. Ten is the base most commonly used. The logarithm of 100 is 2 because 10 must be raised to the second power to equal 100. Similarly, the logarithm of 1000 is 3. The reciprocal of 100 is 0.01. The logarithm of 0.01 is minus 2, and the logarithm of 0.001 is minus 3. If we are going to discuss the pH of acid rain we need to understand about logarithms.
mathematical modeling — a means of simulating the operation of a complex process by solving simultaneously the mathematical equations which describe the process. Sometimes solving the mathematical equations requires computations that tax the capabilities of even the most powerful complifying assumptions which cut down the cost of arriving at the solution. Unfortunately, these assumptions also introduce departures from reality into the solution. These departures may be trivial or catastrophic. On hearing the results of work performed by a mathematical modeler, you are apt to produce tension if you ask about the simplifying assumptions, and their effects on the outcome. A great deal of mathematical modeling has gone into the study of acid rain problems.
microequivalent — you will encounter this word in discussions of the acidity of rain. In chemistry, the number of parts by weight of any element combining with or replacing one atomic weight of hydrogen is called the "equivalent weight" of that element. One thousandth of this number is a

milliequivalent. One millionth of an equivalent is a microequivalent. The concentration of an acid solution can be expressed in terms of the number of microequivalents per liter. There is a direct relationship between the number of microequivalents per liter and pH. One microequivalent of acidity per liter equates to a pH of 6. Ten microequivalents per liter would produce a pH of 5. One hundred would put the pH at 4. The pH 5.6 represents 2.5 microequivalents per liter. That is the acidity once considered to be the starting point for acid rain, but many now consider 5.0 a better boundary.
mole — the amount of a chemical substance that has a weight in grams numerically equal to the molecular weight of the substance. Chemists sometimes describe the strength of an acid solution by specifying the number of moles per liter.
neutron activation analysis — a very precise method of chemical analysis that makes possible the detection of minute quantities of an element in a small sample. After a sample has been irradiated with neutrons produced in a nuclear reactor, the elements that have been made temporarily radioactive exhibit unique radiation decay spectra characteristic of each element. The concentration of the element is deduced by counting the emitted radiation over a standard time interval. Neutron activation analysis has been used to determine when arsenic was administered to a victim by analyzing short segments of a single hair from the head of the victim.
nitrate — a salt of nitric acid. Not to be confused with what AT&T charges for phone calls after 11 pm.
nitrogen — a colorless, odorless gas that makes up about four-fifths of the atmosphere. Under usual conditions it is so inert that it can be used to keep food from spoiling. Under unusual conditions, however, such as high pressures and temperatures, it combines with oxygen to form several oxides of nitrogen. These oxides combine with water to form acids which, sooner or later, turn into nitric acid. If the water is in the form of rain, acid rain results.
oxygen — a colorless, odorless gas that makes up about one-fifth of the atmosphere. It combines readily with most of the other elements to form oxides. Water is an oxide of hydrogen. Oxides of nitrogen and sulfur are becoming increasingly commonplace in the atmosphere. Oxygen makes possible respiration and most of the combustion you'll encounter in everyday life. If we don't start paying more attention to combustion, we may not encounter much respiration in everyday life.
ozone — triatomic oxygen. This faintly blue gaseous form of oxygen is a powerful oxidant with a split-personality. It wears a white hat when it occurs in the ozonosphere at heights between 7 and 35 miles above the Earth's surface. There it absorbs enough of the incoming ultraviolet radiation from the sun to keep us from being a solid mass of skin cancers. At levels near the Earth it is seen as one of the bad guys of pollution. Among other deleterious effects, it can damage tree foliage. Ozone may be responsible for some of the forest effects that are attributed to acid rain.
pH — the negative logarithm of the hydrogen ion concentration. pH can range from 0 to 14. A pH of 7 would apply to a solution that is neutral, that is, neither acidic nor basic. A pH of less than 7 is considered acidic, and a

pH over 7 is considered basic. If rain or snow were composed of pure water, they would have a pH of 7, but snow is almost never pure and neither is rain. Naturally-occurring carbon dioxide dissolves in rain and snow to form a weak solution of carbonic acid that has a pH of 5.6. A pH of 5.6 would be descriptive of rainfall if it didn't encountered much in the way of oxides of nitrogen or sulfur. Many workers in the field today don't consider using the term "acid rain" to describe precipitation until its pH drops below 5.0. You can forget the saying, "As pure as the driven snow."

pollutant — any gaseous, chemical, or organic waste that contaminates air, soil, or water. Many of the substances now spoken of as pollutants have occurred in the atmosphere, as the result of natural processes, since the beginning of time. Long before man began using the atmosphere as a sewer, ozone and the oxides of carbon, nitrogen, and sulfur were atmospheric constituents. Man's contribution to pollution has been essentially additive, but in amounts that are difficult to ignore.

radical — in chemistry this means an atom or group of atoms with at least one unpaired electron. The hydroxl ion, OH, is a radical. While you may encounter this usage in discussions of acid rain, it is more likely that it will be used to refer to an environmentalist who advocates restricting the income of coal executives.

region — a group of states having something in common. That something might be a desire to protect their forests from acid rain, or a desire not to put a lot of coal miners out of work. Acid rain is causing the kind of interregional tension that makes one wonder what the United States of America are united about.

scrubber — an apparatus for removing impurities from a gas. When the gas is air and the impurity is sulfur dioxide, installation of scrubbers receives a lot of attention. Scrubbers are widely advocated for reducing the acid rain problem, especially by people who don't have to raise the money to pay for them.

stack — a cylindrical structure, usually hundreds of feet tall, for transferring smoke and noxious fumes away from the source. The tallest ones are found in connection with smelters that roast sulfur-containing ore and powerhouses that burn sulfur-containing coal. A smelter in Canada has a stack 1250 feet tall. There is an interesting rationale for constructing very tall stacks. The higher the release point for noxious fumes, the greater the chance of dilution before the fumes return to Earth. The clever, but misleading, triplet "Dilution is the Solution to Pollution" has guided a great deal of powerhouse design. Dilution is not an open-ended process. When fumes are diluted by mixing with clean air, the clean air becomes less clean. If enough stacks contribute their output, the clean air soon becomes dirty air. Pollution is created by dilution. The real effects of making a stack taller are to move the point of impact further away, and to increase the time available for operation of adverse atmospheric chemical processes. Dumping your garbage into your next-door neighbor's yard may be hazardous to your health, especially if he is bigger than you, but carrying it into the next block before dumping it doesn't really solve the problem either. When dumping downstream is considered to be the socially acceptable procedure of waste disposal, it is only a matter of time before the dumpees rise up against the dumpers. This is what is happening today with acid rain.

sulfur — a yellow nonmetallic element that occurs widely in nature, in both the free state and in combination with other elements. It was once known as brimstone, and you probably know where one is apt to encounter brimstone. When sulfur combines with oxygen it forms a colorless and extremely irritating gas called sulfur dioxide. Sulfur dioxide combines with oxygen and water to form sulfuric acid. While sulfuric acid is getting a bad press for its role in forming acid rain, it has a socially acceptable side too. It is widely used in chemistry to help manufacture many of the products that make for better living.

testimony — an affirmation of fact or truth such as that given before a congressional committee. Hearings about acid rain, held before the Committee On Environment and Public Works of the United States Senate, produced a lot of testimony in February, 1984.

unanimity — complete agreement or accord. It is not likely that you will need this word in the near future to describe anything connected with acid rain, but it is nice to know it is there in case you need it.

vitriol — sulfuric acid.

waste disposal — a process for unloading your unwanted trash and undesirable chemicals onto someone else. Venting of combustion products into the air is widely practiced. This approach to chemical waste management has been around since cave men discovered fire.

Appendix B: Bibliography

Arnold, John D., *Make Up Your Mind! The Seven Building Blocks to Better Decisions,* New York: AMACOM, 1978.
Cogbill, Charles V., and Gene E. Likens, 1974, *Acid Precipitation in the Northeastern U.S,* Water Resources Research 10:1133-1137.
Cowling, Ellis B., Acid Precipitation in Historical Perspective, *Environmental Science and Technology,* Vol. 16, No. 2 (1982) 110A-123A.
Crocker, T.D., "What Economics Can Currently Say About The Benefits of Acid Deposition Control," in Adjusting to Regulatory, Pricing, and Marketing Realities, H.M. Trebing, ed., Institute of Public Utilities, Michigan State Univ., East Lansing, MI.
Dumanoski, Dianne, 1982. Acid Politics, *Technology Review*, October, 64-65.
Eskow, Dennis, "Acid gardening provides new hope," *Popular Mechanics,* November 1984,14.
Gannon, Robert, "How scientists are tracking acid rain," *Popular Science,* August 1984, 67-71.
Gibson, J. and C. Baker, National Atmospheric Deposition Program: Isopleth Maps, January-December, 1980, National Atmospheric Deposition Program and Canadian Network for Sampling Precipitation, March, 1982.
Gordon, Sid W., *How to Fish from Top to Bottom,* Harrisburg: Stackpole Company, 1955.
Gorham, Eville, "What to Do About Acid Rain," *Technology Review,* October 1982, 58-70.
Hidy, George M., "Source-Receptor Relationships For Acid Deposition: Pure and Simple?" *Journal of the Air Pollution Control Association* 34:518-531
Hoffman, Michael, "Acid Fog," *Engineering and Science,* September 1984, 5-11.
Howard, Ross and Michael Perley, *Acid Rain - The Devastating Impact on North America,* New York: McGraw-Hill, 1982.
Lewis, William M. Jr., and Michael C. Grant, "Acid Precipitation in the Western United States." *Science* 207 (January 11, 1980) 176-177.
Likens, Gene, Richard F. Wright, James N. Galloway, and Thomas J. Butler,

"Acid Rain," *Scientific American,* October 1979, 43-51.
Mandelbaum, Paulette, (ed.), *Acid Rain: Economic Assessment*, New York: Plenum Press, 1985.
Maugh, Thomas H. II., "Acid Rain's Effects on People Assessed," *Science* 226 (December 21, 1984) 1408-1410.
National Academy of Sciences, *Acid Deposition, Atmospheric Processes in Eastern North America,* Washington, D.C., National Academy Press. 1983
National Acid Precipitation Assessment Program, *Annual Report 1983 to the President and Congress,* Washington, D.C., 1984.
National Acid Precipitation Assessment Program, *Annual Report 1984 to the President and Congress,* Washington, D.C., 1985
Natural Resources Council, Board on Agriculture and Renewable Resources, *Committee in the Atmosphere and the Biosphere. Atmosphere-Biosphere Interactions: Toward a Better Understanding of the Ecological Consequences of Fossil Fuel Combustion,* Washington, D.C.:National Academy Press, 1983.
Ostmann, Robert Jr., *Acid Rain: A Plague Upon the Waters,* Minneapolis: Dillon Press Inc., 1982
Record, Frank A., David V. Bubenick, and Robert J. Kindya, *Acid Rain Information Book,* Park Ridge, New Jersey: Noyes Data Corporation, 1982.
Reiquam, H., "European Interest in Acidic Precipitation: A Review." In Precipitation Scavenging, edited by Rudolf J. Engelmann and W. George N. Slinn, U.S. Atomic Energy Commission. December 1970. 289-292.
Samson, Perry J., (ed.), *The Meteorology of Acid Deposition,* The Northwest Atlantic International Section, Air Pollution Central Association, October, 1983.
Siebel, E.P., and R.G. Semonin, 1981, "Acid Rain: What Do We Know?" Illinois State Water Survey, Illinois Institute of Natural Resources, Champaign, Illinois, 11pp.
Stankunas, A.R., D.F. Unites, and E.F. McCarthy., "Air Pollution Damage to Man-Made Materials: Physical and Economic Estimates," Electric Power Research Institute, Palo Alto, CA., 1983.
U.S. Congress, House. Committee on Energy and Commerce, Subcommittee on Health and the Environment, *Acid Rain, A Survey of Data and Current Analyses,* Report prepared by Congressional Research Service, 98th Cong.,2d sess.,1984. Committee Print 98-X.
U.S. Congress, Office of Technology Assessment, *Acid Rain and Transported Air Pollutants: Implications for Public Policy,* 98th Cong., 1984 OTA-O-204,
U.S.Congress, Senate. Committee on Environment and Public Works, Hearings on Acid Rain, 1984. 98th Cong.2d sess. S. Hrg. 98-714.
U.S. Environmental Protection Agency, *Effects of Sulfuric Acid on Two Model Hardwood Forests,* EPA, 600/3-80-014. January, 1980.
U.S. Environmental Protection Agency, *The Acidic Deposition Phenomenon and Its Effects, Critical Assessment Review Papers,* EPA-600/8-83-016 AF. 1983.
U.S. Environmental Protection Agency, *The Acidic Deposition Phenomenon*

and Its Effects: Critical Assessment Document, Prepared by David A. Bennett, Robert L. Goble, and Rick A. Linthurst, EPA/600/8-85/001. 1985

U.S. Geological Survey, *Acid Precipitation: An Annotated Bibliography*, Circular 923. 1984.

Vimont, John C., *Snowpack Acidity in the Colorado Rocky Mountains*, Atmospheric Science Paper No. 347, Department of Atmospheric Science, Colorado State University, Fort Collins, Colorado, 1982.

Yocum, J.E. and A.R. Stankunas, "A Review of Air Pollution Damage to Materials," EPA Environmental Criteria and Assessment Office, Research Triangle Park, N.C., 1980.

Appendix C: Academic Centers of Acid Rain Research

Auburn University, Auburn, Alabama 36830
Colgate University, Hamilton, New York 13346
Colorado State University, Fort Collins, Colorado 80521
New York University, New York, New York 10003
North Carolina State University, Raleigh, North Carolina 27607
Pennsylvania State University, University Park, Pennsylvania 16802
Purdue University, Lafayette, Indiana 47907
Syracuse University, Syracuse, New York 13210
Washington State University, Pullman, Washington 99163
Washington University, St. Louis, Missouri 63130
University of California-Berkeley, Berkeley, California 94720
University of Colorado, Boulder, Colorado 80302
University of Maine, Orono, Maine 04473
University of Nevada, Reno, Nevada 89507
University of New Hampshire, Durham, New Hampshire 03824
University of Rochester, Rochester, New York 14627
University of Washington, Seattle, Washington 98105
University of Wisconsin, Madison, Wisconsin 53706
Virginia Polytechnic Institute, Blacksburg, Virginia 24061
Yale University, New Haven, Connecticut 06520

Appendix D: Statistical Tables

Table 1.
1980 U.S. SO_2 Emissions Estimates (1,000 metric tonnes/year)

State	Electric Utilities	Non-Utility Combus-tion	Non-Ferrous Smel-ters	Trans-porta-tion	Other Sources	State Total
Alabama	492.7	77.7	1.5	12.1	103.5	688.3
Alaska	10.7	2.9	0.0	2.3	1.1	16.9
Arizona	79.4	7.9	699.7	8.5	20.6	816.1
Arkansas	24.1	28.7	12.9	9.2	17.2	92.1
California	70.7	50.6	0.0	91.0	192.7	405.0
Colorado	70.3	21.9	0.0	8.9	18.2	119.3
Connecticut	29.1	31.3	0.0	4.6	0.2	65.2
Delaware	47.6	23.9	0.0	1.9	25.8	99.2
D.C.	4.2	7.7	0.0	0.9	0.6	13.4
Florida	658.5	87.9	0.0	38.6	208.3	993.3
Georgia	668.3	39.6	0.0	19.2	34.6	761.7
Hawaii	37.7	7.6	0.0	2.4	5.3	53.0
Idaho	0.0	10.3	17.2	3.7	11.3	42.5
Illinois	1021.1	171.0	0.0	29.0	113.0	1334.1
Indiana	1396.7	263.1	4.5	19.8	137.4	1821.5
Iowa	209.8	52.1	0.0	10.8	25.5	298.2
Kansas	136.2	10.2	0.0	13.6	42.1	202.1
Kentucky	914.0	60.3	6.3	13.0	23.1	1016.7
Louisiana	22.5	69.4	5.4	27.8	150.9	276.0
Maine	14.8	59.0	0.0	3.2	9.0	86.0
Maryland	202.5	50.9	5.1	13.2	34.9	306.6
Massachusetts	249.9	52.5	0.0	9.3	0.8	312.5
Michigan	512.9	139.6	65.0	18.1	87.1	822.7

Table 1 (continued)

State	Electric Utilities	Non-Utility Combus-tion	Non-Ferrous Smel-ters	Trans-porta-tion	Other Sources	State Total
Minnesota	160.9	39.7	0.0	13.1	22.5	236.2
Mississippi	117.2	43.6	0.0	16.2	81.5	258.5
Missouri	1034.7	49.9	26.8	17.2	51.8	1180.4
Montana	21.2	22.9	78.0	5.0	21.5	148.6
Nebraska	44.9	3.9	0.0	9.2	10.0	68.0
Nevada	30.5	1.6	181.4	2.7	4.0	220.2
New Hampshire	73.0	9.1	0.0	1.4	0.8	84.3
New Jersey	100.0	67.6	0.0	22.9	62.8	253.3
New Mexico	76.8	2.0	57.4	8.5	99.0	243.7
New York	435.7	303.5	5.7	34.5	77.3	856.7
North Carolina	395.0	105.1	1.3	16.4	28.6	546.4
North Dakota	77.8	11.5	0.0	4.1	3.4	96.8
Ohio	1970.1	281.7	6.8	31.3	111.2	2401.1
Oklahoma	34.2	13.5	0.0	11.5	50.2	109.4
Oregon	3.0	22.8	3.6	13.5	11.6	54.5
Pennsylvania	1330.1	230.2	2.7	33.9	237.6	1834.5
Rhode Island	4.7	7.3	0.0	1.5	0.3	13.8
South Carolina	193.3	76.5	0.0	8.9	17.1	295.8
South Dakota	26.0	2.8	0.0	3.6	3.2	35.6
Tennessee	847.1	74.9	5.1	15.7	33.8	976.6
Texas	274.7	96.6	78.6	87.5	620.8	1158.2
Utah	20.1	14.8	4.0	5.4	21.1	65.4
Vermont	0.5	4.4	0.0	1.3	0.0	6.2
Virginia	148.5	128.7	0.0	23.2	27.1	327.5
Washington	63.0	37.5	97.0	19.0	30.2	246.7
West Virginia	856.6	76.6	8.2	6.4	39.0	986.8
Wisconsin	440.6	96.9	0.0	13.2	27.5	578.2
Wyoming	106.7	26.8	0.0	6.2	27.0	166.7
Total	15760.5	3178.8	1374.4	795.8	2982.7	24092.2

Source: United States-Canada Work Group IIIB. Emissions, Costs and Engineering Assessment Final report, 1983.

Table 2.
1980 U.S. NO_x Emissions Estimates
(1,000 metric tonnes/year)

State	Electric Utilities	Non-Utility Combus-tion	Non-Ferrous Smel-ters	Trans-porta-tion	Other Sources	State Total
Alabama	155.8	75.6	0.0	148.7	28.5	408.6
Alaska	0.0	24.7	0.0	24.1	3.4	52.2
Arizona	82.2	35.9	0.0	107.9	7.8	233.8
Arkansas	24.0	40.5	0.0	119.0	13.7	197.2
California	104.7	186.3	0.0	743.7	76.7	1111.4
Colorado	77.9	60.7	0.0	104.0	8.2	250.8
Connecticut	18.5	20.8	0.0	81.5	0.8	121.6
Delaware	17.6	7.8	0.0	19.9	1.8	47.1
D.C.	1.4	5.1	0.0	12.7	0.7	19.9
Florida	194.0	47.2	0.0	314.9	31.9	588.0
Georgia	171.4	35.1	0.0	214.0	27.8	448.3
Hawaii	12.1	2.5	0.0	23.6	2.8	41.0
Idaho	0.0	13.2	0.0	47.0	13.6	73.8
Illinois	377.1	117.1	0.0	385.7	32.1	912.0
Indiana	327.8	89.7	0.0	254.3	29.5	701.3
Iowa	89.3	42.9	0.0	150.1	8.6	290.9
Kansas	77.7	137.4	0.0	159.8	21.7	396.6
Kentucky	246.8	60.6	0.0	166.0	8.6	482.0
Louisiana	88.8	500.7	0.0	172.4	80.3	842.2
Maine	1.0	12.2	0.0	37.7	3.0	53.9
Maryland	55.2	33.5	0.0	129.7	6.7	225.1
Massachusetts	51.8	33.3	0.0	143.1	1.8	230.0
Michigan	215.4	109.4	0.0	274.1	26.7	625.9
Minnesota	101.2	48.1	0.0	181.8	7.7	338.8
Mississippi	45.6	72.0	0.0	113.2	28.0	258.8
Missouri	215.0	44.9	0.0	230.4	24.6	514.9
Montana	20.8	20.0	0.0	56.8	16.4	114.0
Nebraska	36.0	20.0	0.0	112.8	7.7	176.5
Nevada	38.9	3.4	0.0	32.0	1.2	75.5
New Hampshire	22.3	3.4	0.0	24.2	0.7	50.6
New Jersey	59.7	61.9	0.0	223.6	23.1	368.3
New Mexico	72.4	99.2	0.0	87.6	3.6	262.8
New York	117.7	126.5	0.0	348.9	23.4	616.5
North Carolina	194.5	45.0	0.0	229.8	17.2	486.5
North Dakota	48.1	9.6	0.0	54.1	1.3	113.1
Ohio	468.0	147.0	0.0	397.4	26.0	1038.4
Oklahoma	94.9	196.4	0.0	163.8	21.9	477.0
Oregon	2.5	23.0	0.0	130.6	18.1	174.2

Table 2 (continued)

State	Electric Utilities	Non-Utility Combus-tion	Non-Ferrous Smel-ters	Trans-porta-tion	Other Sources	State Total
Pennsylvania	354.2	149.0	0.0	393.9	44.1	941.2
Rhode Island	2.6	4.7	0.0	25.5	0.3	33.1
South Carolina	76.5	35.3	0.0	114.8	9.5	236.1
South Dakota	19.0	3.2	0.0	52.5	6.1	80.8
Tennessee	181.8	62.2	0.0	202.8	22.4	469.2
Texas	473.2	1010.0	0.0	676.2	148.3	2307.7
Utah	35.2	29.9	0.0	59.1	6.6	130.8
Vermont	0.5	1.9	0.0	19.6	0.4	22.4
Virginia	55.8	59.0	0.0	226.8	25.5	367.1
Washington	22.5	28.6	0.0	175.2	35.8	262.1
West Virginia	273.8	49.6	0.0	78.6	8.3	410.3
Wisconsin	131.3	51.8	0.0	188.7	9.6	381.4
Wyoming	93.0	70.5	0.0	62.7	5.2	231.4
TOTAL	5647.5	4168.6	0.0	8500.5	976.5	19293.1

Source: United States-Canada Work Group IIIB. Emissions, Costs, and Engineering Assessment. Final report, 1983.

Table 3.
Global Emission of Sulfur (Teragrams/year)

Item	Eriksson, 1960	Junge, 1963	Robinson and Robbins, 1968	Kellogg et al. 1972	Friend, 1973
Industry, space heating (mainly SO_2 and H_2S)	40 (10)a	40 (14)	70 (30)	50 (27)	65 (23)
Biological Decay, land (H_2S)	110 (29)	70 (24)	68 (29)	90b(49)	58 (20)
Biological Decay, ocean (H_2S)	170 (44)	160 (54)	30 (12)	-b	48 (17)
Sea spray (sulfates)	40 (10)	-c	44 (18)	43 (23)	44 (15)
Volcanoes (SO_2, H_2S, sulfates)	-d	-	-	1.5(1)	2 (1)
Fertilizer (sulfates)	10 (3)	25 (8)	11 (5)	-	26 (9)
Rock weathering (sulfates)	15 (4)	-	14 (6)	-	42 (15)
Total (natural sources)	345	225	167	134.5	220
Total (natural and man-made)	385(100)	295(100)	237(100)	184.5(100)	285(100)

[a]Numbers in parenthesis indicate percent of total emissions (natural and man-made). [b]Kellogg et al. estimate a total of 90 Tg/yr of sulfur from decay of land and ocean biota. [c]Junge's model was for excess sulfur only, so the sea-salt component was not included. [d]Dashes indicate negligible contribution.

Source for Table 3.Jersey: Noyes Data Corporation, 1982. One teragram (Tg)= 1012grams (g)=109kilograms (kg)=106 metric tons=1.1x106 short tons.

Appendix E: Sources of Information About Acid Rain

Acid Rain Information Clearing House — 33 South Washington Street, Rochester, New York 14608.
Air Pollution Control Association — P.O. Box 2861, Pittsburg, Pennsylvania 15230
Alliance for Clean Energy — 1901 N. Ft. Myer Drive. Twelfth Floor, Rosslyn, Virginia 22209, (703) 841-1781.
Center for Environmental Information, Inc. — 33 South Washington Street, Rochester, New York 14608.
Council on Environmental Quality — 722 Jackson Place N.W., Washington, D.C. 20006, (202) 395-5700.
Electric Power Research Institute — 3412 Hillview Avenue, Palo Alto California 94304
Environmental Defense Fund — 444 Park Avenue South, New York, New York 10016 and 1405 Arapahoe, Boulder, Colorado 80302
Environmental Law Institute — 1346 Connecticut Ave. N.W., Washington, D.C. 20036, (202) 452-9600.
Executive Director-National Acid Precipitation Assessment Program — c/o EOP Publications (Room 2200), 726 Jackson Place N.W., Washington, D.C. 20503
Natural Resource Ecology Laboratory, Colorado State University — Fort Collins, Colorado 80523, (303) 491-5571.
National Clean Air Coalition — 530 7th St. S.E., Washington, D.C. 20003, (202) 543-8200.
Superintendent of Documents United States Government Printing Office — Washington, D.C. 20402
United States Congress, Office of Technology Assessment — Washington, D.C. 20510.
United States Environmental Protection Agency — Office of Acid Deposition, Environmental Monitiring, and Quality Assurance, Washington, D.C. 20460
United States General Accounting Office — Document Handling and Information Services Facility, P.O. Box 6015, Gaithersburg, Maryland 20760, (202) 275-6241.

Appendix F: A Fable About Acid Rain

As Told by a Small Boy
To Archie Kahan

Once upon a time there was a land where acids falling from the sky began to cause pain amongst the populace. Some of the pain localized in their minds. Soon after it was generally recognized that taking two aspirin wasn't going to make the acid-deposition headaches go away, serious thought was given to the question of how to go about cutting the problem down to size. The idea of reducing the amount of pollution being released to the atmosphere had a lot of appeal in some circles, but those circles were not heavily populated by people who were going to bear the immediate burden of paying for the required change. It was clear that the adverse effects which were being attributed to acid rain were not uniformly distributed over space or through time. Some areas seemed unaffected. Other areas were very heavily impacted.

"What makes you think that my modest releases are causing a problem?" "Why should I pay to clean up someone else's mess?" These were questions that were frequently asked by people to whom the suggestion had been made that they should participate in underwriting costly emission-reduction efforts. In the absence of persuasive answers, the disputants decided to consult the wise men of the land for advice.

There were a number of wise men whose interests had long been focused on the scientific problems related to acid deposition, but they had been too busy studying the science involved to give much attention to the political processes by which decisions were made in the land. There were, however, other wise men whose credentials were both scientific and political. Obviously, these more astute individuals deserved both to be consulted and listened to.

Because these wise men were truly wise, they soon recognized that they were caught in the middle, between two powerful and angry groups. Some of the less-experienced wise men were in favor of giving a prompt answer to the call for help, and living with the consequences. Others, older and less prone to risk-taking, considered that hasty resolution of the dispute might prove to be extremely hazardous to their hard-won reputations as men of wisdom. "This problem is serious enough to warrant careful study before we attempt to reach a decision," was a position that had won them additional pondering time in the past. "We need better data and more of it before we can understand the problem well enough to offer valid advice," was another position that had stood the test of time. After much deliberation, the conservative position was adopted by the leadership of the land, and a large sum of money was allocated to the proposed data collection and study program, which was expected to last for a period of several years.

As sometimes happens, the announcement of the allocation of the large sum of money attracted the attention of wise men in the land who weren't particularly happy doing what they had been doing before they heard the announcement. They rapidly became experts on acid deposition and eagerly devoted their energies to the prompt expenditure of the allocated funds.

There was a measure of agreement among the wise men that knowing more about when and where acid was being deposited from the atmosphere onto the land certainly couldn't hurt anything, and might even prove useful. The best way to gain this additional knowledge was well-known. It involved establishing observing networks which could provide periodic readouts of whatever data the instruments recorded. Even though there were no instruments available which were capable of accurately measuring total acid deposition, it was possible to collect samples of precipitation which could be subsequently analyzed as to their acidity. Collection of these limited data was generally conceded to be better than not collecting any data at all. Meanwhile, thought could be given to what relevance the amount of acid deposited by precipitation had to the total amount of acid being deposited. Opinions varied widely among the wise men as to the importance of that portion of acid that got to the ground without becoming involved with precipitation. Some said it constituted 20 percent of the total, while others held out for 80 percent of the total. Since averaging extreme values had proven useful for masking past uncertainties, the decision was made to settle on 50 percent and to get on with the program of data collection.

In some informed circles, collection of weather data had long been considered to be a marginally useful activity at best. It was viewed as an activity to be engaged in primarily by lower-strata wise men. Data collection was tolerated by upper-strata wise men, provided that it wasn't allowed to become so costly that it interfered with their modeling activities. The upper-strata wise men were so wise they didn't need observed data to carry out their deliberations. Their thoughts were widely perceived to be well-nigh infallible.

As might be expected, controversy developed over the issue of how to divide the funding pie between the data-collecting function and other, loftier functions. This conflict was resolved by an administrator who sat in a position of power. His management skills, demonstrated in his dealing with budgetary matters, had more to do with his holding his powerful position than did his understanding of science, but he was very good at making his mind up rapidly and rendering prompt decisions. Once rendered, his decisions had a irreversible nature.

Throughout the land, collection of data had traditionally been undertaken with the promise that analysis of the data would follow hard on the heels of its collection, quickly providing interested wise men much-desired additional knowledge. At times this sequence of events actually occurred, and great joy would break out among the wise men. But this did not happen often. Collecting data was usually a lot more fun than was data analysis. Since there was no widely-accepted way of determining how much data was enough data, the data collection process tended to go on and on.

Sometimes, after a considerable period of instrumented network operation, it would come to be recognized that the instruments were producing impressive numbers, but not fully reliable data. A period of feverish consideration of what to do about the instrumented network would follow. Discarding the accumulated numbers was an option, but choosing it involved admission that something less than perfect wisdom had entered in to the design of the original data-collection system. Another option, which offered a generous measure of face-saving, was available for use. If the data-collection effort had any relevance at all to the welfare of the nation, the large body of intermingled information and misinformation could be bound, labeled "Data Report Number One," and shipped off to the sponsor of the research effort, along with a proposal requesting funding for an improved observing network. The sponsor was apt to have very little interest in admitting to the world at large that an inadequately considered program of observation had been supported. Archiving the report, in a manner designed to render retrieval extremely unlikely, could usually be successfully accomplished. Funding of the new proposal tended to bestow a measure of apparent worthiness on the initial effort. All parties concerned found this practice comforting.

But none of this maneuvering was necessary in the case of the acid deposition program. So great was the national interest in learning what should be done to manage the problem that the data were promptly analyzed and plotted onto outline maps of the nation. Lines were drawn on the maps connecting the places that had experienced the same level of acidity in their precipitation. These maps were widely reproduced. They showed up in document after document having to do with acid deposition. Some of these were printed on very high quality paper. There was great joy among the wise men of the land.

One day a small boy chanced to see the acid precipitation maps. What he saw puzzled him. He wondered what the rationale was for connecting places on a map with smoothly drawn lines labeled with values of pH. Did it matter not at all that some of the points received more than twice as much rain in an average year than did other points on the same line? He wondered how the information, so impressively presented, would be used to arrive at the solution to the acid deposition problem. He was genetically inclined to be a disrupter of the peace anyhow, having descended from the boy who first noticed that the Emperor's new clothes were no clothes at all. So he went about the land asking the wise men he encountered to explain to him how the maps would be used. "Stupid child! You have no business asking such a question! Besides the answer is obvious." he was told. Impressed by the scornful, confident manner of the wise men, he returned home and spent the rest of his years wondering why he couldn't understand what was obvious to others. In his spare time, he prayed that several species of acid-resistant plants and animals would soon evolve.

Index